"Recipes such as the bell-pepper-and-clove-spiked Rice and Peas, the unusual Lime Souffle, and a zesty Chicken Curry with Prune Sauce offer a range of intriguing spice combinations while calling only for ingredients American cooks will find easy to locate, making this an easily utilized guide to the unique pleasures of that region's cuisine."

The Midwest Book Review

"I'd recommend this book for anyone interested in 'island hopping.'"

Linda Cicero
The Miami Herald

"The best reference for a previously undocumented cuisine."

The Cleveland Plain Dealer

"The chapters cover appetizers, soups, fish and shellfish, meats and poultry, vegetables and salads, sauces, breads, puddings and other desserts, and drinks. The glossary will clarify unfamiliar terms, while the final chapter deals with the availability of foods needed to cook Caribbean style."

Seattle Post Intelligencer

THE COMPLETE BOOK OF CARIBBEAN COOKING

ELISABETH
LAMBERT ORTIZ

BALLANTINE BOOKS ● NEW YORK

ISBN 0-345-33256-3

This edition published by arrangement with M. Evans and Company, Inc.

Several of the recipes in this book first appeared in *House and Garden* magazine Copyright © 1967 by The Condé Nast Publications, Inc., and *Gourmet* Magazine in (July and September) 1970.

Manufactured in the United States of America

First Ballantine Books Edition: July 1986
Sixth Printing: April 1993

Contents

Foreword

I became interested in Caribbean cooking a long time ago when I was lucky enough to spend several years at school in the West Indies. We left London for Portsmouth by train one grey day in February. It had been snowing, and the trees were lacy black skeletons against the white fields. The sky was pale blue, with a faint yellow winter sun. Coming by ship into Kingston Harbor in Jamaica, with everything a blaze of color, all reds and yellows and deep vivid greens, a sun like fire in a deep blue sky, and the sea—the beautiful Caribbean sea—ranging from jade at the shore, through turquoise to indigo, it was almost more than I could believe.

The market was a sheer delight. The vendors were mostly women, handsome in their full, printed skirts with white blouses. We often saw them coming into market walking with immense grace, their baskets of produce balanced on their heads. And the produce! Great piles of yellow oranges and green limes, and pale yellow grapefruit, papayas ranging from green to orange, scarlet, yellow and black ackees, green and black avocados, mangoes as vivid as a sunset, great green-skinned, yellow-fleshed pumpkins cut to show their quality to the buyer, and huge yams, and little yams, and tiny green okras. Of course, we had most of them in London markets but there they were imported, exotic, and sold in a setting less vivid than the market at Half-way Tree, or Cross Roads.

It was my first journey away from home, and like the rest of the family, I loved it. Mother adopted a number of Jamaican dishes into the family repertoire, and brief excursions taught me that, just as every island has its own character, so do their kitchens. Though I managed a few more island trips later, it was not until 1966 that I was able to settle down to a proper study of the cooking which had earlier captured my imagination as a schoolgirl.

The Caribbean kitchen is above all eclectic, gathering its ingredients and cooking methods from Europe, Asia and Africa, and joining them in happy association with its own native foods. Christopher Columbus in 1492 discovered the West Indies, that chain of islands which runs from Florida in the north to Venezuela in the south, and includes the Greater Antilles, Cuba, Jamaica, Hispaniola (Haiti-Dominican Republic), and Puerto Rico, as well as the smaller islands that make up the Lesser Antilles, the Leeward and Windward Islands and the Virgin Islands. Africa, Spain, Britain, France, the Netherlands, Denmark and the USA, as well as Indian and Chinese settlers, not to mention the Caribs and Arawaks, have all played their part in the development of a cuisine where a Dominican sancocho, a Trinadadian curry and a Keshy Yena from Curaçao are perfectly at home with the Danish-inspired Asparagus Pudding. Though each island has its specialties, they will be met in other islands as welcome resident aliens, and many dishes, such as the banana and coconut desserts, are truly island-wide.

When he first arrived in the Caribbean Columbus is said to have remarked that he saw so many islands he hardly knew to which he should go first. I felt rather the same way when I began serious island-hopping. I solved the problem by dividing the islands into language, or national groups—the Dutch Islands, the French-speaking, the English-speaking, and the Spanish-speaking islands. It worked very well as this way I could much more easily trace the origins of the dishes I encountered; later on I had a great deal of fun tracing a single dish in its migration, for dishes in the Caribbean tend to island-hop as much as tourists do. Nevertheless, there is a permanent

French stamp on the foods of the French islands, a recognizable Spanish stamp on the foods of the Spanish-speaking islands, and so on. I was also extraordinarily lucky to have friends throughout the islands who helped me by letting me into their kitchens. And later island friends here at home who checked my findings. I am deeply in the debt of all and more grateful than I can say. Yet, after almost seven years of intermittent island visiting, I must in all honesty confess that there are still islands whose culinary treasures I have not yet unearthed: Bequia, Barbuda, unvisited.

I have cooked and tested all the recipes in this book, at home, in New York in my own kitchen with ingredients obtained locally, and without any great difficulty. The local ingredients work very well.

I love the Caribbean, and I love Caribbean food. I hope that readers will feel the same, especially about the food, since this book has very much been a labor of love.

New York—1966–1972

Acknowledgments

I would like to thank the friends, old and new, who have given me such generous help with this book. I shall be forever in their debt, and if I have, by some accident, left anyone out, I ask forgiveness in advance.

For help with the cooking of the Netherlands Antilles, Mrs. Evert M. (Bep) Newton, Mr. Van Gign, and Mr. Sixto Felida; for the Cuban kitchen, Mrs. Mirtha Stengel, Mr. and Mrs. Roberto Rendueles, and Venezuelan diplomat Dr. Raúl Nass of the O.A.S., Washington, D.C.; for the Guadeloupe kitchen, Mr. Roger Fortuné, Mr. Mario Petreluzzi, Mr. H. Bade, and Mrs. Jean-Noël Villahaut Ces François; in Jamaica Mrs. Roy A. Lyons, Mr. Richard Lyons, Miss Mary R. Olson, Dr. Alex D. Hawkes, and Mr. Peter Finch; for the Martinique kitchen, Mrs. Yveline de Lucy de Fossarieu, Mr. Elie Ducros, Mr. Jean-Claude Fays, Mr. Henry Joseph, Mr. Jacques Guannel, Miss Verrey, Mrs. Mireille de Lépine, and Mr. Gérard R. de Campeau; for the Puerto Rican kitchen Mrs. Tere de Lomba, Miss Josefina de Román and Mr. Roberto Ramos Rodriguez; for the cooking of St. Kitts and other Leeward Islands, Nevis, St. Martin, Montserrat and Anguilla, Mr. Arthur Leaman of the *Golden Lemon*, St. Kitts, Mrs. Aimie Osborne, and Mrs. Lilian

Johnston; for the cooking of the Dominican Republic, Mrs. Amanda Ornés de Perelló; for the cooking of Trinidad Tobago, Barbados and the Windward Islands, Miss Nonée Osborne, Mr. and Mrs. Raymond Roopchand, Miss Lilian Fraser, Miss Ivy Walke, Mr. and Mrs. Leo Byam; for the cooking of Haïti, Mrs. Nicole Scott and Mrs. Lyonelle Singer.

My special thanks to Olive and Wilma who refused to give me their full names on the grounds that they weren't really doing anything when they let me work with them in their kitchens, giving me in fact most precious help.

My thanks also go to Miss Barbara Sue Ting Len, not only for secretarial help, but for putting at my disposal her knowledge of the influence of the Guyanese kitchen on Trinidad and other islands, and to Miss Sonia Lecca and Miss Yvonne Wong for secretarial help.

Techniques of Caribbean Cooking

Certain techniques used in Caribbean cooking are what give their characteristic flavors to many of the dishes of the region. In the Spanish-speaking islands sofrito, a highly-seasoned tomato-sweet pepper sauce, adapted from the original Spanish version, is widely used, so is lard or oil flavored with achiote (annatto). Dry or wet massala (curry powder or paste) and ghee (butter oil) are used in Trinidad where the Indian influence is strong. An important Amerindian contribution is cassareep, a liquid seasoning made from grated cassava roots. Originally from Guyana on the South American mainland, its use has spread to Trinidad, to Barbados in the Windward Islands, to St. Kitts in the Leeward Islands, and over to Jamaica in the Greater Antilles. A strong French influence can be seen in the use of seasonings, especially on islands which changed hands between Britain and France innumerable times, persisting even when the island ended up English.

1

The islanders themselves travel widely, so that one meets gifted cooks who have introduced the specialties of their island to another island quite far from home base. Our cook, Annie, was, I think, originally from Trinidad, Wilma, in Trinidad, was from St. Lucia, Olive, in St. Kitts, was from Dominica and called her casserole a daubing pot—an historical footnote to the fact that the island was more than once, French. It is this internal migration that gives an overall quality to Caribbean cooking, though what are called in the islands nationality dishes—Colombo in Martinique and Guadeloupe, Saltfish and Ackee, in Jamaica, Asopao in Puerto Rico, Sancochos in the Dominican Republic, Cou-Cou, Jug-Jug and Pudding and Souse, in Barbados, Callaloo and Accra and Floats in Trinidad, and Carne Mechada in Cuba—are still very much alive in their original homelands.

No special cooking equipment is needed except that pots should be of good, heavy quality and not flimsily made. I find enamelled cast-iron ware very satisfactory for most Caribbean dishes, as it is both oven and flame-proof. Puerto Rico has a special cooking pot, the caldero (literally a cauldron), which is a heavy cast-aluminum or iron casserole, round or oval, with a tight-fi.ting lid. Such diverse dishes as fillet of beef and Arroz con Pollo (Chicken with Rice) can be cooked with great success in this. Occasionally an earthenware casserole is advised in which case make sure it is heavy enough not to crack over direct heat. Use one or more asbestos mats under it if necessary.

Any reasonably well-equipped kitchen will have a blender, wire whisks, measuring cups and spoons, and so on; in fact all that is needed for these recipes. A kitchen scale is useful, though not absolutely necessary.

For the recipes in the Drinks section the usual home bar equipment is all that is needed. This should include a variety of glasses, a shaker and mixing glass set with a strainer, a corkscrew, can and bottle opener, a long stirring spoon, or a glass stirring rod, and a jigger measure with an accurate scale of ½ and ¼ ounces. I find particularly useful the double ended measure whose bowls are ¾ ounce at one end and 1 ounce at the other. These double measures come in a variety of sizes: ¾ and 1¼ ounces, ¾ and 1½ ounces, 1 and 1½ ounces, and 1 and 2 ounces.

There are no unusual techniques for preparing foods for cooking. Fruits and vegetables are washed and peeled in the usual way. Meats, poultry, fish and shellfish require no more than ordinary methods of handling and storage.

There are few difficulties facing a determined shopper planning to cook Caribbean. Meats and poultry are the same, except that goat and kid are used more than here. Fish and shellfish vary very little, and where a specific tropical fish is not available a similar fish is given as an alternative. The fruits, vegetables, herbs and spices for the recipes in this book can all be found without much effort. The Glossary explains more exotic ones, though nowadays much that was once regarded as exotic has become commonplace, and available in supermarkets.

When a recipe calls for rum, you will always get a better result if you use the rum of the island, instead of relying on an all-purpose rum. The Drinks sections can be consulted for using up any leftovers.

Recipes for these fundamentals of the Caribbean kitchen, and notes on island seasonings, are grouped here for convenience in the immediately following directions. They will, I think, be helpful for any cooks unfamiliar with the cooking approach of this region, and should be read before starting to cook the various island dishes.

Aceite o Manteca de Achiote

Annatto Oil or Lard

This is made from the orange-red pulp surrounding the seeds of a tropical tree. During cooking the seeds give off a rich, orange color. If they are cooked too long this changes to a lighter, golden color and much of the flavor is lost. It is impossible to give an absolutely precise cooking time as the freshness of the seeds is a factor. Very stale seeds will give off all their color in one minute of cooking. Watch the saucepan carefully and remove it from

*the heat immediately when the color begins to lighten.
The colored and flavored oil or lard is used in a number
of islands. The ground whole seed is widely used as a
spice in Latin America.*

| 1 cup vegetable oil or lard | ½ cup achiote (annatto) seeds |

Heat the oil or lard in a small saucepan, add the seeds
and cook over low heat for about 5 minutes, stirring from
time to time until a rich orange color is obtained. Cool,
strain, and store the oil or lard in a covered jar in the
refrigerator. It will keep for several months. Use as directed
in recipes. Makes about 1 cup.

Cassareep

4 pounds cassava (yuca) roots	½ teaspoon ground cloves
1 cup cold water	4 teaspoons dark brown sugar
½ teaspoon ground cinnamon	

Peel the cassava roots under cold running water. Dry on
paper towels. Grate on the second finest side of the grater,
or cut up coarsely and grate bit by bit in an electric blender.
Add the water to the grated roots and stir to mix well.
Squeeze about a cupful at a time through a dampened
cloth, twisting the cloth to extract as much liquid as possible. When all is squeezed, put the cassava meal in a
plastic bag and store it in the refrigerator for use in recipes
calling for cassava meal.

Combine the liquid which has been squeezed out in a
saucepan with the cinnamon, cloves and sugar. Bring to
a boil, reduce the heat and simmer slowly, stirring from
time to time, until the liquid is thick and syrupy. If the
cassareep is not dark enough some cooks add caramel or
a bottled commercial browning liquid for gravy. Use as
directed in the recipe for Pepperpot. Keep refrigerated.
Makes about 1 cup.

Chicharrones de Puerco   *Spanish Islands*

Pork Cracklings

I have made these with varying degrees of success. The secret lies, I am certain, in the age of the pig. Skin from the back of a young pig is what one needs. Fortunately, ready-made packaged Chicharrones are available in markets in Latin-American neighborhoods.

Have the butcher cut the skin from the back of a young pig leaving about ¾-inch of fat on it. Carefully score the fat in a criss-cross pattern without cutting through to the skin itself. Soak in cold water for 2 or 3 hours, drain and pat dry. Put the pork pieces in a heavy saucepan or kettle with a little melted lard and cook, uncovered, very, very slowly for about 4 hours. When the skin looks transparent, increase the heat a little and cook for about 30 minutes longer until the skins puff up. Drain. Sprinkle with a little cold water, or Seville (bitter) orange juice and cook for a few minutes longer. Lift out and season with salt.

Coconut Milk and Cream

Coconut milk and cream are used a great deal in all the islands. Coconuts are available in tropical markets and increasingly in supermarkets elsewhere. If fresh coconut is not available, try to find packaged coconut cream. Failing this, use dried coconut, available packaged in supermarkets and from health-food stores. Health-food stores also carry canned coconut milk, sometimes called coconut juice. The liquid inside the fresh coconut is called coconut water.

Pierce 2 of the 3 eyes of a coconut and drain out the water. Strain and set aside. Put the coconut, eyes down, on a very hard surface and whack at it with a hammer. It will crack into enough small pieces to make it easy to remove the meat with a knife, levering the pieces out. Do not bother to remove the brown skin from the pieces to make milk or cream. However, if grated coconut is to be used in a recipe, it is necessary to peel this off.

Grate the coconut as fine as possible, or put into a blender with the reserved coconut water. For a very rich coconut milk, squeeze the grated coconut through a damp cloth, twisting the cloth to extract as much liquid as possible. For ordinary use, however, pour one cup boiling water over the grated coconut and let it stand for one hour. Squeeze through a cloth. This process may be repeated with a second cup of boiling water if abundant, not very rich coconut milk is needed.

For Coconut Cream, allow the coconut milk to stand until the cream rises to the top. This is very thick and rich and is wonderful with desserts.

As packaged shredded coconut, and canned moist grated coconut may not be as rich as fresh coconut, hot milk or light cream may be used instead of water to make coconut milk or cream.

Packaged coconut cream should be mixed to the desired consistency with hot water.

The average coconut weighs about 1½ pounds, and yields between 3 and 4 cups of grated meat. If mixed with the coconut water and hot water, this should yield about 3 cups of coconut milk. The amount will vary with the freshness and quality of the coconut.

Ghee   *Trinidad*

1 pound unsalted butter, in 4-ounce (¼-pound) sticks

Put the butter into a heavy saucepan over medium heat. Melt the butter, stirring from time to time, then increase the heat to bring the butter to a boil. Let it boil for about 1 minute. Reduce the heat to the lowest point possible, using 2 or 3 asbestos mats if necessary. Cook the butter, without stirring, for 45 minutes by which time it will be golden and the milk solids in the bottom of the pan will be brown.

Wring a piece of cheesecloth out in hot water and, using it folded into 4 layers, line a sieve. Carefully pour the butter through the cheesecloth. Pour the sieved butter, now Ghee, into a jar and store in the refrigerator. It will keep indefinitely. It will keep at room temperature for 2 or 3 months. Makes about 1½ cups.

Massala   *Trinidad*

Ground Spice Mixture

This mixture of ground spices and hot pepper was brought to Trinidad by migrant Hindu workers. When ground dry it is curry powder. When wet, because of the addition of fresh hot peppers or a liquid, it is curry paste. Commercial curry powder may be used, but since Massala is easy to make, and all the ingredients readily available, it is worth the extra effort. Massala may be used in any island recipe calling for curry powder.

WET MASSALA:

1 teaspoon saffron threads, or ground turmeric
½ cup coriander seeds
2 teaspoons anise seeds
2 teaspoons whole cloves
2 teaspoons cumin seeds
2 teaspoons fenugreek seeds
3 teaspoons black peppercorns
2 teaspoons mustard seeds
1 large onion, finely chopped
4 cloves garlic, chopped
Fresh hot red peppers to taste

Soak the saffron threads in a little water and, using a mortar and pestle, grind into a paste. Grind all the remaining ingredients using a mortar and pestle, or combine in an electric blender, a little at a time, to make a heavy paste. Remove the seeds from the hot peppers unless a very hot curry paste is wanted. Use as directed in recipes, or to taste. Keep refrigerated in jars, but use within a day or so. Makes about 2 cups. Also see Curry Powder I and II.

DRY MASSALA:

Grind the saffron threads dry, or use turmeric. Omit the onion and garlic, and substitute dried red peppers for the fresh ones. Store in airtight glass jars at room temperature. Dry Massala will keep for 6 months. Makes about 1 cup.

Salt Beef and Pork   *All Islands*

Salt beef and salt pork are widely used in the West Indies, largely because, in the old days, there was no refrigeration, and in the hot climate meat spoiled easily. Now that refrigeration has altered the situation, people still use salted meat because they have acquired a taste for it. Fresh meats, poultry, fish and shellfish are, of course, also eaten. But certain dishes still call for salt meat. The meat may be either pickled in brine or dry corned.

PICKLING SOLUTION FOR ABOUT 5 POUNDS OF MEAT:

3 cups coarse salt
2 teaspoons saltpeter
½ cup dark brown
  sugar
4-inch piece stick
  cinnamon

1 tablespoon allspice
  berries
1 tablespoon dry mustard
4 quarts water

Combine all the ingredients in a large enamelware, or stainless steel saucepan or soup kettle. Bring to a boil and boil for 5 minutes. Skim. Allow to cool. Pour into a stoneware crock, or a stainless steel or enamel container with a tight-fitting lid. Add the meat together with 1 teaspoon thyme, 2 or 3 sliced scallions, 1 sliced onion, and 1 or 2 fresh hot red peppers. Store in a cool place for 7 to 10 days, turning the meat daily. Keep refrigerated until needed. Meat should be in one piece. For beef, brisket is the best cut. Rump and chuck can also be used. For pork, use belly or shoulder.

TO DRY CORN BEEF AND PORK:

3 pounds boneless meat	1 teaspoon saltpeter
3 cups coarse salt	2 teaspoons brown sugar

Mix the salt, saltpeter and sugar together in a large glass or china bowl or stoneware crock. Rub mixture well into the meat. Sprinkle a little more dry salt over the meat to cover it well. Each day for 3 days pour away any liquid that collects. The first day there will be a great deal, the other two days hardly any. Sprinkle a little more salt on the meat after draining it, and turn it daily. Refrigerate for 7 to 10 days, turning the meat daily.

To use, wash meat thoroughly. Drain, cover with fresh water and simmer for about 20 minutes to the pound. Keep refrigerated until needed.

Seasoning for Various Dishes   *Dominican Republic*

Sazón Preparado

This is a variation of sofrito, and comes from the Dominican Republic where it is used to flavor stews, beans, rice and vegetables. It is easy to make and is useful to have on hand, especially for the cook in a hurry.

3 medium onions, chopped	½ cup coarsely chopped parsley
1 green bell pepper, seeded and chopped	½ cup chopped fresh green coriander leaves
1 red (ripe) bell pepper, seeded and chopped or 2 canned pimientos, chopped	1 teaspoon Tabasco, or hot pepper sauce
4 large cloves garlic, peeled and chopped	1 tablespoon sweet paprika
1 tablespoon orégano	1 cup tomato paste
1 cup chopped scallions, using green part as well as white	1 cup olive, or vegetable oil
	½ cup vinegar, preferably cane or white distilled
	Salt to taste

Combine all the ingredients and blend, bit by bit, to a purée in an electric blender. Pour into a saucepan and simmer, stirring constantly, for 5 minutes. Cool and bottle. Makes about 6 cups.

Marinade
"Seasoning-Up" Meats and Poultry

Just as sofrito and achiote lard or oil are essential to the cooking of the Spanish-speaking islands, so is the technique of "seasoning-up" meats and poultry essential to the cooking of the English-speaking islands.

The great inventiveness of island cooks makes it difficult to give precise recipes. On returning to the islands, I kept catching echoes of the flavors our family cook, Annie, produced daily. Since my own mother was a very good cook and incorporated a lot of island approaches into her own repertoire, I grew up in a very well-flavored world and my memory of island cooking was kept intact.

Rather than lay down hard and fast rules, I would prefer to give a fairly standard marinade (seasoning-up). My own experience is that if one stays within the limits imposed by these seasoning rules, one can do much as one pleases, always with admirable results.

The herbs and vegetables most commonly used are onion, garlic, chives, scallions, shallots, thyme, marjoram, parsley, (preferably flatleaved parsley), celery leaves, bay leaves, basil, sage, rosemary, tarragon, orégano, ginger and fresh hot peppers. Among the spices, cloves, cinnamon, nutmeg, mace, allspice, and both black and white pepper are used, as are curry powder, cayenne pepper, Spanish (hot) paprika, sweet paprika, soy sauce, Worcestershire sauce, Seville (bitter) orange juice, lime juice, oil, vinegar, and wines such as sherry, Madeira, and red and white table wines. And, of course, rum. It is a formidable list, and gives a great deal of leeway to the creative cook.

In a number of islands the term "herb" refers to the

local chives available in there. Garlic used sparingly with scallions, chives and shallots gives the authentic flavor of island chives, and is much to be preferred to our more usual onion-garlic mixture.

Island cooks are fussy about the appearance of the finished dish, and dislike the use of thyme in a marinade as the leaves tend to leave dark specks in a sauce or gravy. For this reason such herbs as thyme and marjoram are usually tied in a piece of cheesecloth, and added to the pot in which the meat is cooked rather than directly to the marinade. Hot peppers, whole and with the stem on, are added to the pot so that they can be retrieved at the end of cooking, having lent more flavor than heat to the dish. However, peppers are often tied in a square of cheesecloth and removed before serving.

The marinating technique almost certainly goes back to 16th century France and Britain, when meat was often tough, and in the summer months might well be tainted. Spices and herbs not only tenderized and flavored meat, but also preserved it.

The following is a fairly standard marinade and can be used for any meat or poultry which can then be stewed, braised, broiled or roasted. This is sufficient for about 3 pounds of meat.

1 medium onion, grated
1 clove garlic, crushed
4 blades chive, chopped coarsely or, 1 scallion, coarsely chopped
1 sprig celery leaves, coarsely chopped

2 tablespoons cane or malt vinegar
2 tablespoons dry sherry or rum
1 tablespoon soy sauce
1 teaspoon cayenne pepper or Spanish (hot) paprika

Mix all together. Rub well into the meat or poultry and allow to stand at room temperature for at least 1 hour, turning once or twice. Or use as suggested in recipes.

If the meat is to be stewed, it can go straight into the stew pot with water or stock to cover, and all of the marinade. If it is to be braised, the marinade should be scraped off and reserved, and the meat patted dry before braising. Two teaspoons of brown sugar should be rubbed into the meat and it should then be sautéed in a little butter or oil or fat from the meat. Then put it into a casserole with the marinade and stock or water, as well as sliced onions, carrots and so on according to the meat recipe. For boiling or roasting, the marinade should be scraped off and reserved for making a sauce or gravy when the meat is done.

Marinade Variations

Olive, a very gifted cook in St. Kitts, has a slightly different technique which produces a very subtle flavor. It is given in detail in the recipe for Olive's Seasoned-up Pot Roast. The same technique can be used for pork with the addition of a little sage, while the addition of finely grated fresh ginger root, or ground Jamaica ginger, is pleasant with chicken.

Some cooks prefer to crush the stems of fresh herbs, such as parsley, instead of chopping them coarsely; all the island cooks prefer to use fresh herbs rather than dried ones.

Given a sunny window ledge, or similar small space, it is easy enough to grow pot herbs from seed. Many of the annuals will keep going all winter if grown indoors on a ledge with a southern exposure. Many markets sell fresh herbs, and there are always the dried herbs to fall back on.

CARAMEL COLORING:

Island cooks usually make their own caramel coloring from local brown sugar, or rub sugar direct into the meat before searing.

To make the caramel:	**2 tablespoons water**
1 pound island sugar, or	
use granulated sugar	

Combine the sugar and water in a heavy saucepan and cook over medium heat until the sugar is dark brown, stirring from time to time. Add 2 cups cold water, bring to a boil, stir and simmer until the caramel has the consistency of syrup. Cool and bottle. Be careful not to let the caramel burn as it will develop an acid taste.

Undercooked caramel will give a sweet taste to food. If properly made, caramel will color without sweetening.

Seasoning Mixture   *Barbados*

2 medium onions, very
   finely chopped
2 tablespoons finely
   chopped chives
3 cloves garlic, crushed

1 fresh hot red pepper,
   seeded and mashed
1 teaspoon orégano
½ teaspoon ground
   cloves
1 teaspoon salt
1 tablespoon lime juice

Mix all ingredients together thoroughly. Rub well into the inside of a suckling pig prepared for roasting. Makes about 1 cup, enough for a 10 to 12-pound pig.

To season whole cleaned fish, gash two or three times on each side of the backbone, and stuff the seasoning into the incisions. Any fish, or meat, may be seasoned with the mixture. Cook as directed in recipes.

Sofrito

Puerto Rico

½ pound salt pork, diced

2 tablespoons annatto (achiote) seeds

4 medium onions, finely chopped

12 cloves garlic, finely chopped

2 medium green bell peppers, seeded and chopped

½ pound ham, diced

1 pound tomatoes, peeled and chopped, or 2 cups drained canned tomatoes, coarsely chopped

1 tablespoon finely chopped fresh green coriander

1 teaspoon dried orégano

Salt, freshly ground pepper

Fry the salt pork dice in a heavy frying pan over medium heat, stirring from time to time, until they have given up all their fat and are crisp and brown. Lift out of the fat with a slotted spoon and reserve. Add the annatto seeds to the pan and cook, stirring occasionally, over medium heat for 5 minutes. Remove from the heat, strain, discard the seeds and return the fat to the pan.

Add the onions, garlic and green peppers and sauté until the onion is tender but not browned. Add the ham, tomatoes, coriander, orégano, reserved salt pork dice, and pepper to taste. Simmer over low heat for 30 minutes, stirring from time to time. Season to taste with salt. Cool and pour into glass jars, cover tightly and refrigerate until needed. Use as directed in recipes. Makes about 2 cups.

Appetizers

Ackee patties

4 ounces salt codfish
2 tablespoons vegetable
  oil
1 small onion, finely
  chopped
1 fresh hot red pepper,
  seeded and chopped, or
  use hot pepper sauce

Freshly ground pepper
1 tablespoon parsley,
  chopped
1 cup drained canned
  ackees
1 recipe Flaky Pastry (as
  for Meat Patties) (see
  Index)
1 egg white, lightly
  beaten

Pour boiling water over the fish and let it cool. Drain, rinse, and put on to cook with fresh cold water to cover. Cook until tender, about 15 minutes. Drain. Remove any bones and skin and flake fish finely. Heat the oil in a frying pan and sauté the onion until tender, but not browned. Add the fish, hot pepper, pepper to taste, parsley and ackees, and cook for a few minutes, stirring with a wooden spoon. Crush the ackees into the mixture, which should be fairly smooth, but not a purée.

Roll out the pastry about ⅛th-inch thick on a lightly floured board and cut into about twelve 5-inch circles.

15

Add the fillings, damp the edges of the pastry with water and fold each over into a crescent. Seal the edges by pinching together with the fingers, or crimping with a fork. Brush with egg white and prick the tops to let the steam escape.

Bake on an ungreased cookie sheet in a 425° oven for 20 to 30 minutes, or until lightly browned. Serve for lunch with a vegetable or a salad, or as a snack or first course. Makes about 12 patties.

For cocktails, put 1 teaspoon of the mixture on 2-inch pastry circles, fold as described and bake 15 to 20 minutes.

Accra   *Trinidad*

Saltfish Cakes

This is a member of the same family as Barbados Codfish Cakes, Jamaica's Stamp and Go, Puerto Rico's Bacalaitos, Martinique and Guadeloupe's Acrats de Morue and Haiti's Marinades, and illustrates how the same dish changes from island to island. Accra are traditionally served with Floats.

2 teaspoons active dry yeast
½ cup warm water
½ pound boneless salt codfish
1 cup all-purpose flour
1 teaspoon sugar
¼ cup finely chopped onions
Clove garlic, finely chopped

1 tablespoon fresh hot peppers, seeded and finely chopped
1 tablespoon finely chopped chives
Salt, freshly ground pepper
Vegetable oil for deep frying

Sprinkle the yeast on the warm water and let stand for 10 minutes. Pour boiling water over the codfish, and allow to cool. Rinse in cold water, remove any skin and bones, and shred fish very fine. Mix fish with the flour, sugar, onions, garlic, peppers, chives, salt if necessary and a generous amount of pepper. Add the yeast and beat until smooth. Allow to rise for 1½ to 2 hours in a warm draft-free place.

Drop by tablespoon into hot oil (370° on frying thermometer) and fry until golden brown. Drain on paper towels and serve hot with hot Floats (see Index). Makes about 24.

Acrats de Morue *Martinique-Guadeloupe*
Codfish Fritters

1½ cups all-purpose flour	2 scallions, finely chopped
½ teaspoon salt	1 clove garlic, crushed
2 medium eggs	1 tablespoon chopped parsley
3 tablespoons unsalted butter, melted and cooled	½ teaspoon thyme
1 cup milk	1 melegueta peppercorn or 1 allspice berry, ground
½ pound salt codfish	Freshly ground pepper
1 fresh hot pepper, seeded	Oil for deep frying

Sift the flour and salt into a bowl. Beat the eggs with the butter and add. Add the milk gradually, stirring only to mix. Add a little more milk if the batter is too stiff. Cover and allow to stand for 2 or 3 hours.

Meanwhile soak the fish in cold water. The time will depend on the hardness and saltiness of the fish. Drain, remove any bones and skin. Pound fish in a mortar with the hot pepper. Add the scallions, garlic, parsley, thyme, melegueta peppercorn or allspice, and freshly ground pepper to taste. Stir into the batter and allow to stand for 30 minutes. Heat oil in a deep fryer, or large, heavy saucepan (375° on a deep-frying thermometer), and fry the mixture by heaped tablespoonfuls until golden brown. Drain on paper towels and keep warm. Serve hot as a first course. Serves 6 to 8.

Akkra
Jamaica

Bean Fritters

These fritters are known as calas in Curaçao, and in that island are made only from black-eyed peas. Sweet rice fritters made with yeast, called calas, were once very popular in the French Quarter of New Orleans. How the name reached Curaçao, or who has the best right to it, no one knows.

1 cup black-eyed peas, or soy beans	2 teaspoons salt
2 fresh hot red peppers, seeded and chopped	Oil for frying

Soak the beans overnight in cold water. Drain, rub off and discard the skin, cover beans again with cold water and soak for 2 or 3 hours longer. Drain, rinse, and put through a meat grinder using the finest blade, or reduce bit by bit in an electric blender. Grind the peppers. Add the salt and peppers to the beans and beat with a wooden spoon until they are light and fluffy and considerably increased in bulk. Heat the oil in a heavy frying pan and fry the mixture by tablespoonfuls until golden brown on both sides. Drain on paper towels. Serve hot as an accompaniment to drinks. Makes about 24 fritters.

Tostones de Plátano
Puerto Rico

Green Plantain Chips

1 large, green plantain, peeled and cut into diagonal slices ½-inch thick	Salted water Vegetable oil for frying Salt

Soak the plantain slices for at least 30 minutes in the salted water. Drain and pat dry with paper towels. Heat 2 or 3 tablespoons of oil in a heavy frying pan and sauté the plantain pieces until tender, but do not let them get crusty on the outside. Drain on paper towels.

Lay a sheet of waxed paper over the plantain slices and flatten evenly by pressing until about half as thick as before. Dip the pressed plantain in salted water and fry until crusty and golden brown on both sides. Drain on paper towels, salt lightly and serve with meat or fish dishes, or as an accompaniment to drinks. Makes about 15 Tostones.

In the French islands this is known as Banane Pesé. In Haïti it is a traditional accompaniment to Griots de Porc.

Bacalaitos   *Puerto Rico*

Salt Codfish Fritters

½ pound salt codfish
2 cups all-purpose flour
2 teaspoons baking
  powder
1 large clove garlic,
  crushed
1 cup water

1 tablespoon annatto
  (achiote) oil (see Index)
Lard or vegetable oil for
  deep frying

Soak the codfish in cold water for 2 hours or longer, according to the saltiness and hardness of the fish. Drain, rinse and place in a small saucepan. Pour boiling water over the fish and allow to stand for 5 minutes. Drain. Remove any bones and skin and shred the fish.

Sift the flour and baking powder into a large bowl. Add the garlic, water, and annatto oil and mix to a smooth batter. Add the shredded fish and mix well. Heat lard or oil (370° on frying thermometer) in a deep fryer or large, heavy saucepan. Fry the mixture by tablespoonfuls until golden brown. Drain on paper towels, keep warm and serve hot as a first course. Makes about 24.

To serve as an hors-d'oeuvre, use a teaspoon instead of a tablespoon measure. Makes 60 or more small fritters.

Buljol

Trinidad

Salt Codfish Salad

8 ounces salt codfish	Freshly ground black
1 medium onion, finely	pepper
chopped	3 tablespoons olive, or
2 medium tomatoes,	vegetable, oil
peeled, seeded and	1 tablespoon lime, or
chopped	lemon, juice
1 fresh, hot red pepper,	Lettuce leaves
seeded and chopped	1 medium avocado
	(optional)

Place the fish in a bowl and cover with boiling water. Allow to cool. Drain. Remove any skin, and bones, and shred the fish. Pour boiling water over a second time. When cool, drain and press out all the water. Mix the onion, tomatoes and hot pepper with the fish. Season with pepper, oil, and lime or lemon juice. Serve on lettuce leaves. Garnish with slices of peeled avocado, if liked. Serves 3 to 4 as a first course.

In Trinidad this is often served for breakfast.

Cassava Chips

Jamaica

Cassava root	Salt
Oil for deep frying	

Peel the cassava root and slice, crosswise, as thinly as possible. Steep in iced water for 30 minutes, drain and dry on paper towels.

Fry until delicately browned and crisp in deep oil heated to 370° on a frying thermometer. Drain on paper towels, sprinkle with salt, and serve as an accompaniment to drinks.

Chiquetaille de Morue   *Haïti*
Salt Codfish Salad

1 pound dried salt
  codfish
1 cup salad, or olive, oil
½ cup vinegar
¼ cup shallots,
  chopped
1 onion, finely chopped
1 leek, well washed and
  chopped fine
1 clove garlic, crushed

2 carrots, scraped and
  finely diced
½ cup raw green
  beans, finely diced
1 tablespoon parsley,
  chopped
Freshly ground pepper
Hot pepper sauce

Put the codfish in a large bowl and pour boiling water over it. Allow to cool. Drain, remove the bones and skin and shred the fish. Pour boiling water over the fish a second time, and allow to cool. Drain and press out all the water. Return fish to the bowl and mix with all the remaining ingredients, seasoning to taste with pepper and hot pepper sauce. Allow to stand for 2 hours at room temperature for the flavor to develop.

Serve as a spread on canapés, or in sandwiches, as an accompaniment to drinks. Makes about 4 cups.

Coctel de Camarones   *Dominican Republic*
Shrimp Cocktail

1 cup olive oil
¼ cup lime, or lemon,
  juice
½ teaspoon sugar
2 teaspoons
  Worcestershire sauce

1 teaspoon hot pepper
  sauce (see Index)
1 medium onion, grated
Salt, freshly ground
  pepper
1½ pounds medium or
  jumbo shrimp, cooked

Mix the oil, lime juice, sugar, Worcestershire sauce, hot pepper sauce, onion, salt and freshly ground pepper together, beating with a fork to mix thoroughly.

Toss the shrimp with the sauce and serve cold as a first course. Serves 4 to 6.

Empanadas   *Curaçao*
Meat Patties

1 cup masa harina
P.A.N., or other
Venezuelan precooked
corn meal. See below*
1 cup boiling water
1 teaspoon salt
1 teaspoon sugar
1 cup all-purpose flour

1 egg
2 tablespoons sweet
butter, melted and
cooled
Few drops yellow
vegetable coloring
(optional)
⅓ cup grated Edam or
Gouda cheese
1 egg, well beaten

Put the corn meal into a basin. Stir in the boiling water. Cool. Add the salt, sugar, flour and egg, mix and turn out onto a floured board. Knead until smooth. Return to the bowl and add the melted butter, vegetable coloring, and grated cheese, mixing well.

Roll out onto a lightly floured board. Cut into circles about 4-inches in diameter. Put 1 tablespoon of filling on each circle and fold over into a half-moon shape. Brush the edges with beaten egg and seal well. Turn the edges over to the top side to make a quadruple thickness and pinch into scallops with the fingers. Fry in deep hot fat until golden. (370° on frying thermometer). Makes about 20 empanadas.

Serve hot as a first course, or as an accompaniment to drinks.

*NOTE: The corn meal used for the empanadas is similar to the corn meal used for Mexican tortillas. Dried corn is soaked, boiled, ground and dried. However, the Venezuelan corn has a very different flavor from Mexican corn, and it is not possible to substitute Mexican masa harina. Several packaged brands are available in Latin American groceries.

FILLING:

2 tablespoons unsalted
  butter
½ pound beef, ground
1 tablespoon finely
  chopped onion
1 tablespoon finely
  chopped celery
2 tablespoons seeded and
  chopped green bell
  pepper

1 medium tomato,
  peeled, seeded and
  chopped (optional)
Salt, freshly ground
  pepper
Few drops red vegetable
  coloring (optional)

Heat the butter in a frying pan and sauté the beef, onion,
celery and green bell pepper until done, about 15 minutes.
Add the tomato, salt, freshly ground pepper, and vegetable coloring if liked. Cook for 3 to 4 minutes longer.
Cool. Use to stuff the empanadas.

Féroce d'Avocat   *Martinique-Guadeloupe*

*This could be translated as "a fierceness of avocado"
which, while picturesque, would give an unfair impression
since féroce simply refers to how much hot fresh pepper
has been used in the dish. Traditionally this is highly
seasoned but ultimately one pleases oneself and adds hot
pepper to taste.*

4 ounces salt codfish
1 medium-sized avocado,
  peeled, seeded and cut
  into ½-inch cubes
¾ cup vegetable oil
¼ cup lime, or lemon,
  juice
½ medium onion,
  finely chopped
1 clove garlic, crushed
1, or more, fresh hot red
  or green peppers,
  seeded and chopped

1 tablespoon chopped
  parsley
Salt and freshly ground
  pepper to taste
⅛ teaspoon sugar
1 cup farine de manioc
  (cassava meal)
½ cup coconut milk,
  or milk, about

Soak the cod overnight in cold water. Drain thoroughly, refresh with cold water, pat dry and broil until lightly colored on both sides. When cool enough to handle, remove bones and skin and shred as finely as possible. Place fish in a bowl with the avocado. Mix together the oil and lime or lemon juice, add the onion, garlic, hot pepper, parsley, salt and pepper to taste, and the sugar. Be careful not to over-salt as the cod will still be salty. Pour mixture over the cod and avocado.

Mix the cassava meal with the coconut milk to barely moisten it. Add to the cod and avocado and mix all together thoroughly with a wooden spoon to a smooth, heavy paste. Serve as an appetizer, or on canapés to accompany drinks. Makes 3 cups, about.

Lambi Souse   *Grenada*

Pickled Conch

2 pounds conch (see glossary)
1 medium onion, finely chopped
1 cucumber, peeled, seeded and chopped
1 fresh hot red or green pepper
1 cup lime juice
Salt
Red peppers, watercress and parsley for garnish

Pound the conch to tenderize. Put into a saucepan with salted water to cover and simmer until tender, about 1½ hours, or longer. Cool in the stock, drain, cut up into small pieces and put into a jar with the onion, cucumber, hot pepper, lime juice and salt to taste. Refrigerate overnight. Garnish with peppers, watercress and parsley and serve as an accompaniment to drinks, or as an appetizer for 6. Served with boiled breadfruit, it makes a lunch dish for 4.

Marinades

Haïti

Fritters

1 cup all-purpose flour	2 teaspoons unsalted
1½ teaspoons baking	butter, melted and
powder	cooled
1 teaspoon salt	2 teaspoons vegetable oil
4 eggs	2 teaspoons rum

Sift the flour with the baking powder and salt into a bowl. Make a well in the center and add the eggs, butter, oil and rum. Beat thoroughly until the batter is smooth. Let the batter stand 1 or 2 hours before using.

To make the fritters, mix the batter with 4 ounces salt codfish, soaked, shredded and drained, with any skin and bones removed; or use 4 ounces cooked chicken, cut into dice; or add chopped shallots, parsley and hot pepper to the batter; or cooked shrimps, or in fact anything on hand.

For sweet fritters, reduce the salt to ½ teaspoon, add a tablespoon of sugar, and add ¼ pound mashed or sliced bananas, or any suitable fruit.

Heat vegetable oil in deep kettle (to 370° on a frying thermometer). Drop fritter mixtures by tablespoonful into the hot fat. Fry until golden brown on both sides. Drain on paper towels. Makes about 24.

Mero en Escabeche

Puerto Rico

Soused or Pickled Red Grouper

Mero, or red grouper, is a tropical sea bass. Sea bass, striped bass, haddock, shad, mackerel or snapper are all suitable for this dish.

3 pounds fillets of red grouper, or other suitable fish	2 whole cloves garlic
	2 bay leaves
Salt	¼ teaspoon peppercorns
2 cups olive oil	1 cup vinegar
2 medium onions, thinly sliced	1 cup small pitted green olives

Cut the fish fillets into 1½-inch pieces and season with salt. Heat 2 or 3 tablespoons of the olive oil in a frying pan and fry the pieces of fish. Lift out and place in a deep glass or porcelain bowl.

Combine the onions, garlic, bay leaves, peppercorns and vinegar in a saucepan and simmer until the onion is tender. Cool. Add the remaining olive oil and the olives and pour over the fish. Cover the bowl and refrigerate for at least 24 hours before serving.

Serve cold, garnished with lettuce leaves. Serves 6 to 8.

Mofongo

Puerto Rico

Plantain Spread

4 half-ripe plantains	4 cloves crushed garlic (optional)
Lard or oil for frying	
½ pound chicharrón	Salt to taste

Peel the plantains and cut into 1-inch slices. Heat enough lard or oil to cover the bottom of a heavy 10 to 12-inch frying pan and fry the plantain slices, as many at a time as the pan will hold comfortably, until they are golden brown on both sides. Drain on paper towels and grind the cooked plantains in a mortar with the garlic and the chicharrón until the mixture is creamy. Season to taste with salt and serve spread on bread or crackers, or make into small balls. Serve as an appetizer or with drinks.

It is important that the plantains be midway between green and ripe. Green, they will have the sticky consistency they have in foo-foo, ripe they will be too sweet. Chicharrón is Latin American pork cracklings, which can be made at home (see recipe) or bought ready-made in Latin-American and Caribbean markets.

Pastelillos de Carne de Cerdo
Puerto Rico

Little Pork Pies

FOR THE PASTRY:

2 cups all-purpose flour	4 tablespoons unsalted
1 teaspoon salt	butter
½ teaspoon baking	1 egg, lightly beaten
soda	½ cup water, about

Sift the flour, salt and baking soda into a large bowl. Rub the butter into the flour with the fingertips until it has the consistency of a coarse meal. Make a well in the center. Mix the egg with the water and pour gradually into the flour, mixing with a wooden spoon until the dough is smooth. Gather the dough into a ball, wrap in waxed paper and refrigerate for 1 hour.

FOR THE FILLING:

3 tablespoons vegetable oil or lard	2 teaspoons capers
½ pound lean pork, ground	2 tablespoons seedless raisins
2 ounces ham, ground	¼ cup small, pitted green olives
Salt, freshly ground pepper	1 hard-boiled egg, coarsely chopped
1 cup sofrito (See Index)	
2 teaspoons distilled white vinegar	

Heat the oil or lard in a heavy frying pan and add the pork, ham, and salt and pepper to taste. Cook, stirring for about 5 minutes, or until there is no trace of pink in the pork. Add the sofrito and vinegar, stir to mix well, cover and cook over low heat for 30 minutes. Add the capers, raisins, olives and egg and cook for a minute or two longer. Allow to cool.

Cut the dough into 3 pieces. Roll each of the pieces out on a lightly floured board, one at a time, to ⅛-inch thickness or less. Cut into circles about 4-inches in diameter. There will be about 18 circles in all. Place a tablespoon of the meat mixture in the center of each circle of dough, moisten the edges with cold water and fold the circle in half, pressing the edges down with the tines of a fork to seal them securely.

Fry in deep oil at a temperature of 350° on a frying thermometer. When the pastelillos rise to the top of the oil, spoon a little of the hot oil over them to make them puff up, then turn to brown a little more. Drain on paper towels and serve hot, or at room temperature as a first course.

For pastelillos to serve as an accompaniment to drinks, cut the pastry circles 2½-inches in diameter and use 1 teaspoon of filling on each. Makes about 4 dozen of the smaller size.

VARIATION: For Pastelillos de Queso (Cheese Turnovers) Use 1½ cups grated cheddar, Edam or similar cheese in place of the meat filling to stuff the pastelillos.

Pâté de Harengs Saurs   *Haïti*
Pâté of Smoked Herring

Smoked herrings	**Freshly ground pepper**
Milk, or water	**Hot pepper sauce**
Unsalted butter	

Soak the herrings in milk or water for several hours to
remove the salt. Drain and remove the fillets, discard
bones and skin. Put the fillets into a heavy frying pan with
a little milk and butter and cook for about 8 to 10 minutes.
Season to taste with freshly ground pepper and hot pepper
sauce. Using a mortar and pestle, reduce the herring to
a smooth paste using some of the pan juices and more
butter. Spread on fingers of fresh, hot toast and serve as
an appetizer, or as an accompaniment to drinks.

Platanutri   *Puerto Rico*
Plantain Chips

Green or half-ripe	**Oil for deep frying**
plantains	**Salt**

Peel the plantains, and slice crosswise as thinly as possible. Drop into salted ice water and let stand for 30 minutes. Drain, and dry on paper towels. Fry until delicately
browned in deep oil heated to 370° on a frying thermometer. Drain on paper towels, sprinkle with salt and serve
as an accompaniment to drinks.

In St. Kitts green bananas are cooked in this way. The
result is very delicate.

Picklises

Green beans, cut French-
style
Cabbage, very finely
shredded
Cauliflower, separated
into flowerets
Carrots, scraped and
thinly sliced
Onion, thinly sliced

Tender young green peas
Radishes, thinly sliced
Celery, sliced
3 fresh hot red peppers,
pricked in 2 or 3 places
with a fork
Vinegar

Prepare equal amounts of the vegetables and place in a
large crock or jar. Cover with vinegar and allow to stand
in a cool place for 1 week. Serve as a relish with steak
or any roast meat, or with crackers and cheese as an
accompaniment to drinks. Store in the refrigerator, if the
picklises last long enough to store, which they seldom do.

Phulouri

Split Pea Fritters

1 cup split peas
1 medium onion, chopped
1 clove garlic, chopped

Salt, freshly ground
pepper
Oil for deep frying

Soak the split peas overnight in cold water to cover. Drain
thoroughly. Put through the fine blade of a food mill with
the onion and garlic, or reduce to a purée in an electric
blender. Season highly with salt and pepper and beat with
a wooden spoon until light and fluffy. Or use an electric
beater.

Heat the oil in a deep fryer or saucepan (370° on a
frying thermometer). Form the mixture, a tablespoonful
at a time, into balls and drop into the hot oil, about 6 at
a time. Fry until brown all over. Drain on paper towels.

Serve hot, each stuck with a toothpick, as an appetizer. Makes about 24.

If liked, a tablespoon of curry powder may be added to the split peas when they are ground. A hot pepper sauce is often served as a dip for the Phulouri.

Potted Jack Fish

St. Kitts

6 jack fish, or similar
  small fish, weighing 10-
  ounces to 1-pound each
2 tablespoons all-purpose
  flour
½ teaspoon salt

¼ teaspoon freshly
  ground pepper
2 tablespoons unsalted
  butter
½ cup vinegar,
  preferably cane vinegar
2 bay leaves

Have the heads removed from the fish, and have the fish cleaned and split; or do it yourself. Carefully remove the backbone and roll up each fish from the tail, skin outside, like rollmops. Fasten with a toothpick.

Mix together the flour, salt and pepper and roll the fish in this. Arrange the fish in a buttered baking dish, dot with the butter, then pour the vinegar mixed with ½ cup cold water over them. Lay the bay leaves on top of the fish. Cover lightly with a piece of buttered paper and bake in a 350° oven until done, about 15 to 20 minutes. Serve either hot or cold. Serves 6. If served cold, garnish with lettuce and tomato slices.

Run Down

Jamaica

Salt Catfish and Tomatoes

1 pound shad or
    mackerel fillets
¼ cup lime, or lemon
    juice
3 cups coconut milk
1 large onion, finely
    chopped
2 cloves garlic
1 tablespoon finely
    chopped fresh hot
    pepper, preferably red

1 pound tomatoes, peeled
    and chopped
Salt, freshly ground
    pepper
¼ teaspoon thyme
1 tablespoon vinegar,
    preferably malt, or
    cane

Pour the lime juice over the fish and set aside. Cook the coconut milk in a heavy frying pan until it is oily. Add the onion, garlic, and cook until the onion is tender. Add the hot pepper, the tomatoes, salt, pepper, thyme and vinegar, and stir and cook very gently for 10 minutes. Drain the fish, add, and cook until the fish is tender, about 10 minutes. Serve hot with boiled bananas.* Serves 4 as an appetizer, 2 as a main course. Run Down can also be used as a stuffing for breadfruit.

    Salt codfish or rock lobster tails can be used instead of shad or mackerel.

*For cooking instructions for green bananas see BANANE JAUNE AVEC SAUCE BLANCHE (Green Bananas with White Sauce).

Saltfish Cakes

Barbados

1 pound salt codfish
1 pound West Indian
    pumpkin (calabaza), or
    Hubbard squash
1 tablespoon unsalted
    butter
2 eggs, lightly beaten

Salt, freshly ground
    pepper
1 to 2 cups freshly made
    bread crumbs
3 to 4 tablespoons
    vegetable oil or lard

Put the fish in a bowl, cover with warm water and soak for 2 hours or longer, according to the saltiness and hardness of the fish. Drain, rinse and place in a saucepan with boiling water to cover. Simmer gently, covered, until the fish is tender, about 15 minutes. Drain, remove any bones and skin, and shred fish finely.

Peel the pumpkin, remove any seeds, cut into chunks and cook in boiling salted water to cover until tender, about 15 minutes. Drain thoroughly and mash with the butter. Add the fish, mixing well. Beat in the eggs, and season to taste with salt, if needed, and pepper. If the mixture is too loose, stir in bread crumbs until it is firm enough to be formed into cakes.

Form into 12 cakes, about 2-by-1-inch, and roll them in breadcrumbs. Heat the oil in a large, heavy frying pan and fry the cakes, as many at a time as the pan will conveniently hold, until brown on both sides, about 8 minutes. Drain on paper towels and keep warm. Serve hot as a first course. To serve as an accompaniment to drinks, make into 1-inch balls. Makes about 20 larger cakes; twice as many fish balls.

Souscaille   *Martinique*
Fresh Mango Appetizer

This is derived from the fresh mango chutneys of the Hindu agricultural workers who migrated to the north of Martinique in the 19th century. It makes an unusual and refreshing appetizer, or accompaniment to drinks. The mango used in Martinique is usually the mango vert, a rather stringy mango, not considered to be one of the fine dessert mangoes, known as mangue. Other mangoes are used in Martinique and as our choice of mangoes is not very wide, any type will do so long as it is green, that is, underripe. The mango is peeled and cut into slices and

*marinated in the hot sauce for at least 10 minutes, longer
if desired, then eaten by hand.*

Sauce Piquante

Hot Sauce

1 cup cold water
2 cloves garlic, crushed
½ teaspoon salt
Freshly ground pepper

1 or more fresh hot green
   peppers, finely
   chopped
¼ cup lime juice

Mix all the ingredients together. Add sliced green mangoes and marinate for at least 10 minutes. Eat by hand.

Sweet Potato Chips   *St. Vincent*

1 pound white (boniato)   **Oil for deep frying**
  sweet potatoes

Wash and peel the sweet potatoes and slice as thinly as possible. Soak for 1 hour in cold, salted water. Drain and dry on paper towels. Fry until delicately browned in deep oil heated to 370° on frying thermometer. Drain on paper towels, sprinkle with salt and keep warm in the oven until ready to serve, or serve at room temperature, as an accompaniment to drinks. Serve with a dip, if liked. Serves 4 or more.

Stamp and Go

Jamaica

Codfish Cakes

½ pound salt codfish
1 cup all-purpose flour
1 teaspoon baking
  powder
½ teaspoon salt
1 egg, lightly beaten
¾ cup milk
1 tablespoon butter,
  melted

1 tablespoon annatto
  coloring*
1 onion, finely chopped
1 fresh hot pepper,
  chopped
Vegetable oil or lard for
  deep frying

Put the codfish in a bowl, cover with warm water and soak for 2 hours or longer, according to the saltiness and hardness of the fish. Drain, rinse and place in a saucepan with boiling water to cover. Simmer gently, covered, until the fish is tender, about 15 minutes. Drain, remove bones and skin, and shred fish finely.

Sift the flour, baking powder and salt together. Combine the egg, milk, butter and annatto coloring and stir into the dry ingredients. Add the fish, onion and pepper and mix well. Drop by tablespoonful into hot oil (370° on a frying thermometer) and fry until golden brown. Drain on paper towels and serve hot. Makes about 24.

*Soak ½ teaspoon annatto seeds in 1 tablespoon boiling water for an hour, or until the water is a deep orange color. Strain. Discard seeds. Use liquid. Or use the butter in the recipe to make some coloring according to the recipe for Achiote Oil or Lard, (see Index).

Soups

Ackee Soup

Our cook, Annie, used to make a wonderful ackee soup, which I have never come across anywhere but in her kitchen. I suspect she invented it, using broken ackees left over from the salt fish and ackee that characterized our Fridays. Annie's salt fish and ackee was of an elegance, largely I think to beat down our resistance to salt fish, since, being English, we were devoted to the fresh caught article, or failing that, Finnan Haddie. Since canned ackees tend to have a number of broken pieces of the vegetable, it is ideal for ackee soup.

1 can ackees (1 pound 3 ounces), about 4 cups	Salt, freshly ground pepper to taste
1½ cups chicken stock	Pickapeppa hot pepper sauce, or Tabasco, to taste
½ cup tomatoes, peeled and chopped	
¼ cup shallots, chopped	½ cup heavy cream

Put the ackees together with the liquid from the can into a saucepan with the chicken stock, tomatoes, shallots,

36

salt and pepper to taste, cover and simmer gently until the shallots are tender. Purée in an electric blender. Return to the saucepan, season to taste with hot pepper sauce, stir in the cream and heat through. The soup is also very good served chilled. Serves 6.

The soup may be garnished, if liked with chopped chives or chopped parsley, or with sweet paprika.

Bouillon   *Haïti*

Modestly called bouillon, this is really a pot-au-feu.

1 stewing chicken, weighing 4–5 pounds	2 or 3 sprigs parsley
2 pounds shin of beef, cut into 2-inch cubes	½ teaspoon thyme
1 calf's foot, split	1 pound sweet potatoes, preferably white type, peeled and sliced
4 quarts water	1 pound potatoes, peeled and sliced
2 carrots, scraped and sliced	2 ripe plantains, or 3 underripe bananas, peeled and cut into 2-inch slices
2 stalks celery, sliced	
1 large onion, chopped	
2 cloves	
3 medium tomatoes, peeled, seeded and chopped	2 medium potatoes, peeled and left whole
1 bay leaf	Salt, freshly ground pepper

Put the fowl, with its giblets, the beef and the calf's foot into a large saucepan, or soup kettle. Add the water and bring to a boil. At the end of 10 minutes skim the surface thoroughly. Reduce to a simmer, cover and cook for 2 hours. Add the vegetables and seasonings, bring back to a simmer, cover, and cook for 1 hour longer. Lift out the two whole potatoes and mash. Stir into the soup. Remove the bay leaf, cloves, and parsley sprigs.

Cut the chicken into serving pieces. Take out and discard the bones in the calf's foot. Cut the meat into serving pieces.

Serve the hot bouillon in large, rimmed soup plates making sure each one gets some of the chicken, meat, and vegetables. Or arrange the hot meats and vegetables on a warmed platter and pour the soup into a warmed tureen. Serve meat, vegetables and soup in soup plates. Serves 8 to 10.

Black Bean Soup   *Trinidad*

1 pound (about 2 cups) black beans	2 small stalks celery with leaves, chopped
½ pound corned beef, or 1 pig's tail	4 scallions, chopped, using white and green parts
1 medium onion, chopped	Bay leaf
2 cloves garlic, crushed	6 cups beef, or chicken, stock
2 sprigs parsley	Freshly ground pepper
1 sprig thyme, or ½ teaspoon dried	Salt
	Pepper Wine (see Index)

Soak the beans overnight in cold water. Drain, and discard water. Put the beans into a large saucepan or soup kettle. Add the corned beef, left in one piece, or the pig's tail, the onion, garlic, parsley, thyme, celery, scallions, bay leaf, stock, and pepper. Bring to a boil, lower the heat, cover and simmer until the beans are very tender, about 2 hours. Discard bay leaf. Remove the corned beef, or the pig's tail. Purée the soup in an electric blender, or put through the fine blade of a food mill. Return the soup to the saucepan, and taste for seasoning, adding a little salt, if necessary. Heat through.

The corned beef may be chopped and added to the soup, if liked, or discarded. If using a pig's tail, discard. A little Pepper Wine may be added to each serving of the soup, if liked. Serves 6.

Bisque de Cribiches   *Martinique*
Freshwater Crayfish Bisque

*Ecrevisses, freshwater crayfish, abound in both Marti-
nique and Guadeloupe, and though not always available
in the Eastern part of the U.S. are easy to find in the
West and parts of the Midwest. In most of the English-
speaking islands, as in parts of the US., "crayfish" have
become "crawfish." In Martinique and Guadeloupe
"ércrevisses" have been transformed into "cribiches."*

4 tablespoons unsalted butter	1 small, fresh hot pepper, left whole
2 pounds crayfish, cleaned and shelled	4 cups water
1 onion, finely chopped	1 cup coconut milk
2 cloves garlic, chopped	2 egg yolks, or 1 tablespoon arrowroot
Sprig fennel (optional)	Salt

Heat the butter in a heavy saucepan and add the crayfish,
onion and garlic. Sauté over medium heat until the crayfish have changed color, about 5 minutes. Add the fennel,
hot pepper and water. Cover and cook at a gentle simmer
for 30 minutes. Remove and discard the fennel and the
hot pepper. Remove the crayfish and pound in a mortar
and push through a fine sieve, or reduce to a purée in an
electric blender with a little of the stock. Return the puréed crayfish to the saucepan. Add the coconut milk and
heat through. Beat the egg yolks with a little of the soup
and stir into the saucepan. Cook over low heat, stirring
constantly, until the soup is lightly thickened. Or mix the
arrowroot with a little water, add to the soup, and stir
over low heat until thickened. Serves 6.

   I like to simmer the crayfish shells for about 15 minutes
to make a stock instead of using plain water as this gives
a richer flavor.

Breadfruit Vichyssoise   *Grenada*

2 tablespoons unsalted
  butter
2 medium onions, finely
  chopped
1 clove garlic, chopped
½ pound fresh
  breadfruit, or ⅓ can
  (1-pound 10-ounce)
  breadfruit (see
  Glossary)

1 quart chicken stock
½ pint (1 cup) light
  cream
Salt, freshly ground
  white pepper to taste
Chopped chives

Heat the butter in a heavy saucepan and sauté the onions
and garlic until tender but not browned. If using fresh
breadfruit, peel the breadfruit, remove core and dice. If
using canned breadfruit, chop coarsely. Add the onions
and garlic with the chicken stock and cook, covered, at
a gentle simmer until the breadfruit is tender. Cool. Put
into an electric blender and blend until smooth, adding
the cream while blending. Season with salt and pepper.
Chill thoroughly. If the soup is too thick, thin with a little
milk. Serve soup sprinkled with chopped chives. Serves
6.

Cream of Pumpkin Soup   *Jamaica*

4 tablespoons unsalted
  butter
2 large onions, finely
  chopped
2 pounds West Indian
  pumpkin (calabaza), or
  use Hubbard squash
5 cups chicken stock

1 cup light cream
Salt, freshly ground
  pepper
Dash Pickapeppa hot
  pepper sauce, or
  Tabasco
Freshly ground nutmeg,
  if liked

Heat the butter in a large, heavy saucepan and sauté the
onions until tender but not browned. Pare the pumpkin,

remove any seeds and strings, and cut into 1-inch cubes.
Add the pumpkin and chicken stock, cover and simmer
until the pumpkin is disintegrating, about 45 minutes. Cool
slightly and put through sieve, or purée quickly in an
electric blender. Be careful not to overblend. Return to
saucepan, season to taste with salt and pepper, add the
cream and the hot pepper sauce and reheat gently. Pour
into a warmed soup tureen and sprinkle with nutmeg.
Serves 6.

Callaloo

This is perhaps the most famous of all the créole soups
and there are even more versions of it than there are ways
of spelling its name. It turns up as Calaloo, Callilu and
Callaloo. Trinidad is most generally credited with it, but
it also turns up in other islands, Jamaica, Grenada, Haïti,
Martinique, Guadeloupe, to name a few.

Essential to the dish is callaloo, which is a name given
the young leaves of certain aroids, such as taro. And here
one really runs into trouble with names since this refers
to a diverse group of tropical plants with edible tubers,
and sometimes edible leaves.

Everyone knows this family's inedible members: the
anthuriums, philodendrons, and calla lilies. Leaves of the
edible plants are variously known as dasheen, dachine,
eddoe, taro, elephant ear, tannia, taniers and yautía. Various members of the family are carefully distinguished
one from the other but really it makes very little difference
what either leaf or tuber is called, as they taste much the
same. One further complication: Chinese spinach, which
can often be found in Chinese markets, under that name
in English, or as hon-toi-moi or yin-choi, is also called
callaloo or bhaji in some of the islands. It can be bought
canned in markets that sell Caribbean foods, and fresh in
Chinese markets. Since taro leaves are seldom, if ever,
available, it is useful to have authentic substitutes, and I
have found that fresh garden spinach and Swiss chard
have much the same flavor and texture. No one needs go

without Callaloo for want of the right ingredients.

Usually just served as a soup, Callaloo is sometimes presented in a much more elaborate form in the French islands of Martinique and Guadeloupe. The soup is served in a tureen with riz créole and a chiquetaille of salt codfish, in separate dishes. Large old-fashioned rimmed soup plates would be ideal for serving this as a meal in itself.

Le Calalou   *Guadeloupe*

This is a much more elaborate version of callaloo soup. It is served with riz créole (rice) and chiquetaille de morue (codfish salad), as a complete meal.

3 pounds callaloo leaves, or spinach, Chinese spinach, or Swiss chard
½ pound okra, sliced
1 pound eggplant, peeled and coarsely chopped
4 tablespoons vegetable oil
4 ounces lean salt pork, cut into ½-inch cubes
3 green (unripe) bananas peeled and chopped

2 onions, finely chopped
2 cloves garlic, minced
½ teaspoon thyme
¼ teaspoon ground cloves
2 tablespoons chopped chives
1 fresh hot pepper, seeded and chopped
1 tablespoon white vinegar
Salt, pepper to taste
1 cup coconut milk

Wash, drain and coarsely chop the greens. Place in a large, heavy saucepan with the okra and eggplant and a quart of water. Cover and cook until the vegetables are very tender. Set aside.

In a heavy casserole heat the oil and try out the salt pork. Add the bananas, onions and garlic. Cover and cook gently until the bananas and onions are tender. Add all the rest of the ingredients and cook for a few minutes longer. Take out the cubes of salt pork and reserve. Rub mixture through a sieve. Add the cooked vegetable mixture and beat thoroughly with a *lélé*, if you have one. Or with an electric mixer or any beater until you have a light purée. If the mixture is very thick, add a little chicken stock or water. Return the cubes of pork to the casserole and heat through. The soup should be a thick, smooth purée. Serves 6.

Callau
St. Lucia

This is callaloo again as interpreted by the island of St. Lucia, called LOO-sha by its inhabitants. It can be seen, green and pretty, from the south of Martinique. Though the island changed hands 14 times between Britain and France, there seems little French, or indeed British, influence in the recipe.

1 pound callaloo leaves, or spinach, Chinese spinach, or Swiss chard
12 small okras
4-ounce slice corned beef
4-ounce piece of salt pork
½ pound crab meat
2 or 3 sprigs parsley

1 stalk celery, with leaves, chopped
4 scallions, chopped, using green and white parts
¼ teaspoon dried thyme
Freshly ground black pepper
1 fresh hot red pepper, left whole (optional)

If using callaloo leaves, cut into 1-inch lengths, wash and drain thoroughly, and blanch for 2 or 3 minutes by immersing in boiling water. Put the greens into a large saucepan or soup kettle with the okras, beef and salt pork left whole, crab meat, seasonings, using a generous amount of pepper, and 6 cups of water. Bring to a boil, cover, and simmer until the meats are tender and the soup quite thick. Slice the meat and put some into each soup bowl. Serve in rimmed soup plates. Serves 6.

Le Calalou
Martinique

This may be served as a soup, or if liked accompanied by riz Créole (white rice) and Morue grillée (grilled or broiled salt cod).

2 pounds callaloo leaves, or spinach, Chinese spinach, or Swiss chard	1 clove garlic, chopped
½ pound okra, sliced	4 scallions, chopped, using green and white parts
½ pound ham	1 tablespoon chopped parsley
1 fresh hot green pepper, seeded and chopped	Salt, freshly ground pepper
½ teaspoon thyme	1 quart water

Put all the ingredients in a large saucepan. Cover and simmer for an hour. Remove the ham and reserve. Beat the soup to a purée with a *lélé*, or a wire whisk. Chop the ham and return it to the soup which should be a smooth, fairly light purée. The ham may be kept for some other use. The soup, with the ham, may be puréed in an electric blender. Serves 6.

Le Calalou
Haïti

2 ounces salt pork, cut into ½-inch cubes	½ pound callaloo or spinach, Chinese spinach, or Swiss chard, coarsely chopped
3 slices bacon	
½ pound fillets of any white fish, cut into 1-inch pieces	1 teaspoon thyme
½ cup all-purpose flour	1 bay leaf
1 cup sliced okra	Salt, freshly ground pepper to taste
	6 cups chicken stock

Try out the salt pork in a frying pan. Add the bacon and fry until crisp. Lift out the bacon, drain on paper towels and crumble. Set aside.

Dust the fish with the flour. In the fat remaining in the pan, sauté the fish until golden on both sides. Transfer the fish, with the fat and any bits of salt pork, to a large, heavy saucepan. Add the okra, spinach, thyme, bay leaf, salt and pepper to taste and stock, and simmer gently until done, about half an hour. Sprinkle with the crumbled bacon. Serves 6.

Callalo
Trinidad

1 pound callaloo leaves or spinach, Chinese spinach, or Swiss chard
6 cups chicken stock
1 onion, finely chopped
1 clove garlic, chopped
2 or 3 scallions, chopped, using green and white parts
¼ teaspoon thyme
4 ounces lean salt pork, cut into ½-inch cubes

½ pound fresh, canned, or frozen crab meat
½ cup coconut milk
½ pound young okras, or 10-ounce package frozen okra, sliced
Salt, freshly ground pepper to taste
Pickapeppa hot pepper sauce, Tabasco or any similar sauce, to taste

Wash greens and chop coarsely. Put greens into a large heavy saucepan with the chicken stock, onion, garlic, scallions, thyme and salt pork. Cover and cook at a gentle simmer until the pork is tender. Add the crab meat, coconut milk, and okras and cook until the okras are done, about 10 minutes. Season to taste with salt, pepper and hot pepper sauce. Serves 6.

Serve with Foo-foo (See Index).

Coconut Soup

St. Kitts

8 ounces freshly grated coconut	2 tablespoons unsalted butter
6 cups chicken stock	½ cup heavy cream
2 tablespoons all-purpose flour	Salt, freshly ground white pepper

Combine the coconut and chicken stock in a heavy saucepan. Cover and cook at a gentle simmer for 30 minutes. Strain through a sieve. Discard the coconut after pressing down to extract all the liquid. Cream the flour and butter together and stir into the stock with the heavy cream, stirring over low heat until the soup is thickened. Season to taste with salt and pepper. Serves 6.

Consommé à L'Orange

Haïti

Orange Consommé

This is a good example of how the same idea results in different recipes from island to island. This was certainly the original orange soup, which turns up in Grenada transformed into Jellied Orange Consommée.

4 cups rich chicken stock, clarified and well seasoned	2 cloves
2 cups strained orange juice	1 orange, thinly sliced

Combine the chicken stock, orange juice and cloves in a saucepan, cover, and bring to a simmer over very low heat. Simmer for 2 or 3 minutes. Strain into bouillon cups and garnish with the orange slices. Serves 6. The soup may be served chilled.

VARIATION: Jellied Orange Consommé, Grenada.
Increase the orange juice to 3 cups and use ½ cup of it

to soften 2 envelopes (2 tablespoons) unflavored gelatin. Combine with all the other ingredients, except the sliced orange, in a saucepan and simmer, stirring, until the gelatin is dissolved. Take out and discard the cloves. Refrigerate until set. Serve in chilled bouillon cups, breaking up the gelatin before serving. Garnish with orange slices. Serves 6.

Crème de Navets
Cream of Turnip Soup

Northern Martinique

This recipe is from the family collection of Charles and Yveline de Lucy de Fossarieu, who have recently restored the De Leyritz Plantation as an Inn, at Basse Pointe in the north of Martinique. I was amused when Mme. de Fossarieu explained that it was a Northern dish. I realized I was being arrogant. An island of 50-by-19 miles is as entitled to a regional kitchen as anywhere else. The Colombos, curries brought in by Indian plantation workers, are also considered Northern dishes, developed and modified by the genius of France in the kitchen.

1 pound white turnips	6 cups rich whole milk
1½ tablespoons	(3 pints)
unsalted butter	Salt
	White pepper

Peel the turnips and slice thinly. Heat 1 tablespoon of the butter in a saucepan large enough to hold all the ingredients, and toss the turnips in the butter for 2 or 3 minutes. Add the milk, salt and pepper to taste and cook, partially covered, stirring from time to time, and taking care not to let the milk boil over. The turnips will be tender in about 20 to 25 minutes. Purée in an electric blender, or push through a sieve or the fine blade of a food mill. Adjust the seasoning and heat through. Serves 6.

Chip-Chip Soup

Trinidad

Chip-chips are small tropical clams, with hatchet-shaped shells about ¾-of-an-inch long on the straight sides. Their flavor, perhaps less pronounced, is very similar to that of the clams available in the U.S., though Chip-chip soup is very different from either New England or Manhattan Clam Chowder. Local clams are an excellent substitute for chip-chips.

4 dozen clams
¾ pound potatoes, or tannias, peeled and cut into ½-inch cubes
1 large onion, finely chopped
2 scallions, halved
½ teaspoon thyme

1 whole fresh green or red pepper, or Pepper Wine (see Index) to taste
Salt, freshly ground pepper
1 tablespoon tomato paste
2 tablespoons unsalted butter
1 tablespoon lime or lemon juice

Wash and scrub clams in several waters to remove any sand. Rinse well. Place in a large saucepan with about 1-inch of water, cover pan tightly and cook until the shells open. Discard any with unopened shells. Remove the clams from the opened shells, discard necks and reserve clams. Strain the liquor from the pan through cheese cloth. Measure and add chicken stock or water to make 6 cups. Return liquid to the saucepan, add the potatoes, onion and scallions. Tie the thyme and hot pepper in a piece of cheesecloth and add to the pan. Season to taste with salt and pepper and cook, covered, until the potatoes are tender. Remove and discard the scallions and the cheesecloth bag. Put the potato mixture through a sieve, or purée it in an electric blender. Return to the saucepan, add the tomato paste and sweet butter and heat gently. Stir in the lime juice. Put the clams into a warmed tureen, or individual soup plates, and pour the hot soup over them. Serves 6.

Instead of using clams in the shell, substitute three 1½-pint cans of steamed clams in their shells. Strain and measure the liquid making up the quantity, if necessary, and follow the recipe.

Cream of Crab Soup   *Barbados*

2 tablespoons unsalted
  butter
2 tablespoons all-purpose
  flour
2 hard-boiled eggs
Juice and finely grated
  rind 1 lime, or lemon
3 cups fish stock

2 cups milk
1 cup light cream
½ pound crab meat,
  flaked
Salt, freshly ground
  pepper
Dash Angostura bitters
¼ cup dry sherry

Melt the butter in a saucepan and add the flour. Cook, stirring, for a minute or two. Remove from the heat and add the eggs, mashing them to a smooth paste. Add the juice and rind of the lime, the fish stock, milk, cream and crab meat. Return the saucepan to the heat and simmer gently, stirring from time to time, for 10 minutes. Season with salt and pepper, add the bitters and sherry and reheat gently. Serves 6.

Chilled Cream of
Cucumber Soup   *Barbados*

3 medium cucumbers,
  about 1½ pounds,
  peeled and chopped
1 medium onion, finely
  chopped
5 cups chicken stock

Salt and white pepper to
  taste
2 teaspoons arrowroot
1 cup heavy cream
1 tablespoon chopped
  chives

Put the cucumbers, onion and stock into a heavy saucepan, cover, and simmer gently for 15 minutes. Cool a little, then pour into an electric blender and reduce to a purée. Strain and return to the saucepan. Season to taste with salt and pepper. Mix the arrowroot with 1 tablespoon of water and stir into the soup, simmer, until lightly thickened, but do not boil. Stir the cream into the soup. Chill and serve garnished with the chives. Serves 6.

Trident Pumpkin Soup   *Jamaica*

This very elegant version of pumpkin soup was created by John Macy, at Trident Villas & Hotel, *Port Antonio.*

1½ pounds West
   Indian pumpkin
   (calabaza) or use
   Hubbard squash
6 cups chicken stock
Salt, freshly ground
   pepper to taste

⅜ cup dry sherry
½ pound or ½ pint
   shelled oysters, and
   their liquor
1 cup heavy cream

Peel the pumpkin, remove any seeds and strings, and cut into 1-inch cubes. Put into a large saucepan with the stock. Cover and simmer gently, stirring with a wooden spoon from time to time, until the pumpkin is disintegrating, about 45 minutes. The texture of this soup should be nice and lumpy; if the pumpkin lumps are too large, mash them with the spoon against the sides of the saucepan. Season to taste with salt and pepper, stir in the sherry, add the oysters and the cream and cook just long enough for the edges of the oysters to curl and to heat the soup. Serves 4 to 6.

    Shrimp cut into ½-inch pieces, or diced lobster, or crab meat can be used instead of the oysters.

Eggplant Soup   *Nevis*

2 eggplants, each
  weighing about
  1-pound
4 ounces unsalted butter
1 medium onion, finely
  chopped

2 scallions, sliced, using
  both green and white
  parts
4 cups chicken stock
¼ teaspoon dried
  thyme
Salt, freshly ground
  pepper
1 cup heavy cream

Peel the eggplants and cut into ¼-inch slices. Cut enough
eggplant into ¼-inch cubes to make 2 cups and set aside.
Heat half of the butter in a saucepan large enough to hold
all the ingredients and sauté the onion and scallions until
tender, but not browned. Add the sliced eggplant, the
stock and the thyme. Season to taste with salt and pepper
and cook, covered, at a simmer until the eggplant is tender,
about 15 minutes. Purée in an electric blender, or put
through the fine blade of a food mill. Return to the saucepan and adjust the seasoning. Stir in the cream, and heat
the soup through.

Meanwhile, heat the remaining butter in a heavy frying
pan and sauté the 2 cups of eggplant cubes, stirring frequently, until they are browned all over. Add to the hot
soup and serve immediately. Serves 6.

Groundnut Soup
                                                    St. Kitts

Peanuts are often called groundnuts in the English-speaking islands.

4 ounces (¾ cup) peeled and roasted peanuts	1 cup heavy cream, or evaporated milk
5 cups chicken stock	1 tablespoon Angostura bitters
Salt, freshly ground pepper	Dry sherry, or dry vermouth (optional)
Pickapepper hot pepper sauce, or Tabasco	Croutons, or chopped chives

Put the peanuts and enough chicken stock to cover in an electric blender and blend on high speed to a smooth paste. Pour into a heavy saucepan, add the rest of the stock, season to taste with salt and pepper and hot pepper sauce. Cook over low heat, stirring from time to time, for about 15 minutes. Stir in the cream and cook, stirring, until heated through. Stir in the Angostura bitters.

A tablespoon of dry sherry, or dry vermouth, may be added to each serving. Garnish with croutons and serve hot. Or chill and serve sprinkled with chives. Serves 6.

Lobster Chowder with Foo Foo
                                                    Jamaica

Botanist, columnist and cookbook author, Dr. Alex D. Hawkes, a friend who now lives and works in Jamaica, was kind enough to let me have his favorite Jamaican Lobster Chowder recipe. The lobsters are, of course, Jamaican crawfish or crayfish, better known here as rock or spiny lobsters.

4 1-pound rock lobsters,
   or lobsters, or use
   frozen rock lobster
   tails
½ cup coconut, or
   vegetable, oil
6 cups rich fish stock
⅓ cup chopped
   scallions using green
   and white parts
⅓ cup scraped and
   chopped carrots
2 tablespoons finely
   chopped parsley
2 teaspoons sweet
   paprika

3 tablespoons tomato
   paste
Salt
6 whole peppercorns
⅓ cup brandy
2 tablespoons unsalted
   butter
2 tablespoons all-purpose
   flour
1½ cups coconut
   cream (see Index)
¼ cup Madeira
Foo Foo Balls (see Index)
   for garnish

Cut the lobsters in halves, lengthwise. Heat the oil in a large saucepan, or soup kettle, and add the lobster halves. Sauté, stirring constantly, until the shells turn red. Drain off and discard the oil. Add the fish stock, scallions, carrots, parsley, paprika, tomato paste, salt to taste, and peppercorns.

Cover and simmer gently for 10 minutes. Remove the lobsters, and when cool enough to handle take the meat from the shells and cut it into bite-size pieces. Set aside.

Pound the shells, using a mortar and pestle, until they are reduced to a fine powder. Place in a small, heavy saucepan. Warm the brandy and pour over the shells, and ignite. When the flames die down, add to the chowder. Stir to mix, cover and simmer for 30 minutes. Strain, rinse the saucepan and return the chowder to it.

In a small, heavy saucepan, melt the butter, stir in the flour, and cook, stirring constantly for 1 or 2 minutes. Gradually stir in coconut cream, and cook, stirring constantly, until the mixture has thickened. Add the Madeira, then pour into the chowder. Add the reserved lobster meat and heat through. Adjust the seasoning and serve in soup bowls, garnished with the Foo Foo Balls, one or more according to taste. Serves 6 to 8.

Pumpkin Soup

Trinidad

1½ pounds West
    Indian pumpkin
    (calabaza) or use
    Hubbard squash
½ green pepper,
    seeded and coarsely
    chopped
1 onion, finely chopped
1 clove garlic, chopped
Bouquet garni of sprig
    thyme, sprig
    marjoram, sprig celery
    with leaves, 2 or 3
    sprigs parsley, 1 bay

leaf, and 3 or 4 blades of
    chive tied in piece of
    cheesecloth.
1 medium tomato,
    peeled, seeded and
    chopped
5 cups chicken stock
Salt and freshly ground
    pepper to taste
1 cup heavy cream
Pepper Wine (see Index)

Peel the pumpkin and cut it into 1-inch cubes. Place the pumpkin in a large saucepan with the bell pepper, onion, garlic, *bouquet garni*, tomato, and chicken stock. Cover, simmer gently until the pumpkin pieces begin to disintegrate, about an hour. Remove the *bouquet garni* and discard it. Rub the soup through a sieve, or purée in an electric blender. Return to the saucepan, season to taste with salt and pepper, stir in the cream and heat through without letting the soup come to a boil. Add a dash of Pepper Wine to each serving. Serves 6.

Jigote

Cuba

Chicken Consommé

Traditionally served at elegant parties and receptions in Cuba, this rich consommé, in bouillon cups, was handed to guests at midnight, and indicated that refreshments, usually a lavish buffet, were about to be served. The custom, though no longer wide-spread, still lingers on, and I have met it in several countries of Latin-America.

1 stewing chicken,
weighing 4–5 pounds

3 pounds shin of beef, cut
into 2-inch cubes

2 or 3 veal bones

4 quarts water

2 carrots, scraped and
sliced

2 small white turnips,
peeled and sliced

1 stalk celery, with leaves

1 large onion, peeled and
stuck with 2 cloves

4 medium tomatoes,
sliced

1 clove garlic

1 bay leaf

2 or 3 sprigs parsley

Salt, freshly ground
pepper

½ teaspoon allspice

1 cup dry sherry

Put the fowl, with its giblets, the beef and veal bones into a large saucepan or soup kettle. Add the water and bring to a boil. At the end of 10 minutes skim the surface thoroughly.

Reduce to a simmer, cover and cook for 3 hours. Add the vegetables and seasonings, bring back to a simmer, cover, and cook for 2 hours more. The broth should by now be reduced to about 3 quarts. Strain, cool, and refrigerate.

Remove the fat from the surface, then strain the consommé through a sieve lined with a dampened linen napkin to remove any remaining traces of fat. Return the consommé to the saucepan, add the sherry and heat through.

Grind the tender parts of the cooked gizzard, liver, and chicken breast together. Put a teaspoonful of this in the bottom of each bouillon cup in which the soup is to be served, and add the hot consommé. Serves 12.

Red Bean Soup
with Dumplings
St. Croix

1 pound (about 2 cups),
  red kidney, chili, or
  California pink beans
2 quarts water
½ pound pork or ham,
  cubed
1 medium onion, finely
  chopped
½ teaspoon thyme
1 or 2 sprigs parsley

Small celery stalk with
  leaves
1 medium tomato,
  peeled, seeded and
  chopped
1 teaspoon sugar
Salt, freshly ground
  pepper
1 ripe plantain
Dumplings

Put the beans into a large saucepan or soup kettle with
the water, pork or ham, onion, thyme, parsley, celery,
tomato and sugar. Cook, covered, at a simmer until the
beans are tender, 2 to 3 hours. Season to taste with salt
and freshly ground pepper. Peel and slice the ripe plantain
and add to the soup. Continue cooking until the plantain
is tender, and the beans have disintegrated, about half an
hour. Remove the parsley and celery. Add the dumplings
and cook 15 minutes longer. The beans should disintegrate
to form a purée, but not a very smooth one. The soup
should retain some texture. Serves 6 to 8.

DUMPLINGS:

1 cup all-purpose flour
¼ cup corn meal
1 teaspoon sugar
1 teaspoon salt

½ teaspoon pepper
2 tablespoons unsalted
  butter

Sift the dry ingredients together. Rub the butter into the
dry ingredients with the fingertips until the mixture is
crumbly. Add enough water to make a fairly stiff dough.
Form into balls about half the size of a walnut and drop
into the hot bean soup. Cover and cook until the dumplings are done, about 15 minutes. Makes about 30 dumplings.

Traditionally both dumplings and plantain are added to this soup, making it almost a meal in itself. Either or both may be omitted for a lighter soup.

Red Pea Soup   *Jamaica*

The red peas in this soup are not the red kidney bean, though this may be used. They are a close relative, slightly smaller and marketed under a variety of names, sometimes as California pink beans, sometimes as Mexican chili beans. This is one of the most famous of the Jamaican soups.

1 pound (2 cups, about) red beans
2 quarts water
¼ pound salt pork, diced
1 medium onion, finely chopped
2 or 3 sprigs parsley

½ teaspoon dried thyme
Small stalk celery with leaves
1 fresh hot red pepper, seeded and chopped, or Pickapepper hot pepper sauce
Salt

Wash the beans thoroughly, drain and put on to cook with 2 quarts water, salt pork, onion, parsley, thyme, celery and fresh hot pepper. Cover, and cook at a simmer until the beans are very tender, about 2½ to 3 hours. Remove the parsley, and celery. Purée the bean soup quickly in an electric blender, or put through the coarse blade of a food mill. The purée should retain some texture.

Return the soup to the saucepan and season to taste with salt. If using Pickapepper hot pepper sauce, add to taste at this point. Heat through and serve. If the soup is too thick, thin with a little hot water. Serves 6.

Pepperpot Soup

Jamaica

This soup should not be confused with the pepperpot stew, containing cassareep, which comes originally from Guyana and has spread to Trinidad, Barbados and beyond. A very similar soup is popular in Antigua.

1 pound shin of beef, cubed
½ pound corned beef or salt pork, cubed
2 quarts water
1 pound kale, or collard greens, chopped
1 pound callaloo, or spinach, or Chinese spinach, chopped
1 onion, chopped
1 clove garlic, chopped
4 scallions, chopped using green and white parts
½ teaspoon dried thyme

1 fresh hot green pepper, chopped
½ pound yam, peeled and sliced
½ pound coco (taro) peeled and sliced
Salt, freshly ground pepper
1 dozen okras
1 tablespoon unsalted butter
4 ounces small cooked shrimp
1 cup coconut milk

Put the meats on to cook in a large saucepan, or soup kettle with 6 cups of water. Simmer, covered for 1 hour. Put the kale and callaloo with 2 cups of water into another saucepan and cook until tender, about 30 minutes. Rub the kale and callaloo through a sieve, or purée in an electric blender. Then add, with all the liquid to the meats, together with the onion, garlic, scallions, thyme, pepper, yam, coco, and salt and pepper to taste. Cover, and simmer until the meats are tender and the coco and yam are done.

Slice the okras. Heat the butter in a small frying pan and sauté the okras until lightly browned. Add to the soup. Add the shrimp and the coconut milk and simmer for 5 minutes longer. Dumplings (see Index) may be added to the soup in the last 15 minutes of cooking, if liked. Serves 6 to 8.

Pâté en Pot   *Martinique*
Lamb Soup

This is a traditional Martinique party soup and is served at engagement parties, weddings, baptisms, and first communion parties as the first course of the meal. It is also served at a special barbecue called a mechoui, when a whole lamb, or sheep, is roasted on a spit. In this way nothing of the lamb is wasted.

Head, liver, tripe and feet of lamb, cleaned ready for cooking
1 onion, chopped
2 cloves garlic, chopped
2 or 3 sprigs parsley
1 sprig celery with leaves
4 cloves
3 bay leaves
Salt, freshly ground pepper
½ cup vegetable oil
1 pound carrots, scraped and diced
1 pound West Indian pumpkin (calabaza), or use Hubbard squash, peeled and cubed

1 pound white turnips, peeled and cubed
1 pound potatoes, peeled and cubed
3 leeks, washed and chopped, or 6 scallions using green and white parts
1 pound cabbage, chopped
1 pound ham, cut into 1-inch cubes
4 ounces bacon, chopped
2 cups dry white wine, or 1 cup Madeira
1 small bottle capers (about ½ cup)

Put the lamb parts into a large saucepan, or soup kettle with the onion, garlic, parsley, celery, cloves, bay leaves, and salt and pepper. Add enough cold water to cover by about 1½ inches, bring to a boil and simmer, uncovered, for about 10 minutes, skimming from time to time. Then cover and cook briskly for 30 minutes longer.

Lift out the meat, remove and discard the bones. Cut into small pieces. Strain the stock and set aside.

Rinse out and dry the saucepan. Add the oil and when it is hot add the lamb meat and the carrots, pumpkins, turnips, potatoes, leeks, cabbage, ham and bacon. Sauté, stirring, for about 5 minutes. Add the reserved stock, cover and simmer for 2 hours. Add the white wine or Madeira, and the capers, undrained. Adjust the seasoning, and heat through. Serve hot in soup bowls. The soup should be very thick; if it is too thin, cook, uncovered for part of the cooking time to reduce the liquid. Serves 12.

Saucochi di Gallinja   *Aruba*

Chicken Soup

3-pound chicken
2 pounds beef and veal soup bones
2 quarts water
2 medium tomatoes, peeled, and coarsely chopped
1 pound onions, chopped
2 medium potatoes, peeled and sliced
2 sweet potatoes, peeled and sliced
½ pound West Indian pumpkin (calabaza), or use Hubbard squash, peeled and diced

2 ears sweet corn, each cut into 3 pieces
1 ripe plantain, peeled and cut into ½-inch slices
3 carrots, scraped and sliced
2 fresh hot red or green peppers, left whole
½ cup peas
½ teaspoon thyme
Salt, freshly ground pepper
Olives and capers for garnish (optional)

Put the chicken, left whole, into a large soup kettle or saucepan. Add the soup bones and the water. Cover and simmer gently for 30 minutes. Add all the rest of the ingredients (except olives and capers) and continue to cook, covered, until the chicken and vegetables are tender, about 30 minutes longer. Discard the soup bones. Remove the chicken and cut into 6 to 8 serving pieces. Place these in a large warmed soup tureen. Pour in the hot soup. Garnish with olives and capers if liked. Serve in rimmed soup plates. Serves 6 to 8.

Sopa de Camarones
Shrimp Soup

Cuba

1 pound medium shrimp	Bay leaf
3 tablespoons unsalted butter	2 cloves
1 medium onion, finely chopped	6 new potatoes, scraped and halved
1 clove garlic, minced	4 cups milk
3 large tomatoes, peeled, seeded and coarsely chopped	2 ears sweet corn, each cut into 6 slices
	2 egg yolks
	6 poached eggs (optional)

Shell the shrimp and set aside. Heat 1 tablespoon of the butter in a small frying pan and sauté the shrimp shells for 2 or 3 minutes. Transfer to a small saucepan, add 2 cups water and boil until reduced in half. Strain and set the stock aside. Discard shells.

Heat the remaining 2 tablespoons of butter in a larger pan and sauté the onion and garlic until the onion is tender but not browned. Add the tomatoes, bay leaf, cloves and shrimp shell stock. Cover and cook for 15 minutes. Strain. Return to the saucepan and add the potatoes. Cover and simmer until the potatoes are almost done, about 15 minutes. Add the milk, shrimp, and corn and cook, covered for 5 minutes.

Beat the egg yolks lightly. Beat 3 or 4 tablespoons of the hot soup into the yolks, then stir the egg mixture into the soup over low heat until it thickens slightly. Serve in rimmed soup plates with a potato, 2 slices of corn and some shrimps in each plate.

A poached egg may be added if liked, in which case poach the eggs during the last few minutes of cooking the soup, as overcooking will toughen the shrimp. Serves 6.

This soup makes an admirable lunch if followed by a green salad, cheese and fruit.

Sopa de Frijol Negro   *Cuba*
Black Bean Soup

2 cups black beans	Salt, freshly ground
1 cup sofrito (see Index)	pepper
½ teaspoon ground	Finely chopped white
cumin	onion for garnish
4 cups, about, of beef or	Pepper Wine (see Index)
chicken stock	

Wash the beans thoroughly, drain and put into a large saucepan or soup kettle with the sofrito, cumin, and enough water to cover by about 2 inches. Bring to a boil, lower the heat, cover and simmer for 2 to 3 hours, or until the beans are very tender. If necessary add a little hot water from time to time.

Drain the cooked beans. Measure the liquid and add enough stock to bring the quantity up to 6 cups. Purée the beans in an electric blender with some of the liquid, or put through a food mill or sieve. Return the beans and liquid to the saucepan, taste for seasoning adding salt and pepper to taste. Simmer gently for 15 minutes longer. Serve in soup bowls with a little chopped white onion as garnish. Pepper Wine may be added at table as liked. Serves 6 to 8.

VARIATION: Sopa de Habichuelas Negras (Black Bean Soup) Puerto Rico.
Put the beans on to cook with the sofrito and 8 cups of chicken stock. Simmer gently, covered, for 2½–3 hours. Season to taste with salt and freshly ground pepper, and serve. The soup should be quite thick, the beans still whole but on the point of disintegrating. If the beans absorb so much liquid during cooking that the soup is drying out, add hot stock or water.

Sopa de Gandules *Puerto Rico*
Green Pigeon Pea Soup

1 pound green pigeon peas, fresh or canned	use Hubbard squash, peeled and cut into 1-inch cubes
6 cups chicken stock	1 cup sofrito (see Index)
1 pound West Indian pumpkin (calabaza), or	Salt, freshly ground pepper

Combine the pigeon peas, stock, pumpkin and sofrito in a large saucepan, cover and simmer gently until the pigeon peas are tender and the pumpkin has disintegrated and thickened the soup, about 20 minutes. Season to taste with salt and pepper if necessary. Serves 6.

Sopa de Plátanos Verdes *Puerto Rico*
Green Plantain Soup

2 green plantains	6 cups rich beef stock
Salt	Grated Parmesan cheese
4 tablespoons vegetable oil or lard for frying	

Peel the plantains and cut into ½-inch slices. Soak in cold, salted water for 20 minutes. Drain and pat dry with paper towels. Heat the lard or oil in a heavy frying pan and sauté the plantain slices until they are tender, about 15 minutes. Lift out and drain on paper towels. Crush in a mortar so that they break into bits. Heat the beef stock in a saucepan and add the plantain bits. Simmer for 15 minutes longer. Serve sprinkled generously with the cheese. Serves 6.

Sopa de Pollo

Dominican Republic

Chicken Soup

3-pound chicken, cut into
  8 pieces
¼ cup Seville (bitter)
  orange juice, or use
  ⅔ orange and ⅓
  lemon juice mixed
Chicken giblets
½ pound West Indian
  pumpkin (calabaza), or
  use Hubbard squash,
  peeled and cubed
2 quarts chicken stock
Bay leaf
2 grains melegueta
  pepper (Grains of
  Paradise), or 2 allspice
  berries
1 fresh hot red or green
  pepper, left whole

1 sprig each coriander
  and parsley, preferably
  flat type parsley
1 large onion, chopped
3 cloves garlic, mashed
½ pound carrots,
  scraped and sliced
1 pound potatoes, peeled
  and sliced
1 pound (about 4
  medium) tomatoes,
  peeled, seeded and
  chopped
2 ounces vermicelli
Salt
1 tablespoon cane
  vinegar, or white
  distilled

Put the chicken pieces in a large bowl and pour the Seville orange juice over them. Let stand for 5 minutes, drain, discarding the juice. Transfer the chicken to a soup kettle or large saucepan with the giblets, pumpkin, stock, bay leaf, melegueta pepper or allspice, hot pepper, coriander, parsley, onion and garlic. Cover and cook at a gentle simmer for 45 minutes.

Remove the chicken pieces and reserve. Strain the broth, rinse out the kettle and return the chicken pieces and the broth to the kettle together with the carrots, potatoes, tomatoes and vermicelli and cook covered, over low heat for 20 minutes, or until all the ingredients are tender. Add a little salt if necessary. Add the vinegar and cook for 1 or 2 minutes longer. Serve in rimmed soup bowls with a piece of chicken in each serving. Serves 8.

Sopito

Curaçao

Fish and Coconut Soup

½ pound corned beef
1½ pounds whole fish,
   such as red snapper,
   sea bass, or striped
   bass, cleaned and
   scaled
2 medium onions, finely
   chopped
2 tablespoons chopped
   shallots
2 stalks celery, chopped
1 green bell pepper,
   peeled, seeded and
   chopped

2 bay leaves
2 leaves fresh basil, or 1
   teaspoon dried
3 cloves
½ teaspoon ground
   cumin
Salt
3 tablespoons yellow corn
   meal
1 cup coconut cream

Cover beef with boiling water and let stand until cold. In a large saucepan or soup kettle bring 2 quarts of water to a boil with 1 of the onions, 1 tablespoon of the shallots, 1 of the stalks of celery, the green pepper, bay leaves, basil, cloves, cumin and a little salt. Simmer, covered for 20 minutes. Add the fish and poach until it flakes easily with a fork. Strain, reserving the fish and other solids. Remove and discard the cloves and bay leaves. Reserve the fish stock.

Drain the beef, and rinse with fresh cold water. Cut into ½-inch cubes, and put into the pan with the strained fish stock, and the remaining onion, shallots and celery. Cook, covered, until the meat is tender, about 1½ hours. Sprinkle the corn meal over the soup and stir for a minute or two. Stir in the coconut cream.

Bone the fish, and cut it into 1½-inch pieces. Return it and the other strained out solids to the soup, taste for seasoning, and heat through, but do not let it boil. Serve with Funchi (see Index). Serves 6.

Soppi Mondongo

Curaçao

Tripe Soup

2 pounds tripe
¼ cup lime juice
2 pig's feet, split and
    cleaned for cooking
Salt
½ pound corned beef
1 onion, coarsely chopped
¼ cup chopped
    shallots
1 stalk celery, coarsely
    chopped
1 pound West Indian
    pumpkin (calabaza), or
    use Hubbard squash,
    peeled and cut into 1-
    inch cubes
1 sweet potato,
    preferably white type,
    peeled and cubed

3 potatoes, peeled and
    cubed
6 pitted green olives
1 tablespoon capers
1 tablespoon seeded
    raisins
1 green bell pepper,
    seeded and coarsely
    chopped
1 fresh hot green pepper,
    seeded and chopped
Freshly ground pepper
¼ teaspoon grated
    nutmeg
¼ teaspoon ground
    cloves

Wash and drain the tripe. Pour the lime juice over it and let it stand for 10 minutes. Transfer the tripe to a large saucepan, or soup kettle. Add the pig's feet and 3 quarts salted water. Cook until tender about 2½ to 3 hours. Meanwhile, pour boiling water over the corned beef, and allow to stand for ¾ hour. Drain, rinse and add to the cooking tripe. When the meats are tender let cool. Cut the tripe into strips about ¾-inch wide, and the corned beef into ½-inch cubes. Remove the meat from the pig's feet and discard the bones. Put all the vegetables into the stock, with the meats, and seasonings. Simmer gently until the vegetables are tender. About 30 minutes.

Cooks in Curaçao say the soup should be left to cool and stand for 3 hours or so after it is cooked, then reheated, as this improves the flavor. They often add a tablespoon of dry sherry or brandy to each soup plate. Serve with crusty French bread. Serves 10 to 12.

Soupe au Poisson   *Martinique-Guadeloupe*

Fish Soup

Fish soup is popular in both islands and, though there is a standard recipe, each cook adds his or her special touch. M. Mario Petrelluzzi, the moving spirit of La Pergola Restaurant *at Gosier, in Guadeloupe, used to add half a cup of Ricard to his soup. And the cooks at the* Bakoua Hotel *at Trois Ilets in Martinique, add croutons and grated Gruyère cheese to theirs. In both cases with admirable results.*

3 tablespoons plain, or annatto olive oil or unsalted butter (see Index)

2 medium onions, finely chopped

4 scallions, chopped, using green and white parts

1 pound tomatoes, peeled, seeded and chopped

⅛ teaspoon ground saffron if using plain oil or butter, otherwise omit

½ teaspoon ground ginger

2½ quarts water

3 pounds whole fish, such as snapper, sea bass, striped bass or other white fish, cleaned and scaled

2 fresh hot red peppers, left whole

2 cloves garlic, crushed

2 cloves

2 melegueta pepper berries or 2 allspice berries

1 bay leaf

1 pound potatoes, peeled and sliced

Heat the oil or butter in a large saucepan and sauté the onions and scallions until the onions are golden. Add the tomatoes and cook, stirring, for 1 or 2 minutes. Add the remaining ingredients, bring to a boil, lower the heat and cook, uncovered, at a brisk simmer for 30 minutes.

Lift out the fish, remove and discard the bones and set the fish aside. Put the soup through a sieve, pressing down to extract all the juices. Return the fish and soup to the

saucepan and heat through. If preferred, the fish may be
pressed through the sieve. Serves 6 to 8.

Tannia Soup   *Dominica*

*This root vegetable, tannia, has a bewildering variety of
names but is best known in U.S. markets as dasheen and
yautia. There are slight differences between the members
of this vegetable family but they are not great enough to
seriously alter the taste or texture of a dish. The plants
are sometimes called Elephant Ear or Purple Elephant
Ear. The leaves are used to make callalou soup.*

2 tablespoons unsalted
   butter
½ pound lean salt
   pork, cut into
   ½-inch cubes
1 onion, finely chopped
2 quarts chicken or beef
   stock
2 pounds tannias, peeled
   and cubed

1 cup tomatoes, peeled,
   seeded, and coarsely
   chopped
⅛ teaspoon thyme
Salt, fresh ground pepper
   to taste
1 tablespoon chopped
   parsley

Heat the butter in a heavy saucepan, add the salt pork
and onion and sauté until the onion is tender but not
browned. Add the stock, tannias, tomatoes, and thyme,
and season to taste with salt and pepper. Cook at a gentle
simmer until the tannias are tender and have thickened
the soup. Stir from time to time to prevent the soup from
burning. The tannias will partly disintegrate but the soup
should not be cooked down to a purée. Sprinkle with
chopped parsley. Serves 6.

If liked, a cup of chopped spinach may be added with
the tannias.

Fish and Shellfish

Arroz Con Camarones   *Dominican Republic*
Shrimp and Rice

4 tablespoons achiote oil (see Index)	1 tablespoon fresh coriander, chopped
1 large onion, finely chopped	1 bay leaf
2 cloves garlic, minced	Salt, freshly ground pepper
2 cups long grain rice	Oil or butter
4 cups chicken stock	1 pound raw shrimp, peeled, deveined and cut into ½-inch pieces
2 medium tomatoes, peeled, seeded and chopped	

Heat the achiote oil in a heavy 10 to 12-inch covered frying pan. Sauté the onion and garlic until the onion is tender but not browned. Add the rice, stir and cook until the rice has absorbed all the oil, taking care not to let it brown. Add the chicken stock, tomatoes, coriander, bay leaf, and salt and pepper to taste. Cover, and cook at a gentle simmer until the rice is tender and all the liquid absorbed.

Heat a little oil or butter in a frying pan and toss the shrimp in the fat over fairly high heat until they are pink,

3 or 4 minutes. Add the shrimp to the rice, mixing gently and cook, covered, for a minute or so longer. It is important not to overcook the shrimp, as this toughens them. Serve with a fresh hot pepper sauce. I like to shell the shrimp and set them aside, then make a stock from the shells. Used in place of the chicken stock, this gives the rice a very rich shrimp flavor. Serves 4.

TO MAKE SHRIMP STOCK

In a small saucepan, heat 1 tablespoon of oil or butter and toss the shells in this until they turn pink. Add a sprig of parsley, a leaf of basil, ⅛ teaspoon orégano or marjoram, ⅛ teaspoon thyme, a clove of garlic, sprig of celery leaves, 1 or 2 cloves of allspice, and salt and pepper to taste, add 5 cups of water, bring to a boil, reduce the heat and simmer, covered for 30 minutes. Strain and measure, making up the quantity to 4 cups with water.

Ackee and Shrimp   Jamaica

1 pound medium size raw
    shrimp
1 can ackee (1-pound
    3-ounces), or 1 pound
    fresh ackees
2 tablespoons butter
1 onion, finely chopped
1 clove garlic, minced
½ teaspoon marjoram
2 tablespoons golden rum

1 cup ackee-shrimp stock
1 tablespoon mixed
    mustard, preferably
    Dijon type
1 teaspoon Pickapeppa
    hot pepper sauce, or
    Tobasco
½ cup tomato purée
Salt, freshly ground
    pepper to taste
2 teaspoons arrowroot

Shell and devein the shrimp. Drain the ackees and add water to make the liquid up to 2 cups. Put the shrimp shells and the ackee liquid on to cook. Simmer until liquid is reduced to 1 cup. Strain and set stock aside.

Heat the butter in a heavy frying pan and sauté the onion, garlic and marjoram until the onion is tender but not browned. Add the shrimp and cook for 2 or 3 minutes. Heat the rum, pour over the shrimp, light and let the flame burn out. Add the ackee-shrimp stock, the ackees, the mustard mixed with the hot pepper sauce, the tomato purée, and salt and pepper to taste. Simmer gently until heated through. Mix the arrowroot with 1 tablespoon of water, stir into the shrimp mixture and cook until lightly thickened. Pile hot shrimp mixture in the center of a warmed platter. Surround with plain boiled white rice. Serves 4 to 6.

Bombas de Camarones y Papas
Dominican Republic

Shrimp and Potato Balls

2 pounds potatoes
6 tablespoons sweet
  butter
2 egg yolks
4 ounces Muenster
  cheese, grated
1 tablespoon chopped
  parsley
Salt, white pepper
1 medium onion, finely
  chopped

2 pounds cooked shrimp,
  shelled, deveined, and
  coarsely chopped
Flour
1 egg, lightly beaten
1 cup bread crumbs
Vegetable oil for deep
  frying
Lemon slices for garnish

Peel and cook the potatoes until tender in salted water. Drain thoroughly, then mash with 4 tablespoons of the butter, the egg yolks, grated cheese, parsley, and salt and white pepper to taste. Set aside.

Heat the remaining 2 tablespoons of butter in a frying pan and sauté the onion until tender, but not browned. Cool slightly and stir in the shrimp, mixing well. Form the potato mixture into balls about the size of a small egg then stuff each with about 1 tablespoon of the shrimp mixture. Roll each lightly in flour, dip in beaten egg and then in bread crumbs. Place on a piece of waxed paper and refrigerate for at least 30 minutes.

Deep fry balls in hot oil (375° on a frying thermometer) 3 or 4 at a time, until all are golden brown all over. Drain on paper towels and keep warm until all the bombas are done. Makes about 30.

Serve garnished with lemon slices and a Salsa Tártara or Tomato Sauce (see Index) as a luncheon dish, for 6. Or as a first course for 12.

The bombas, made smaller and served on toothpicks, with the sauces for dipping, are an excellent accompaniment to drinks.

Baked Lobster   *Jamaica*

When we lived in Jamaica, this was our cook Annie's great company dish. It was always served as a fish course. When we had visitors, Annie insisted on the formalities, and nothing less than four courses was acceptable. However, it makes an excellent main course for either lunch or dinner. Lobsters in Jamaica are really crayfish (crawfish), delectable creatures with the best flesh in the tail rather than in the claws. It makes no great matter which is used, and I have found crab meat a splendid variation.

4 cups fresh lobster meat, cut into 1-inch chunks, or 2 14-ounce cans lobster meat	2 cloves garlic, finely chopped
Juice 2 large limes, about ½ cup	1 tablespoon fresh hot red or green peppers, seeded and chopped
10 tablespoons (4 ounces plus 2 tablespoons) unsalted butter	1½ cups freshly made bread crumbs
2 medium onions, finely chopped	Salt, freshly ground pepper
	2 teaspoons Worcestershire sauce
	Lime wedges

Mix the lobster meat with the lime juice and leave for 15 minutes. Heat all but 2 tablespoons of the butter in a heavy 10-inch frying pan and sauté the onions lightly with the garlic and peppers until the onions are tender but not browned. Add 1 cup of the bread crumbs and cook, stirring from time to time, until the bread crumbs are golden. Add the lobster meat and lime juice, season to taste with salt, pepper and Worcestershire sauce and turn into a buttered 1-quart soufflé dish. Top with remaining bread crumbs and dot with remaining 2 tablespoons of butter.

Bake in a preheated 350° oven for half an hour, or until the top is golden.

Serve with lime wedges. Serves 4 to 6 according to appetite.

Asopao de Langosta y Camarones

Puerto Rico

Rice, Lobster and Shrimp Stew

Asopao is Puerto Rico's special contribution to the Caribbean kitchen. It can be made with various shellfish or chicken, and the finished product is slightly soupy, which is what asopao means.

2 cups long grain rice
2 cups sofrito (see Index)
1 pound raw shrimp, shelled and deveined and cut into ½-inch pieces
1 pound rock lobster tails, or lobster meat, cut into ½-inch chunks

1 pound green peas, shelled, or 10-ounce package frozen peas
6 cups chicken stock
1 tablespoon capers
½ cup small pitted green olives
2 pimientos, cut in strips

Put the rice on to soak for 30 minutes in 2 cups cold water. Heat the sofrito in a heavy casserole, stir in the shrimp and lobster and cook, stirring from time to time, for 5 minutes. Drain the rice and add to the casserole with the peas and chicken stock, stir and cook, covered, at a gentle simmer until the rice is tender, about 20 minutes. If using frozen peas, add according to package directions. Stir in the capers, olives and pimientos and cook just long enough to heat through. Serves 6.

If liked, the Asopao may be garnished with asparagus tips.

For Asopao de Mariscos (Shellfish Stew) use a mixture of shellfish such as shrimp, crab, lobster, and clams and finish it with ½ cup dry sherry stirred in just before serving.

For Asopao de Calamares, use squids, cleaned and cut into 1-inch pieces.

Asopao de Jueyes is made with land crabs. Use lump crab meat instead.

Camarones à la Criolla   *Dominican Republic*
Shrimp Creole Style

4 tablespoons sweet butter	½ teaspoon sugar
1 large onion, finely chopped	1 tablespoon lime, or lemon, juice
1 clove garlic, chopped	Bay leaf
1 or 2 fresh hot red or green peppers, seeded and chopped	1 tablespoon parsley, finely chopped
1 cup chopped celery	1 teaspoon Worcestershire sauce
4 medium tomatoes, peeled, seeded and chopped	1½ pounds shelled, deveined, raw medium shrimp
Salt, freshly ground pepper	Parsley for garnish
	Grated Parmesan cheese

Heat the butter in a large, heavy frying pan. Add the onion, garlic, hot pepper, and celery and sauté until the onion is tender, but not browned. Add the tomatoes, salt and pepper to taste, sugar, lime juice, bay leaf and parsley and simmer, uncovered, until the sauce is well blended and slightly reduced. Remove the bay leaf. Stir in the Worcestershire sauce and the shrimp and cook until the shrimp have lost their translucent look, about 3 minutes. Garnish with chopped parsley and serve on a bed of white rice, accompanied by the Parmesan cheese in a separate bowl. Serves 6.

Camarones Guisados   *Puerto Rico*

Shrimp Stew

2 pounds raw shrimp	Bay leaf
1 ounce salt pork, cut in ⅛-inch cubes	1 tablespoon capers
1 tablespoon achiote oil (see Index)	12 pitted green olives, sliced
1 onion, finely chopped	⅛ teaspoon orégano
1 clove garlic, chopped	½ teaspoon sugar
1 green bell pepper, seeded and coarsely chopped	Salt, freshly ground pepper
2 ounces ham, coarsely chopped	1 tablespoon lime, or lemon, juice
4 medium tomatoes, peeled, seeded and chopped	1 canned pimiento, sliced
1½ pounds potatoes, peeled and cut in 1-inch cubes	1 tablespoon coarsely chopped fresh coriander

Shell the shrimp, devein, and set aside. Put the shells into a saucepan with 3 cups cold water, bring to a boil and simmer briskly, uncovered, for 15 minutes. Strain, measure the liquid and reduce, if necessary, to 1 cup. Set aside.

Try out the salt pork with the achiote oil in heat-proof casserole until the pork is browned all over. Add the onion, garlic and green pepper and cook until the onion is tender, but not browned. Add the ham, tomatoes, potatoes, bay leaf, capers, olives, orégano, sugar, shrimp stock, and salt and pepper to taste. Cover and simmer until the potatoes are done, about 20 minutes. Add the shrimp and cook until the shrimp have lost their translucent look, about 2 minutes for small shrimp, up to 5 minutes for jumbo. Stir in the lime juice, and garnish with the pimiento and coriander. Serve with white rice. Serves 6 to 8.

Camarones Rellenos   *Dominican Republic*

Stuffed Shrimp

24 jumbo shrimp	2 tablespoons lime, or
4 tablespoons anchovy	lemon, juice
paste	2 tablespoons onion juice
4 tablespoons unsalted	½ teaspoon freshly
butter, creamed	ground pepper
1 cup freshly made bread	1 cup all-purpose flour
crumbs	

BATTER:

1 cup all-purpose flour	Oil for deep frying
1 teaspoon salt	Freshly grated Parmesan
1 tablespoon unsalted	cheese
butter, melted	Salsa Tártara (Tartare
1 cup flat beer	Sauce) (see Index)
1 egg, separated	

Peel and devein the shrimp, making an extra deep and long incision to serve as a pocket for the stuffing. Combine the anchovy paste, butter, bread crumbs, lime juice, onion juice and pepper. Refrigerate for 30 minutes.

To make the batter, sift the flour and salt into a bowl. Make a well in the center and add the butter, beer, and the yolk of the egg. Mix quickly and thoroughly, and set aside in a warm place.

Stuff each shrimp with about 1 teaspoon of the anchovy stuffing, and dust lightly with flour. Beat the egg white

until stiff and fold into the batter. Dip the stuffed shrimp
into the batter and fry in deep oil, 350° on a frying thermometer, two or three at a time. Drain on paper towels
and keep warm. When all the shrimp have been fried,
sprinkle them with grated cheese and serve immediately
with Salsa Tártara Tartare Sauce served separately. Serves
4 to 6.

NOTE: Beer gives a lighter batter, but milk or water may be used.

Cangrejos Enchilados   *Dominican Republic*

Crabs in Pepper Sauce

1 pound lump crab meat	3 tablespoons tomato
¼ cup olive oil	purée
1 large onion, finely	Salt, freshly ground
chopped	pepper
4 cloves garlic, chopped	¼ teaspoon sugar
1 green bell pepper,	1 tablespoon lime, or
seeded and chopped	lemon, juice
4 hot green peppers,	½ cup dry sherry
seeded and chopped	2 tablespoons chopped
4 medium tomatoes,	parsley
peeled, seeded and	
chopped	

Pick over the crab meat and remove any cartilage. Set
aside. Heat the oil in a heavy frying pan and sauté the
onion, garlic and peppers until the onion is tender but not
browned. Add the tomatoes, tomato purée, salt, pepper
and sugar and cook until well blended and quite thick,
about 10 minutes, stirring from time to time. Stir in the
lime juice and sherry, then add the crab meat, stir, cover
and cook over the lowest possible heat until the crab meat
is heated through, 3 or 4 minutes. Be careful not to overcook as the crab meat will shred and lose its texture.
Sprinkle with parsley and serve with white rice. Serves
4 to 6.

Court Bouillon de Poisson

Martinique-Guadeloupe

Fish Poached in Tomato Sauce

The name court bouillon should not mislead. It does not mean court bouillon in the sense of a poaching liquid; here it means fish cooked in a special sauce. With poisson en blaff this is probably the most characteristic dish of the French Islands.

7 tablespoons lime juice
1 fresh hot red pepper, pounded
3 cloves garlic, crushed
1 tablespoon salt
2 cups cold water, about
2 1-pound white-fleshed fish, 1 of them a red snapper, if possible, cleaned but with heads left on
¼ cup annatto oil (see Index)
1 cup shallots, finely chopped
4 scallions, finely chopped

2 teaspoons finely chopped garlic
3 medium tomatoes, peeled and chopped
Salt, freshly ground pepper
1 fresh hot red pepper, left whole
2 sprigs parsley
1 bay leaf
1 sprig thyme
1 cup dry white wine, or ½ cup wine, ½ cup water
2 tablespoons olive oil

In a large shallow dish combine 6 tablespoons of the lime juice, the pounded pepper, crushed garlic, salt and water. Add the fish and a little more water, if necessary, to cover. Marinate for 1 hour. Drain, discard the marinade, and cut each fish in half, crosswise.

In a heavy frying pan, large enough to hold the fish comfortably, heat the annatto oil, add the shallots, scallions and 1 teaspoon of the chopped garlic. Sauté until the shallots are tender, but not browned. Add the tomatoes, salt and pepper to taste and cook for a few minutes longer. Add the fish and cook for two minutes, turning once. Add the whole pepper, parsley, bay leaf and thyme, all tied in a square of cheesecloth, and the wine. Cook, uncovered, at a gentle simmer for 10 to 15 minutes, or until the fish is done. Remove and discard the bouquet garni. Mix the olive oil, with the remaining tablespoon of lime juice and teaspoon of garlic, beating well with a fork. Pour over the fish and serve immediately. Serves 2.

Serve with Riz Créole (Rice Creole-style) or with two or three local vegetables, plainly cooked, such as breadfruit, plantains or bananas, yams, West Indian pumpkin, and sweet potatoes, served separately. Annatto, known as rou cou in the French islands, is sometimes omitted, more usually in Martinique.

Crab Pilau   *Tobago*

1 pound fresh, canned or frozen crab meat, picked over to remove any cartilage
3 tablespoons lime juice
2 tablespoons vegetable oil
2 tablespoons unsalted butter
2 medium onions, finely chopped
1 clove garlic, chopped

1 fresh hot pepper, seeded and chopped
2 tablespoons curry powder
2 cups raw long-grain rice
4 cups coconut milk
Salt, freshly ground pepper
1 tablespoon chopped chives

Put the crab meat into a bowl, add the lime juice and set aside. In a heavy casserole, heat the oil and butter and sauté the onions, garlic and hot pepper until the onions are tender but not browned. Add the curry powder and cook, stirring for 3 or 4 minutes, being careful not to let the curry powder burn. Stir in the rice and cook for about a minute longer, just to coat the grains. Add the coconut milk, season to taste with salt and pepper, stir, and cook, covered, over low heat until the rice is almost done, about 15 minutes. Fold in the crab meat and any liquid, and the chives. Cover and cook for about 5 minutes longer, or until the liquid is all absorbed and the crab heated through. Serves 6.

Crabes Farcis   *Martinique-Guadeloupe*

Stuffed Crabs

Land crabs are used for this dish in the islands.

6 live, hard-shelled crabs
1½ cups freshly made
   bread crumbs
1 fresh hot pepper,
   seeded and chopped
   fine, or hot pepper
   sauce to taste
3 tablespoons chives,
   chopped
2 tablespoons parsley,
   chopped

2 cloves garlic, crushed
1 tablespoon lime juice
Salt, freshly ground
   pepper
¼ teaspoon allspice
3 tablespoons Madeira,
   or dark rum,
   preferably Martinique
   or Guadeloupe *rhum
   vieux*
Butter

Plunge the crabs into boiling water and boil for 8 to 10 minutes. Remove and cool. Carefully take out the meat from the shells and claws, and chop fine. Discard spongy fiber. Scrub the empty shells and reserve.

Mash 1 cup of the bread crumbs into the crab meat until the mixture is quite smooth. Add the hot pepper, chives, parsley, garlic, lime juice, salt, pepper, allspice, and Madeira or rum, mixing thoroughly. Stuff the reserved crab shells with the mixture. Sprinkle with the remaining ½ cup of bread crumbs and dot with butter. Bake in a 350° oven for 30 minutes, or until lightly browned. Serves 6 as an appetizer, 2 to 3 for lunch.

If live crabs are not available, buy 1 pound fresh, frozen, or canned crab meat and stuff scallop shells.

Crapaud
Fried Frogs' Legs

Dominica and Montserrat

Crapauds, also called Mountain Chickens, are a special type of frogs found in Dominica and Montserrat. They are much larger than the usual type of frog and have a very delicate flavor. They are worth a trip to the islands, especially to Dominica which produces the most remarkable limes, whose juice, mixed with the local rum, makes a memorable punch for sipping while waiting for one's crapauds.

1 medium onion, grated
3 cloves garlic, crushed
½ teaspoon ground cloves
1 teaspoon salt
½ teaspoon white pepper

1 tablespoon malt vinegar
12 pairs medium sized frogs' legs, defrosted if frozen, and split in half
1 cup vegetable oil
1 cup flour
Lime wedges

Mix together the onion, garlic, cloves, salt, pepper, and vinegar in a large mixing bowl. Add the frogs' legs and allow to stand for at least 1 hour, turning the frogs' legs from time to time.

Heat the oil in a heavy frying pan. Pat the frogs' legs dry with paper towels and dip in flour. Fry half a dozen or so at a time, for about 5 minutes on each side. Drain on paper towels and serve with lime wedges on the side. Serves 6.

Daube de Poisson

Martinique-Guadeloupe

Fish Stew

½ cup lime, or lemon, juice
1 fresh hot red pepper, pounded
3 cloves garlic, crushed
1 tablespoon salt
2 cups cold water, about
3 pounds fresh tuna, or similar fish, cut into 6 steaks
All-purpose flour
4 tablespoons olive oil

1 onion, finely chopped
4 scallions, chopped, using green and white parts
2 medium tomatoes, peeled and chopped
Salt, freshly ground pepper
Bay leaf
¼ teaspoon thyme
1 tablespoon olive oil

In large bowl mix together 6 tablespoons of the lime juice, the hot pepper, 2 cloves of the garlic, the salt and water. Add the fish and, if necessary, a little more water to cover. Allow to stand for 1 hour. Drain thoroughly and discard the marinade.

Pat the fish dry with paper towels and dust lightly with flour. Heat the 4 tablespoons of oil in a heavy frying pan and sauté the fish lightly until golden on both sides. Lift out and keep warm.

In the oil remaining in the frying pan, adding a little more if necessary, sauté the onion and scallions until the onion is tender but not browned. Add the tomatoes, salt and pepper to taste, the bay leaf and thyme and cook, stirring occasionally, for 5 minutes.

Add the fish and enough water barely to cover. Cover and cook for 10 to 15 minutes, or until the fish is tender. Discard the bay leaf. Just before serving beat together the remaining clove of garlic, the remaining 2 tablespoons of lime juice and the 1 tablespoon of olive oil and pour over the fish. Serves 6.

Escovitch or Caveached Fish   *Jamaica*

This is the Jamaican version of the Pescado en Escabeche of the Spanish islands.

3 green bell peppers,
    seeded and sliced
2 medium onions, thinly
    sliced
3 carrots, scraped and
    thinly sliced
Bay leaf
½-inch slice fresh
    ginger root, finely
    chopped
6 peppercorns
⅛ teaspoon mace
Salt
2 cups water
2 tablespoons olive oil
½ cup vinegar,
    preferably malt or cane
¼ cup olive oil for
    frying
2 pounds snapper, or
    other white fish fillets
Olives and pimientos for
    garnish

Combine the peppers, onions, carrots, bay leaf, ginger, peppercorns, mace and salt with the water. Cover and simmer for 30 minutes. Add the olive oil and vinegar and simmer for a minute or two longer. Strain.

Heat the ¼ cup olive oil in a large, heavy frying pan and sauté the fish fillets until lightly browned on both sides; be careful not to overcook. Drain the fish and arrange in a warmed serving dish. Pour the hot sauce over the dish and serve hot. Or chill the fish in its sauce and serve cold, garnished with olives and pimientos.

Serves 4 as a main course, 8 as a first course.

Fish Pudding

St. Croix

1 pound poached red
   snapper, or sea bass
   fillets
1 pound poached fresh
   salmon
1 cup dry bread crumbs
½ cup chopped
   shallots
1 fresh hot red pepper,
   seeded and chopped
   (optional)

4 eggs, separated
4 tablespoons unsalted
   butter, melted
1 tablespoon lime, or
   lemon, juice
Salt, freshly ground
   pepper

Flake the poached and drained fish and mix lightly with
the bread crumbs, shallots and hot pepper. Beat the egg
yolks until thick, and combine with the butter, lime juice,
salt and pepper. Fold into the fish mixture. Beat the egg
whites until stiff and fold gently but thoroughly into the
fish mixture. Pour into a 6-cup buttered soufflé dish and
bake in a 350° oven for about 35 minutes, or until the
pudding is firm. Serves 6.

    Serve with either Lemon Butter Sauce or Curry Sauce.
See Asparagus Pudding. Omit the red pepper if the Curry
Sauce is to be served.

Flying Fish Pie

Barbados

*Unhappily flying fish are not a routine item in fish shops
or supermarkets here, but rather than lose this attractive
dish altogether, substitute fillets of any white fish. Be
careful to get real yams, not the sweet potatoes known
as Louisiana yams.*

12 flying fish, or 1½
   pounds white fish fillets
Salt, freshly ground
   pepper
4 tablespoons unsalted
   butter
2 pounds yams
1 large onion, very finely
   sliced
1 large tomato, peeled
   and thinly sliced

2 hard-boiled eggs, sliced
FOR THE SAUCE:

2 egg yolks
2 tablespoons vegetable
   oil
2 tablespoons sweet
   butter, melted
1 tablespoon
   Worcestershire sauce
½ cup dry sherry

Season the fish with salt and pepper. Heat 2 tablespoons
of the butter in a frying pan and sauté the fish lightly on
both sides. Cut in halves. Peel the yams and cook in salted
water until tender. Cool and slice thinly. Butter a deep
dish, or soufflé dish. Arrange half the fish fillets in one
layer. Make a layer of half the onion, tomato, and 1 of
the eggs. Cover with a layer of yams, using half. Then
the rest of the fish, the rest of the onion, tomato and the
egg. Top with the other half of the sliced yams. Dot with
the remaining 2 tablespoons of butter.

Beat the egg yolks, then thoroughly mix in the oil,
melted butter, Worcestershire sauce and sherry. Pour over
contents of the baking dish. Bake in a 350° oven until the
top of the pie is golden brown and heated through, about
30 minutes. Serves 4 to 6.

Fricasseé D'Escargots 1755
Northern Martinique

Fricasse of Snails, 1755

This snail dish was created in the kitchens of the De
Leyritz Plantation *in 1755 to celebrate a domestic event
connected with the building of a* petit chateau bordelais,
*the main house of the plantation, built near Basse Pointe,
in the north of Martinique, by Michel de Leyritz at the
beginning of the 18th century. It is still in the repertoire*

of the restored plantation, now a restaurant and small hotel, and is another example of the good cooking of the north of the island.

4 tablespoons sweet butter	**Salt, freshly ground pepper**
1 medium onion, finely chopped	**Dash of hot pepper sauce (optional)**
1 clove garlic, chopped	**8-ounce can (4 ounces drained weight) *escargots* (snails)**
1 tablespoon parsley, chopped	**½ cup heavy cream**
¼ pound sliced mushrooms	

Heat the butter in a heavy, medium-sized frying pan and sauté the onion, garlic, parsley, and mushrooms until the onion is tender and the mushrooms cooked. Season to taste with salt and pepper, and a dash of hot pepper sauce, if liked.

If the snails are very large, cut them into halves or quarters. Add the snails to the mushroom mixture and cook over low heat for 5 to 8 minutes. Stir in the cream and cook for a minute or two longer.

Serve with Riz Créole (see Index), or with any plainly cooked starchy vegetable such as potatoes, sweet potatoes, breadfruit, yams, etc. The recipe may be successfully doubled, or trebled. Serves 2.

Keshy Yena coe Cabaron   *Curaçao*
Stuffed Cheese with Shrimp Filling

4-pound Edam cheese
1½ pounds cooked shrimp, shelled and chopped
2 tablespoons unsalted butter
1 large onion, finely chopped
1½ cups tomatoes, peeled, seeded and chopped

Salt, freshly ground pepper to taste
⅛ teaspoon cayenne pepper
1 cup freshly made bread crumbs
¼ cup seedless raisins
2 tablespoons finely chopped sweet pickles
½ cup chopped black olives
2 eggs, well beaten

Peel the red wax covering from the cheese, cut a 1-inch slice from the top, hollow out and reserve for use as a lid. Scoop out the cheese, leaving a shell about ½-inch thick. Cover the shell and lid with cold water and soak for an hour. Grate the scooped out cheese and reserve 2 cups. Store the remaining cheese for another use.

Heat the butter in a frying pan and sauté the onion until tender. Add the tomatoes, salt and pepper and cayenne pepper and cook until the mixture is smooth and fairly thick. Add the bread crumbs, raisins, pickles, olives, grated cheese, and the shrimp. Fold the eggs gently but thoroughly into the shrimp mixture.

Remove the cheese shell and lid from the water and pat dry. Stuff with the shrimp mixture. Replace top of cheese. Put the stuffed cheese into a greased 3-quart casserole and bake in a 350° oven for 30 minutes. Do not overcook as the cheese becomes tough, instead of soft and bubbly. Slide the cheese out of the casserole onto a warmed serving dish. Cut into wedges and serve immediately. Serves 6 to 8.

VARIATION: For Keshy Yena coe Pisca (Stuffed Cheese with Fish Filling) prepare the cheese in the same way, and stuff with the following filling.

1 pound red snapper or
    kingfish fillets
2 tablespoons unsalted
    butter
1 large onion, finely
    chopped
2 medium tomatoes,
    peeled and chopped
Salt, freshly ground
    pepper to taste

⅛ teaspoon cayenne
    pepper
1 cup freshly made bread
    crumbs
¼ cup seedless raisins
2 tablespoons finely
    chopped sweet pickles
10 small pimiento-stuffed
    green olives, chopped
2 eggs, well beaten

Place the fish fillets in a frying pan, cover with cold water, bring to a simmer, cover and cook for about 6 minutes, or until the fish flakes easily with a fork. Cool in the stock, remove and flake. Set aside. Discard the stock, rinse out and dry the pan.

Heat the butter in the pan and sauté the onion until tender but not browned. Add the tomatoes, salt and pepper and cayenne pepper and cook, stirring, until the mixture is smooth and fairly thick. Add the bread crumbs, raisins, olives, fish and grated cheese. Fold the eggs gently but thoroughly into the fish mixture. Stuff the cheese and bake as above.

Herring Gundy   U.S. Virgin Islands

This dish obviously derives from the period, before 1917, when the islands, St. Thomas, St. Croix and St. John, were Danish. The name is a corruption of salmagundi, a word of unknown origin used as early as 1674 to describe a dish of chopped meat, anchovies, eggs, onions, oil and seasonings. A similar term, salmigondis, is used in the French kitchen to describe a ragout of several meats, reheated.

2 pounds salt herring
2 pounds potatoes
2 medium onions, finely
  chopped
1 green bell pepper,
  seeded and chopped
1 teaspoon finely chopped
  hot red or green
  pepper
½ cup small pitted
  green olives, chopped

1½ cups diced, cooked
  beets
1 cup freshly grated
  carrots
4 hard-boiled eggs
1 cup salad oil
¼ cup vinegar,
  preferably cane or malt
Freshly ground pepper
Parsley sprigs
Lettuce leaves

Wash the herrings, drain and soak overnight in cold water to cover. Drain, pat dry with paper towels, remove the skin and bones, and put the fish through the coarse blade of a food mill. Peel the potatoes and cook until tender in salted water. Drain, mash and combine with the herring. Add the onions, bell pepper, hot pepper, olives, ½ cup of the beets, ¼ cup of the carrots and 1 of the eggs, finely chopped. Add the oil, vinegar and a generous amount of freshly ground pepper. Mix well. Chill, if liked. Mound on a serving platter and surround with small heaps of diced beets, grated carrot and chopped egg. Garnish with parsley sprigs and lettuce leaves. Serves 6 as a main course, 12 as a first course.

Langosta Enchilada   *Cuba*

Lobster in Pepper Sauce

The lobsters of the Caribbean are really salt water cray-fish, spiny or rock lobsters. Frozen lobster tails, or lob-sters may equally be used.

3 2-pound lobsters,
  uncooked
2 tablespoons oil
2 cups sofrito (see Index)

1 tablespoon lime juice
6 slices bread
Oil or butter for frying

Set aside the tomalley or coral (if any). Remove all the meat from the lobsters and set aside. Heat 2 tablespoons of oil in a heavy frying pan and sauté the lobster shells over high heat, turning them constantly, until they turn pink. Transfer the lobster shells to a large saucepan and pour in 2 cups of water. Bring to a boil and cook, covered, until the liquid is reduced to 1 cup. Pour off most of the oil from the frying pan, add the lobster meat, the sofrito, and the stock from the shells. Cook, covered, for 20 minutes. Stir in the lime juice, and the tomalley and coral, rubbed through a sieve. Cook mixture for a minute or two longer.

In the meantime, cut the slices of bread into triangles and fry in oil or butter until browned on both sides. Transfer the lobster and sauce to a warmed platter with the triangles of fried bread arranged as a decorative border. Serves 4 to 6.

Langosta Habanera   *Cuba*

Lobster Havana Style

2 1½-pound boiled lobsters	¼ teaspoon cayenne pepper
3 tablespoons sweet butter	4 egg yolks
1½ tablespoons all-purpose flour	3 tablespoons dry sherry
1½ cups heavy cream	3 tablespoons light rum, preferably Bacardi
Salt, freshly ground pepper	Arroz blanco, or Arroz con Ajo (see Index)

Remove the meat from the lobsters and cut into chunks. Reserve the tomalley and the coral (if any). Heat the butter in a saucepan, stir in the flour, and cook, stirring with a wooden spoon, for about 2 minutes but without letting the flour take on any color. Add the cream and cook very gently, stirring constantly, until thick. Season with salt, pepper and cayenne. Beat the egg yolks until light and lemon colored and fold into the sauce, off the heat. Fold in the lobster meat and the coral. Add the sherry, and rum, and the tomalley pushed through a sieve. Cook just long enough to heat through. Pile into the center of a warmed platter and surround with the rice. Serves 4.

Matoutou de Crabes   *Martinique*

This is the Carib word for a dish that was originally made with cassava meal but is now more often cooked with rice. In Guadeloupe the dish with rice is called matété, with cassava meal, matoutou.

2 pounds crab meat, fresh, canned or frozen, picked over to remove any shell or cartilage
4 tablespoons olive oil
½ cup shallots, chopped
4 cloves garlic, crushed
2 tablespoons chopped chives
¼ teaspoon thyme
1 bay leaf
1 tablespoon chopped parsley
3 tablespoons lime juice
Salt, freshly ground pepper
1 teaspoon fresh hot red peppers, seeded and chopped
2 cups rice

Heat the oil in a heavy casserole, add the crab meat, and cook for a few minutes, stirring from time to time. Add all the ingredients, except the rice, and sauté for a minute or two longer. Add the rice and 4 cups of water, cover and cook over low heat until the rice is tender and all the liquid absorbed. Serves 6.

Pargo Asado

Cuba

Baked Red Snapper

5 to 6-pound red snapper, cleaned and scaled
½ cup lime juice
Salt, freshly ground pepper
½ cup olive oil
1 large onion, finely sliced
½ teaspoon thyme
½ teaspoon orégano

1 bay leaf, crumbled
1 medium onion, finely chopped
2 cloves garlic, chopped
1 fresh hot red or green pepper, seeded and chopped
1 tablespoon chopped parsley
½ cup toasted almonds, ground

Cut the head off the fish and use to make 1½ cups stock.

Mix the lime juice with salt and pepper to taste and rub into the fish, inside and out. Set aside. Pour 6 tablespoons of the olive oil into a baking dish large enough to hold the fish comfortably. Arrange the sliced onion on the bottom of the dish and sprinkle with the thyme, orégano and bayleaf. Season with salt and pepper. Drain the fish and pour the marinade over the onions together with 1 cup of the fish stock. Place the fish in the baking dish.

Make the following dressing. Heat the remaining 2 tablespoons of oil in a frying pan and sauté the chopped onion and garlic until the onion is tender but not browned. Add the hot pepper, parsley and almonds and the remaining ½ cup of fish stock. Spread the dressing over the top of and sides of the fish. Bake, uncovered, in a 400° oven for 40 to 45 minutes. Serves 6.

Striped bass may also be used.

TO MAKE FISH STOCK: Put the fish head into a saucepan with 3 cups of water, or half water, and half white wine. Add a small onion, coarsely chopped, some parsley stalks and simmer, uncovered, for about 30 minutes, or until the liquid is reduced to half. Strain and season to taste with salt.

Molondrones
con Camarones

Dominican Republic

Okra with Shrimp

4 tablespoons unsalted
  butter, clarified
1 large onion, finely
  chopped
1 pound young okra
  pods, cut into ½-
  inch slices
8 medium tomatoes (2
  pounds, about), peeled,
  seeded and chopped

Salt, freshly ground
  pepper
1 bay leaf
1 teaspoon sugar
1 tablespoon lime, or
  lemon, juice
2 pounds raw shrimp
1 cup rice

Heat the butter and sauté the onion until tender but not
browned. Add the okra and tomatoes, salt and pepper to
taste, bay leaf, sugar and lime juice, and simmer, covered
for 10 minutes, stirring occasionally. Remove the bay leaf
and set the mixture aside.

Shell and devein the shrimp. If they are large, cut into
1-inch slices; if small, leave whole. Set aside. Put the
shrimp shells into a medium-sized saucepan with 3 cups
of cold water and bring to a boil. Cook, uncovered, for
about 15 minutes. Drain. Discard shells. There should be
2 cups of stock. Reduce over brisk heat, if necessary.
Wash the rice, drain and add to the saucepan with the
shrimp stock. Season with salt, cover, bring to a boil,
reduce the heat as low as possible and cook for about 20
minutes, or until the rice is tender and all the liquid
absorbed.

Fold the rice into the okra and tomato mixture, add
the shrimp and cook, covered, for 5 minutes or until the
shrimp have lost their translucent look. Be careful not to
overcook the shrimp. Serves 6.

Pargo Asado con
Salsa Esmeralda   *Cuba*

Baked Snapper with Green Sauce

2 teaspoons salt
¼ teaspoon freshly
  ground pepper
4 cloves garlic, crushed
¼ teaspoon orégano
¼ teaspoon ground
  cumin
½ cup lime juice
5 to 6-pound red
  snapper, cleaned and
  scaled, but with head
  and tail left on

Butter
2 pounds potatoes, peeled
  and cut into ½-inch
  slices
1 cup olive oil
½ cup parsley,
  chopped
2 pimientos, cut into
  strips

Mix together the salt, pepper, garlic, orégano, cumin and lime juice and rub into the fish, inside and out. Set aside for half an hour. Butter an oven proof dish large enough to hold the fish comfortably. Arrange the potatoes on the bottom of the dish, place the fish on top, pouring the marinade over the fish. Pour the oil over fish and potatoes. Cook in a 400° oven for 40 to 45 minutes. Decorate with parsley and pimientos and serve with the Salsa Esmeralda. Serves 6. Striped bass may also be used.

SALSA ESMERALDA:

Green Sauce

3 cloves garlic, crushed
2 tablespoons chopped
  capers, preferably
  Spanish
Yolks of 4 hard-boiled
  eggs, mashed
1 teaspoon salt
¼ teaspoon white
  pepper

2 tablespoons chopped
  parsley
½ cup toasted
  almonds, ground
¾ cup olive oil
¼ cup distilled white
  vinegar

In a mortar mash together the garlic, capers, egg yolks, salt, pepper, parsley and almonds. Beat in the oil little by little and at the last minute add the vinegar. Makes about 1½ cups.

Pargo con Salsa de Aguacate   *Cuba*
Red Snapper with Avocado Sauce

1 onion, sliced	6 peppercorns, bruised
1 clove garlic, crushed	½ cup lime juice
1 bay leaf	5 to 6-pound red
½ teaspoon thyme	snapper, cleaned and
½ teaspoon orégano	scaled but with head
Sprig celery leaves	and tail left on
2 or 3 sprigs parsley	

Place all the ingredients, except the fish, in a large saucepan. Add 4 quarts of water, bring to a boil and simmer, partially covered, for half an hour. Cool. Wash the fish, drain and wrap in a long, double-thick piece of cheesecloth. Lay the fish in a roasting pan or fish poacher large enough to hold it comfortably, with the ends of the cheesecloth hanging over the two ends of the pan. If the pan has handles, tie the cheesecloth ends to the handles. Pour in the poaching liquid, which should cover the fish by at least an inch. If necessary add a little water. Bring the liquid to a bare simmer, cover tightly, flipping ends of cheesecloth, if untied, on top of the lid, and cook for 30 to 40 minutes, or until the thickest part of the fish feels firm when pressed with a finger.

When done, using the ends of the cheesecloth, lift the fish onto a large board. Open the cheesecloth and gently peel off the fish skin in strips. Using the cheesecloth, carefully turn the fish onto a serving platter. Discard cheesecloth. Remove the skin from the up-turned side.

The fish may be eaten hot or cold. If it is to be eaten hot, the sauce should be served separately. If served cold, the fish should be masked with 1 cup of the sauce, the rest of the sauce served separately. The cold platter should be garnished with olives, both green and black, cherry tomatoes, radishes, parsley sprigs, tiny lettuce leaves and wedges of lime. Serves 6. Striped bass may also be used.

SALSA DE AGUACATE:

Avocado Sauce

2 large avocados	1 teaspoon salt
1 tablespoon lime juice	Freshly ground black
3 tablespoons vegetable oil	pepper to taste

Peel, pit and mash the avocados with a fork. Add the lime juice, oil, salt and pepper and beat until the sauce has the consistency of mayonnaise.

Pescado con Salsa de Coco   *Dominican Republic*

Fish with Coconut Milk Sauce

3 cloves garlic	½ cup peanut oil
2 teaspoons salt	1 onion, finely chopped
3 tablespoons lime juice	1 fresh hot green pepper,
1 teaspoon orégano	sliced
⅛ teaspoon freshly ground pepper	Bay leaf
2½ pounds white fish fillets	2 cups coconut milk
Flour	3 tablespoons tomato paste

Crush 1 of the garlic cloves with the salt, add 2 table-spoons of the lime juice, ½ teaspoon of the orégano, and the freshly ground pepper. Mix well, allow to stand for about 30 minutes, strain and pour over the fish fillets. Allow to stand for 1 hour. Dry the fish and dust with flour. Heat the oil in a frying pan and fry the fish until tender and golden brown. Keep warm.

Chop the remaining 2 cloves of garlic and sauté with the onion and hot pepper in the oil remaining in the frying pan, until the onion is tender. Add the bay leaf, remaining ½ teaspoon orégano, coconut milk, and tomato paste. Cook, stirring, for 3 minutes. Add the remaining 1 table-spoon of lime juice and cook for 2 minutes longer. Pour over fish. Serves 6.

Pescado Relleno   *Cuba*

Stuffed Fish

3-pound red snapper, sea bass, or similar fish, cleaned and scaled	¼ teaspoon allspice
2 cups freshly made bread crumbs	Salt, freshly ground pepper
Milk	¼ teaspoon orégano
2 hard-boiled eggs, finely chopped	2 eggs
1 cup chopped shallots	4 tablespoons lime, or lemon, juice
2 tablespoons chopped chives	1 large onion, thinly sliced
1 fresh hot red pepper, seeded and chopped	1 large carrot, scraped and thinly sliced
	2 tablespoons olive oil
	2 tablespoons sweet butter

Cut the head off the fish and split the fish in half, length-wise. Remove the backbone and set one half of the fish aside. Remove the skin and any remaining bones from the other half and put this half through the coarse blade of a food mill. Moisten all but 2 tablespoons of the bread crumbs with a little milk and add to the ground fish with the hard-boiled eggs, shallots, chives, hot pepper, allspice, salt, pepper, and orégano, mixing gently but thoroughly. Reserve the two tablespoons of crumbs. Beat the eggs, add 2 tablespoons of the lime juice and stir into the fish mixture.

In a heavy, shallow baking pan or casserole, arrange the onion and carrot and pour the olive oil over them.

Arrange the reserved half of the fish, skin down, on this bed of vegetables. Sprinkle with the remaining lime juice and cover with the stuffing, molding it to the shape of the fish. Sprinkle with the reserved bread crumbs and dot with the butter. Bake in a 400° oven for 30 to 40 minutes. Serves 6.

Serve hot with Tomato Sauce (see Index), or cold with mayonnaise.

Pilau de Camarones   *Dominican Republic*

Rice with Shrimp and Tomatoes

6 slices bacon, coarsely chopped
1 large onion, finely chopped
1 tablespoon finely chopped garlic
1 tablespoon fresh hot red or green pepper, seeded and chopped
2 cups long-grain rice
2 pounds tomatoes, peeled, seeded and chopped

3 cups chicken stock
Salt, freshly ground pepper to taste
2 tablespoons unsalted butter
1½ pounds raw shrimp, peeled, deveined and cut into ½-inch pieces
2 tablespoons finely chopped parsley
Freshly grated Parmesan cheese

In a heavy 10-inch frying pan that has a lid, fry the bacon until the pieces are crisp and brown. Remove with a slotted spoon, drain on paper towels and keep warm.

Sauté the onion, garlic and hot pepper in the bacon fat remaining in the pan until the onion is tender, but not browned. Add the rice and cook, stirring, for 2 or 3 minutes until the fat is absorbed, being careful not to let the rice brown. Add the tomatoes, stock, and salt and pepper to taste. Bring to a boil, cover, reduce the heat to the lowest possible point and cook for 20 minutes.

Meanwhile in another frying pan heat the butter and

sauté the shrimp until they turn pink, about 5 minutes. By this time the rice should be tender and all the liquid absorbed. If necessary cook the rice for a few minutes longer, keeping the shrimp warm. Add the shrimp, bacon, and parsley to the rice, mixing lightly but thoroughly. Cover and cook for a minute or two until the mixture is heated through but take care not to overcook the shrimp as this makes them tough. Serve with plenty of grated Parmesan cheese in a separate bowl. Serves 6.

Revuelto de Cangrejo   *Dominican Republic*
Crab and Cod with Scrambled Eggs

This translates literally as "scrambled of crab." Hence the more descriptive English name.

1 pound salt codfish	2 tablespoons chopped parsley
3 tablespoons olive oil	
2 pounds lump crab meat, picked over to remove any cartilage	Salt, freshly ground pepper
4 cloves garlic, finely chopped	6 eggs, lightly beaten

Soak the cod in cold water, the time depending on the hardness and saltiness of the fish. Drain, rinse in fresh water and put on to cook in cold water. Simmer gently for 15 minutes, or until the fish is tender. Drain thoroughly, remove any bones and skin and shred.

Heat the oil in a large, heavy frying pan. Add the shredded cod, the crab meat, and the garlic and cook, stirring from time to time, for 5 minutes. Add the parsley. Season to taste with salt and pepper. Fold in the eggs and cook, stirring as for scrambled eggs, until the eggs are lightly set. Serves 6.

Lobster may be used instead of crab.

Poisson en Blaff   *Martinique-Guadeloupe*
Poached Fish

One theory of the term blaff is that when a freshly caught fish is thrown into the poaching liquid it makes the sound "blaff." Unprovable as a linguistic theory, but very plausible. This is one of the most characteristic dishes of the French islands.

7 tablespoons lime juice
1 fresh hot red pepper, pounded
3 cloves garlic, crushed
1 tablespoon salt
2 cups cold water, about
2 1-pound white-fleshed fish, 1 of them a red snapper, if possible, cleaned and scaled, with heads and tails left on
1 cup dry white wine

1 medium onion, finely chopped, or 2 to 3 scallions, sliced, using the green and white parts
1 clove garlic, crushed
2 whole cloves
1 fresh hot red pepper, left whole
2 melegueta peppercorns (see Glossary) or use 2 allspice berries
2 melegueta leaves, or use bay leaves

In a large, shallow dish combine 6 tablespoons of the lime juice, the pounded pepper, 3 cloves of crushed garlic, salt, and water. Add the fish and a little more water, if necessary, to cover. Marinate for 1 hour. Drain, discard the marinade, and cut each fish in half, crosswise.

Pour the wine and 1 cup of water with the remaining tablespoon of lime juice into a heavy frying pan, large enough to hold the fish comfortably. Add the onion or scallions, garlic, cloves, whole pepper, and melegueta peppercorns and leaves, or allspice and bay leaves. Bring to a boil, and simmer for 5 minutes. Add the fish and cook, uncovered, at a simmer until it is done, about 10 minutes. Serve in individual deep oval dishes, dividing the fish so that each dish contains one head, and one tail portion. Pour the poaching liquid over the fish. The red snapper makes an attractive contrast with the other fish.

Serve with Riz Créole (Creole Style rice), Pois et Riz (Rice and Beans), or fried ripe plantains or bananas. Serves 2.

Salt Fish and Ackee   *Jamaica*

1 pound salt cod
2 dozen ackees or
  1-pound 2-ounce can
  ackees
4 ounces salt pork, diced
  fine
2 medium onions, finely
  chopped
1 green bell pepper,
  seeded and chopped
  (optional)
1 teaspoon finely chopped
  fresh hot pepper,
  seeded

4 scallions, chopped using
  the green and white
  parts
¼ teaspoon thyme
4 medium tomatoes
Freshly ground pepper
6 slices bacon, fried crisp
Parsley sprigs, or
  watercress for garnish
  (optional)

Soak the salt cod in cold water. The length of time will depend on the hardness and saltiness of the fish. Drain, and cook in fresh cold water. Simmer until tender, adding the fresh ackees 15 minutes before the fish is done. Drain and set the ackees aside. Remove any bones and skin from the fish, flake and add to the ackees.

In a heavy frying pan fry the salt pork until it has given up all its fat and the dice are crisp and brown. Lift out the brown pieces with a slotted spoon and set aside with the fish and ackees. Sauté the onions and bell pepper in the fat until they are tender and very lightly browned. Add hot pepper, the scallions, thyme, and 3 of the tomatoes, peeled and coarsely chopped and sauté for about 5 minutes. Add the flaked cod, ackees, and salt pork dice and heat through. If using canned ackees, drain and add at this point.

Transfer to a heated serving dish, season with freshly

ground pepper, and garnish with the crisp bacon slices, the remaining tomato cut into 8 wedges, and if liked, parsley sprigs or watercress. Serves 4.

Salmorejo de Jueyes   *Puerto Rico*
Land Crab Stew

Land crabs are a feature of the Puerto Rican kitchen but are seldom available elsewhere. Their flavor is rather more pronounced than that of sea crabs which, nonetheless, make an excellent substitute. Salmorejo is a traditional Spanish sauce of water, vinegar, oil, salt and pepper.

1½ pounds crab meat, picked over to remove any cartilage
2 cloves garlic, crushed
1 onion, finely chopped
4 pimientos
1 fresh hot red pepper, seeded and chopped
4 tablespoons achiote oil, made with olive oil (see Index)

4 tablespoons lime, or lemon, juice
4 tablespoons vinegar
Salt, freshly ground pepper
24 small, pitted green olives
1 pound fresh green peas, or 10-ounce package frozen peas, thawed

Place all the ingredients except the peas in a heavy saucepan, cover and simmer very gently for 20 minutes. Simmer the fresh peas in salted water to cover until tender, about 10 minutes, or cook frozen peas according to package instructions. Add to the crab mixture just before serving. Serve with rice, and tostones or fried plantains (see Index). Serves 6.

Salt Fish in Chemise   *Dominica*

1½ pounds salt codfish
6 tablespoons unsalted
  butter
2 medium onions, finely
  chopped
2 cloves garlic, chopped
2 tablespoons finely
  chopped chives

3 tomatoes, peeled and
  chopped
½ teaspoon thyme
1 teaspoon fresh hot red
  or green pepper,
  seeded and chopped
Salt, freshly ground
  pepper
6 eggs

Put the salt fish in a bowl, cover with warm water and
soak for 2 hours or longer, according to the saltiness and
hardness of the fish. Drain, rinse and pat dry. Remove
any skin and bones, and shred the fish. Heat the butter
in a frying pan and sauté the onions, and garlic until the
onions are tender but not browned. Add the chives, tomatoes, thyme, hot pepper, salt, if necessary, and pepper to
taste. Add the shredded fish, and a little water if the
mixture is too dry to cook the fish. Simmer, covered, for
15 minutes.

Butter a casserole and pour in the mixture, or divide
among 6 individual casseroles. Break the eggs over the
fish mixture and place in a large frying pan with about an
inch of water. Cover and steam until the eggs are done.
Serves 6.

Salt Fish Soufflé   *Jamaica*

3 tablespoons unsalted
  butter
3 tablespoons all-purpose
  flour
1 cup milk
Salt, white pepper
4 eggs, separated

1 cup cooked and flaked
  salt codfish
1 teaspoon lime juice
Dash Pickapepper hot
  pepper sauce, or
  Tabasco

Melt the butter in a medium-sized heavy saucepan, add the flour and cook, stirring with a wooden spoon, for about 2 minutes, without letting the mixture brown. Heat the milk and pour on to the flour mixture all at once, stirring vigorously. As soon as the mixture has thickened, remove from the heat. Add salt, if necessary, and pepper to taste. Beat the egg yolks into the sauce, one by one. Stir in the fish, lime juice and hot pepper sauce. Beat the egg whites until they stand in peaks. Stir one quarter of the whites into the sauce, then fold in the rest of the whites with an undercutting motion. Pour into a buttered, 6-cup soufflé mold and bake in a 350° oven for 30 to 35 minutes. Serve immediately with Curry Sauce (see Index). Serves 4.

Serenata   *Dominican Republic*

Salt Codfish Salad

1 pound salt codfish	¾ cup olive oil
1 pound potatoes	¼ cup vinegar
1 large avocado, peeled and sliced	Salt, freshly ground pepper
2 medium tomatoes, peeled and sliced	Boiled vegetables, such as yams, sweet potatoes,
1 medium onion, finely chopped	or fried or boiled plantains, to taste
18 pitted green olives	

Soak the cod in cold water for several hours, according to the hardness and saltiness of the fish. Drain and put on to cook in fresh cold water. Simmer for about 15 minutes, or until the fish is tender. Drain thoroughly, remove any skin or bones and cut the fish into small cubes, or shred it.

Arrange the fish in a heap in the center of a serving dish. Meanwhile, peel the potatoes, cut into cubes and cook in salted water until tender, about 15 minutes. Drain and arrange round the salt codfish. Garnish the platter with the avocado, tomatoes, onion and olives.

Mix the oil and vinegar together and season to taste with salt and pepper. Pour over the fish, and serve at room temperature, with freshly cooked hot vegetables such as yams, etc. Serves 4 to 6.

Shrimp Curry   *Trinidad*

1½ teaspoons
    coriander seeds
1½ teaspoons cumin
    seeds
1½ teaspoons brown
    mustard seeds
1½ teaspoons whole
    black peppercorns
½ teaspoon crushed
    hot red pepper
2 bay leaves
3 tablespoons vegetable
    oil
3 tablespoons unsalted
    butter
2 large onions finely
    chopped

2 cloves garlic, crushed
1 tablespoon fresh ginger
    root, finely chopped
4 medium tomatoes,
    peeled and chopped, or
    2 cups chopped,
    drained canned
    tomatoes
2 tablespoons lime juice
1 tablespoon chopped
    lime pickle (optional)
Salt
2 pounds large raw
    shrimp, peeled and
    deveined

In a mortar, or in an electric blender, pulverize the coriander, cumin, and mustard seeds with the peppercorns, hot pepper and bay leaves. Set aside. Heat the oil and butter in a large, heavy skillet and sauté the onions until very lightly browned. Add the garlic, ginger root and the ground spices and cook, stirring for 2 or 3 minutes longer. Add the tomatoes, lime juice, and lime pickle, if liked. This is very hot. Season to taste with salt, cover and cook for 30 minutes over very low heat, stirring from time to time. If necessary add a little stock or water. The sauce should be quite thick. Add the shrimp, and cook, covered, for 5 minutes, or until the shrimp are firm and pink. Be careful not to overcook the shrimp. Serves 4. Serve with boiled rice and mango chutney, and rot (see Index).

For an informal lunch for six, divide the mixture equally among 6 hot roti, fold the roti over to make a neat package and serve as one would a sandwich.

Spanish Fish
St. Kitts

Why this is called Spanish fish is anyone's guess. Perhaps because the tomatoes and peppers originated in Mexico, once a part, by conquest, of imperial Spain. Or perhaps it is a recognition of the Spanish love of salt codfish.

1 pound salt codfish
Flour
Freshly ground pepper
1 cup peanut oil
4 medium onions, finely chopped
4 medium tomatoes, peeled and coarsely chopped
Salt
4 ripe red bell peppers, seeded and chopped, or use canned pimientos
1 cup bread crumbs
2 tablespoons parsley, chopped

Soak the fish in cold water, the time depending on the hardness and saltiness of the fish. Drain, rinse in fresh cold water and drain. Pour boiling water over the fish and allow it to stand until cold. Drain, and pat the fish dry with paper towels. Remove any skin and bones. Cut the fish into 1-inch pieces. Roll in flour, seasoned with pepper. Heat 3 tablespoons of the oil in a frying pan and sauté the fish until lightly browned all over. Set aside.

Add the rest of the oil to the frying pan and sauté the onions and the bell peppers until the onion is tender but not brown. If using pimientos instead of bell peppers, do not sauté them. Simply add them with the tomatoes. Add the tomatoes, salt, and pepper to taste and simmer until very soft. Be careful not to oversalt as the fish will still be quite salty. Rub the tomato mixture through a sieve. Grease or butter a baking dish and pour in half of the resulting purée. Arrange the fish on top of the purée, and cover with the rest. Sprinkle with the bread crumbs and chopped parsley and bake in a 350° oven until the top is lightly browned and the dish heated through, about 20 minutes. Serves 4.

The Conch

Conches are large Antillean marine mollusks of the gastropod class, 9-inches to a foot long. They live below the low tide line. They have heavy spiral shells which are yellow shading to a beautiful pink inside and, held to the ear, one hears the sound of the sea. Fishermen in the islands sometimes use the shell as a trumpet to announce their catch.

The horny plate which seals the shell serves the conch as a clawlike foot, so that while other gastropods creep about the sea floor, the Antillean conch jumps and leaps. This does not prevent it from being caught, and made into a variety of delicious dishes.

Its Carib name is lambi or lambie, in Spanish it is concha, in English conch and in French conque. The French name may explain why it is so often pronounced conk in English.

Cleaning it is a nuisance, but fortunately in U.S. markets it comes already cleaned. Like abalone, the fish needs a thorough beating to tenderize it. There is a creole saying about men who beat their wives, "I bat li con lambi," which means, "I beat her as if she were a conch."

Some cooks have found the pressure cooker the answer to the conch's toughness and give it 30 minutes. Others have found that a go-round in the washing machine, batted at by the paddles, does very well indeed. Otherwise bash at with the flat of a cleaver, a wooden pestle, the bottom of a bottle, or whatever you have handy. The result is well worth the effort.

Daube de Lambis   *Martinique-Guadeloupe*

Conch Stew

2 pounds conch, about 10
½ cup lime, or lemon,
  juice
3 tablespoons olive oil
2 ounces salt pork cut
  into ½-inch dice
A *bouquet garni* of 4
  sprigs of parsley, a
  sprig of thyme, or ½
  teaspoon dried thyme,
  a sprig of celery leaves,
  2 or 3 basil leaves, 1
  whole fresh hot pepper,
  and a bay leaf, tied in
  a square of cheesecloth

2 cloves garlic
2 scallions, chopped using
  green and white parts
⅛ teaspoon cinnamon,
  if liked
Salt, freshly ground
  pepper to taste
Juice of 1 lime or lemon

Put the conch to marinate for several hours in the lime juice. Drain, rinse and beat thoroughly to tenderize. Cut into ½-inch pieces and put into a heavy saucepan, cover with water and simmer gently until tender, about an hour and a half, or cook in a pressure cooker for 30 minutes. Cook, partially covered during the last half hour of cooking, to reduce the liquid.

Heat the olive oil in a heavy covered casserole. Add the salt pork, the *bouquet garni*, garlic, scallions, cinnamon, if liked, and salt and pepper to taste. Stew gently for 5 minutes, then add the conch and their cooking liquid. Cover and simmer for 15 minutes. Remove and discard the *bouquet garni*, add the lime juice and serve accompanied by Riz Créole. Serves 4.

In Guadeloupe the Daube may be thickened with a roux made of 1 tablespoon flour mixed with 1 tablespoon butter. Boiled yams, dasheen or breadfruit may be served with it, or the dish may be turned into Lambi au Riz (Conch with Rice) by making the sauce up to 2 cups with water and adding 1 cup of rice when the conch is added to the casserole with the oil and seasonings. Cook for 20 to 30 minutes, or until the rice is tender.

Daube de Lambis aux Haricots Rouges *Guadeloupe*

Conch Stew with Red Kidney Beans

This variation of the basic Daube, or, as it is also called, Ragoût de Lambis, is popular in Guadeloupe.

Make a Daube de Lambis (Conch Stew) according to the preceding recipe.

Meanwhile put 1½ cups of red kidney beans on to cook in cold water to cover by about 2 inches. Cover, and simmer until they are about half done, about 1 hour. Add *fines herbes* generously, about ¼ cup chopped scallions, 1 tablespoon of finely chopped chives, a teaspoon of minced garlic, ½ teaspoon thyme, ½ teaspoon marjoram, 2 or 3 leaves of basil, and finely chopped and seeded fresh hot pepper. Add salt and continue cooking, partially covered, until the beans are tender and the liquid just about evaporated. Pile the beans in the center of a warmed serving platter and surround them with the conch stew. Serves 4.

Matété de Lambis *Martinique-Guadeloupe*

Rice and Conch Stew

It is impossible to translate matété, which is a Carib word sometimes spelled matoutou. That very useful English word, stew, describes it perfectly adequately. What is interesting is that it would seem that when it is spelled matété, one uses rice in the preparation. When spelled matoutou, one uses farine de manioc, cassava flour. The latter is closer to the original Carib, this being a very ancient dish indeed. It has also undergone considerable refinement in the past couple of hundred years.

2 pounds conch, about 10	1 bay leaf
½ cup lime or lemon juice	3 or 4 melegueta peppercorns
¼ cup olive oil	1 fresh hot red pepper, seeded and chopped
½ cup shallots, chopped	1 tablespoon chopped parsley
4 cloves garlic, minced	2 cups long grain rice
2 tablespoon chopped chives	Salt to taste
¼ teaspoon thyme	

Put the conch to marinate for several hours in the lime juice. Drain, rinse and beat thoroughly to tenderize as described in Conch Stew. Cut into ½-inch pieces.

Heat the oil in a heavy, covered casserole and add the conch, shallots and garlic, and sauté until the conch is golden and the shallots are tender. Add the chives, thyme, bay leaf, melegueta peppercorns, hot pepper, parsley and enough water to cover. Cover and simmer until the conch is tender, about 1½ hours. Measure the liquid and make it up to 4 cups. Add the rice, season to taste with salt, bring to a boil, cover, and cook over low heat until the rice is tender and has absorbed all the liquid. Serves 6.

If liked, cook the rice as in the recipe for Riz Créole and toss it lightly with the cooked conch, which should be cooked partially covered for the last half hour to reduce the liquid.

Meats

Annie's Creole Rabbit

This was a specialty of Annie, our brilliant and gifted Jamaican cook, but whether one can call it pure Jamaican is another matter. There seems to be considerable Spanish influence here, which isn't surprising with Cuba next door, as it were.

2 2-pound rabbits, cleaned, ready to cook, and cut into serving pieces
4 ounces salt pork, cut into cubes
1 onion, finely chopped
2 cloves garlic, chopped
2 tablespoons brandy
1 cup dry sherry
1 cup peeled and chopped tomatoes, or Italian canned plum tomatoes
1 canned pimiento, chopped, and 1 tablespoon juice from can
1 fresh hot green pepper, seeded and chopped
1 bay leaf
⅛ teaspoon orégano
1 cup chicken or rabbit stock, about
Salt, freshly ground pepper to taste

In a heavy frying pan try out the salt pork. Sauté the rabbit pieces in the fat until browned all over. Transfer

111

to a heavy, covered casserole. Fry onion and garlic until browned, and add to the casserole. Pour the brandy into the pan, stir and scrape up all the brown bits. Pour over the casserole contents and ignite. Add all the other ingredients, using enough stock to cover the rabbit pieces. Cover the casserole and cook in a 350° oven for about 2½ hours, or until the rabbit is tender. Serves 6.

Annie's Holiday Tripe
Jamaica

3 pounds tripe
4 tablespoons annatto oil
   (see Index)
3 carrots, scraped and
   finely sliced
1 green bell pepper,
   seeded and coarsely
   chopped
2 scallions, chopped,
   using green and white
   parts
½ cup coarsely
   chopped shallots
2 cups raw rice
2 tablespoons light rum
1 tablespoon chopped
   chives
12 pimiento-stuffed green
   olives, halved

1 tablespoon chopped
   capers, preferably
   Spanish
1 teaspoon vinegar from
   capers
1 pimiento, coarsely
   chopped
1 cup peeled and coarsely
   chopped tomatoes
1 teaspoon tomato paste
1 teaspoon Pickapeppa
   hot pepper sauce, or
   Tabasco
Salt, freshly ground
   pepper to taste
Grated Parmesan cheese

Place the tripe in a large saucepan, cover with cold water, bring to a boil and simmer, covered, until tender, about 2 hours. Drain the tripe and reserve the stock. Cut tripe into 1-inch squares. Heat the oil in a heavy frying pan and sauté the pieces of tripe until golden. Lift out with a slotted spoon into heavy, covered casserole. In the oil remaining in the pan sauté the carrots, bell peppers, scallions and shallots. Lift out and add to casserole. In the oil remaining, adding a little more if necessary, sauté the rice until it has absorbed the oil, being careful not to let it burn. Add to casserole.

Stir the rum into the pan, scraping up all brown bits. Add to the casserole together with the chives, olives, capers, vinegar, pimiento, tomatoes, tomato paste, hot pepper sauce or Tabasco, salt and pepper and about 4 cups of the tripe stock. Simmer gently for 30 minutes.

Serve in rimmed soup bowls with crusty bread, and cheese separately. Serves 6.

Arroz con Carne de Cerdo
Dominican Republic

Rice with Pork

3 cloves garlic, crushed
1 medium onion, finely chopped
1 fresh hot red or green pepper, seeded and chopped
1 bay leaf, crumbled
1 tablespoon chopped parsley, preferably flat Italian type
2 tablespoons distilled white vinegar
Salt to taste
1 pound lean boneless pork, cut into 1-inch cubes

2 slices bacon, coarsely chopped
1 ounce boiled ham, coarsely chopped
4 tablespoons lard
¼ cup tomato purée, freshly made or canned
2 cups raw long-grain rice
1 tablespoon capers, preferably Spanish type
12 small pimiento-stuffed green olives, halved

Mix together the garlic, onion, pepper, bay leaf, parsley, vinegar, salt, pork, ham and bacon and marinate for about an hour.

In a heavy saucepan heat the lard and sauté the marinated mixture for 2 or 3 minutes. Add the tomato purée, the rice, capers and olives and add 4 cups cold water. Stir to mix, bring to a boil, cover and cook over very low heat until the rice is tender and has absorbed all the liquid. Serves 4 as a main course.

Beef Curry   *Trinidad*

4 tablespoons vegetable
    oil
3 pounds beef round or
    chuck, cut into 1-inch
    cubes
2 onions, finely chopped
2 cloves garlic, finely
    chopped
1 tablespoon finely
    chopped chives

1 tablespoon finely
    chopped ginger root
1 small fresh hot pepper,
    seeded and chopped
2 tablespoons curry
    powder
2 cups coconut milk
Salt

Heat the oil in a heavy casserole and add the onions, garlic, chives, ginger root, pepper and curry powder and cook, stirring constantly over medium heat for about 5 minutes, being careful not to let the curry powder burn. Add the beef cubes and cook, stirring, for a few minutes longer. Add the coconut milk, cover the casserole and simmer gently until the meat is tender, about 1½ hours. Season to taste with salt. Serve with boiled white rice and side dishes of grated coconut, mango chutney, raisins, chopped cucumber, chopped tomato, peanuts, and sliced bananas. Serves 6.

Bifteck à la Créole   *Martinique-Guadeloupe*
Steak, Creole Style

3 pounds round or rump
    steak about
    1-inch thick
2 tablespoons olive oil
2 tablespoons red wine
    vinegar

3 cloves garlic, crushed
Salt, freshly ground
    pepper to taste
⅓ cup dark rum

Mix the oil, vinegar, garlic, salt and pepper. Marinate the steak at room temperature in the mixture for 2 or 3 hours, turning several times. Drain well, reserving the marinade.

Broil the steak to the required degree of doneness, basting it with the marinade during the cooking. All of the marinade should be used. Put the steak on a warmed serving platter, pour the juices from the broiling pan over it, heat the rum, pour over the steak and flame it. Slice and serve. Serves 6.

If preferred to the rum, a lump of maître d'hotel butter may be placed on each steak. For this blend ½-cup softened butter with 1 tablespoon of finely chopped parsley. Chill well before using.

Bisté a la Criolla   *Cuba*

Beefsteak, Creole Style

6 tournedos (slices of
  fillet of beef cut from a
  section near the end,
  1½-inches thick)
1 onion, finely chopped
2 cloves garlic, minced
1 heaping teaspoon
  chopped parsley

Juice of 1 lemon
1 teaspoon salt
Several grinds of black
  pepper
6 tablespoons clarified
  unsalted butter

Mix the onion, garlic, parsley, lemon juice, salt and pepper and marinate the tournedos in the mixture for one hour. Remove the steaks and pat them dry with paper towels. Reserve the marinade.

Using a heavy frying pan large enough to hold the meat comfortably, heat the butter, which should cover the bottom of the pan generously. Brown the meat over high heat for 2 to 4 minutes on each side, depending on the degree of doneness desired. Remove to a warmed serving platter. Cook the reserved marinade in the butter remaining in the pan, for 2 or 3 minutes. Pour over the steaks and serve. Serves 6.

Aubergines Toufés ou Toufay   *Haïti*
Beef with Eggplant

2 tablespoons olive or vegetable oil	1 fresh hot green pepper, sliced or 1 teaspoon crushed hot pepper sauce
4 ounces salt pork, cut into ¼-inch dice	1 large clove garlic, crushed
3 pounds beef chuck or bottom round, cut into 1-inch cubes	1 tablespoon tomato paste
6 eggplants, each weighing about 1 pound	Salt, freshly ground pepper
	½ cup beef stock, or water

Heat the oil in a large, heavy casserole and fry the salt pork dice until they have given up all their fat and are quite crisp. Lift out with a slotted spoon and reserve.

Dry the beef cubes on paper towels and sauté, a few at a time, in the fat in the casserole, until they are browned all over. Return the salt pork dice to the casserole with all the beef cubes, cover, and cook over very gentle heat for an hour. Do not add any liquid. Stir from time to time to make sure the beef is not scorching.

Peel and slice the eggplants and add to the casserole with the hot pepper, garlic, tomato paste, salt and pepper to taste and ½ cup beef stock, or water. Stir to mix, cover and cook for about 1¼ hours, or until the beef is tender and the eggplants almost disintegrating. Mash the eggplants to a purée with a wooden spoon, taste for seasoning.

Serve accompanied by rice and beans, either cooked together or separately, (see Index). Serves 6.

Bistec en Cazuela

Puerto Rico

Casseroled Beefsteak

*It is worth going to some trouble to find Seville (bitter)
oranges for this dish. The juice gives an unusual and
delicate flavour which substitutes cannot reproduce.*

6 small steaks, such as
    rump or round, each
    weighing about 8
    ounces
Salt, freshly ground
    pepper
1 cup Seville (bitter)
    orange juice

4 tablespoons lard, or
    vegetable oil
3 medium onions, finely
    chopped
2 cloves garlic, chopped
½ teaspoon orégano
¼ cup beef stock

Have the butcher flatten the steaks, or do it yourself with
a meat cleaver. Season to taste with salt and pepper on
both sides. Place in a bowl and pour in the orange juice.
Cover, and refrigerate overnight, turning once or twice.

Lift the steaks out of the adobo (marinade) and pat
dry. Reserve the adobo. Heat the lard or oil in a heavy
frying pan and sauté the onions and garlic with the orégano. When the onions are tender, but not browned, push
them to one side and sauté the steaks until lightly browned
on both sides. Add the adobo and beef stock. Cover and
cook until the steaks are tender. Serves 6.

Bisté en Cazuela a la Criolla   *Cuba*

Casseroled Beefsteak, Creole Style

6 small steaks such as
  rump, round or sirloin,
  each weighing about 8-
  ounces
2 teaspoons salt
½ teaspoon freshly
  ground pepper
2 cloves garlic, crushed
¼ cup lime, or lemon
  juice
3 tablespoons lard, or
  vegetable oil
1 onion, finely sliced

1 green bell pepper,
  seeded and chopped
1 fresh hot pepper, left
  whole
6 medium tomatoes,
  peeled, seeded and
  pushed through a sieve
Bay leaf
Sprig fresh coriander
¼ cup dry red wine,
  or red wine vinegar
1 cup beef stock

Season the steaks with the salt, pepper, garlic and lime juice and allow to stand for an hour or two. At the end of that time, lift out of the seasonings, pat dry and reserve any juices.

Heat the lard or oil in a heavy frying pan and sauté the steaks, one by one, on both sides until lightly browned. Transfer to a casserole, preferably earthenware*. In the fat remaining in the pan, adding a little more if necessary, sauté the onion and bell pepper. Add to the steaks together with the seasoning juices, the hot pepper, tomatoes, bay leaf and coriander. Add the wine or vinegar to the pan, stir and scrape up any brown bits and add to the casserole. Add the beef stock, cover and simmer gently until the steaks are tender, about 1½ hours. Transfer the steaks to a serving platter and keep them warm. Reduce the sauce if necessary and pour over the steaks. Serve with a purée of boniato (white sweet potato), or other puréed root vegetable. Serves 6.

* NOTE: If using earthenware make sure it is heavy enough not to crack over direct heat. Use one or more asbestos mats if necessary.

Bisté en Rollo   *Cuba*

Rolled Steak

2½-pound flank steak
Salt, freshly ground
  pepper
¼ cup lime, or lemon
  juice
1 clove garlic, crushed
4 ounces ham, cut into
  strips
1 carrot, scraped and
  thinly sliced
1 teaspoon sugar
1 tablespoon unsalted
  butter
1 tablespoon red wine
  vinegar

3 tablespoons dry red
  wine
3 tablespoons vegetable
  oil
1 bay leaf
1 large onion, thinly
  sliced
1 green bell pepper,
  seeded and chopped
½ teaspoon orégano
4 medium tomatoes,
  peeled, seeded and
  chopped
1 pimiento, chopped

Rub one side of the steak with salt and pepper to taste,
1 tablespoon of the lime juice, and the garlic. Cover the
steak with a layer of ham strips. Pour the remaining lime
juice over the carrot slices and leave for a minute or two.
Drain and arrange the carrot slices over the ham. Sprinkle
with the sugar and dot with the butter. Roll the steak with
the grain, fasten with toothpicks, then tie with kitchen
string at both ends and in the middle. Pour the vinegar
and wine over the steak and let it stand for half an hour.

Lift the steak out of the marinade and pat dry with
paper towels. Heat the oil in a heavy casserole and brown
the steak all over. Add the bay leaf, onion, bell pepper,
orégano, tomatoes, pimiento and the marinade. Cover and
cook over low heat until the steak is tender, about 2½
hours, and most of the liquid has evaporated leaving a
thick but not abundant sauce. Serve the steak with the
sauce poured over it. Serve with mashed potatoes, or any
boiled and mashed root vegetable. Serves 4 to 6.

Carne Mechada   *Dominican Republic*
Stuffed Meat

3-pound bola,* or any
   boneless beef such as
   chuck or top round
¼ pound boiled ham,
   chopped
1 tablespoon large
   Spanish capers
2 carrots, scraped and
   finely chopped
1 medium onion, finely
   chopped
1 green bell pepper,
   seeded and finely
   chopped
3 cloves garlic, finely
   chopped

1 tablespoon finely
   chopped parsley
Salt, freshly ground
   pepper
½ teaspoon orégano
¼ cup vegetable oil
4 cups beef stock
3 tablespoons tomato
   paste
1 tablespoon
   Worcestershire sauce
1 tablespoon cider
   vinegar

With a steel, or with a sharp narrow knife make six evenly spaced holes, about the thickness of one's thumb, in the roast almost to the center of the meat. Divide the ham, capers, carrots, onion, pepper, garlic and parsley into six portions, season to taste with salt, pepper and orégano and stuff into holes, ending with the ham. In a heavy casserole large enough to hold the meat comfortably, heat the oil and brown the meat on all sides. Mix the beef stock, tomato paste, Worcestershire sauce and vinegar together and add to the casserole.

Bring to a boil, reduce the heat, cover and cook at a very gentle simmer until the meat is tender, about 2 hours. Remove the meat to a warmed platter, and slice. Pour half of the cooking liquid over the meat. Serve the remaining sauce separately. Serves 6.

* Bola, or boliche, is a Latin American cut of meat from the thigh. It is available in Latin American markets.

Brazo Gitano de Yuca   *Cuba*
Stuffed Baked Cassava Roll

1 pound corned beef
6 tablespoons unsalted
  butter
1 medium onion, finely
  chopped
2 cloves garlic, chopped
2 fresh hot red or green
  peppers, seeded and
  chopped
4 medium tomatoes,
  peeled and chopped

Salt, freshly ground
  pepper to taste
2 pounds cassava root
6 tablespoons unsalted
  butter
3 eggs
1 cup all-purpose flour,
  about

Put the corned beef into a large saucepan, add cold water
to cover. Simmer, covered, until the meat is tender, about
2½ hours. When the meat is cool enough to handle take
it out of the stock, drain and shred it in strips about ⅛-
by 1-inch. Set aside.

In a heavy frying pan heat 2 tablespoons of the butter
and sauté the onion and garlic until the onion is tender.
Add the tomatoes and hot pepper, salt and pepper to taste,
and cook until the mixture is well blended, about 5 minutes. Add the meat, stirring to mix and set aside.

Meanwhile peel the cassava, cut into slices and put on
to cook in salted water, covered, until the cassava is tender,
about 45 minutes. Drain, mash. To make the dough add
the remaining 4 tablespoons of butter, 2 eggs well beaten,
the flour ½ cup at a time, and 1 teaspoon of salt. If the
dough is sticky, add more flour. Roll out on a lightly floured
sheet of waxed paper to a rectangle about 12- by 18-inches
and ½- inch thick.

Spread the meat mixture on the cassava dough to within
about an inch of the edges. With the help of the waxed
paper, lift the long side of the dough and roll it up lengthwise into a compact cylinder. Using large spatulas, transfer the roll to a greased baking sheet. Beat the remaining
egg and brush it on the top and sides of the roll.

Bake in a preheated 350° oven for 1 hour, or until the crust is golden brown. Transfer to a warmed platter, surround with fried ripe plantains. Serve freshly made tomato sauce separately. Serves 6.

This is sometimes made with a dried beef filling. In which case pour boiling water over 1 pound of dried beef. Let stand 5 minutes. Drain and shred. Use in exactly the same way as the corned beef.

Carne de Cerdo Mechada

Dominican Republic

Stuffed Leg of Pork

5 to 6-pound leg of pork	4 cloves garlic, crushed
4 ounces raw ham, coarsely chopped	2 tablespoons white vinegar
1 medium onion, finely chopped	3 tablespoons lard, or vegetable oil
20 small, pitted green olives, chopped	1 fresh, hot pepper, seeded and chopped
2 tablespoons capers	1 cup dry white wine
6 slices bacon, coarsely chopped	2 teaspoons arrowroot, or potato starch
Salt, freshly ground pepper	

With a steel, or with a sharp, narrow knife make evenly spaced holes in the meat, about the thickness of one's little finger, almost to the center of the leg. Stuff each hole with a little of the ham, onion, green olive, capers and bacon. Season the meat with salt and pepper, garlic and vinegar and leave for about an hour.

Heat the lard or oil in a Dutch oven or casserole large enough to hold the meat comfortably. Brown the meat all over. Add the pepper and the wine, and any of the marinade. Cover and cook over low heat until the meat is tender, about 2½ to 3 hours.

Remove the meat to a serving platter and keep warm.

Dissolve the arrowroot in a little water and stir into the
liquid in the casserole. Cook over low heat until lightly
thickened. Adjust the seasoning and serve in a sauce bowl.
Serve with rice, or a starchy vegetable. Serves 6 to 8.

Carne Fiambre   *Dominican Republic*
Cold Beef, Ham and Shrimp Sausage

*This is a traditional dish for a Día del Campo (picnic) or
for an outdoor Sunday buffet luncheon. It is served with
pickled cucumbers and pimiento-stuffed olives, and lettuce and tomatoes with an oil and vinegar dressing.*

1 pound lean ground
  beef, preferably
  ground round
4 ounces lean, boneless
  ham, coarsely chopped
½ pound raw shrimp,
  shelled, deveined and
  coarsely chopped
1 medium onion, coarsely
  chopped
1 clove garlic, coarsely
  chopped

1 fresh hot red or green
  pepper, seeded and
  chopped
Salt, freshly ground
  pepper
2 eggs
Saltine crackers
½ cup tiny frozen
  peas, defrosted
1 egg, well beaten, for
  coating
1 onion, sliced
Bay leaf

Put the ground beef, ham, shrimp, onion, garlic and hot
pepper through the finest blade of a meat grinder. Or,
chop everything as fine as possible and combine. Season
to taste with salt and pepper. Add the 2 eggs, one at a
time, mixing thoroughly. Coarsely crumble enough saltine
crackers to make about 1½ cups, then crush with a rolling
pin. Beat the crackers, half a cup at a time, into the meat
mixture with a wooden spoon, until the texture is smooth.
It should not be sloppy, but firm enough to hold its shape.
Use only the amount of cracker crumbs necessary. Last
of all, fold in the peas as gently as possible. Shape the

mixture into a roll about 10-inches long and about 3-inches in diameter.

Cover a piece of waxed paper generously with more cracker crumbs. Roll the sausage in the crumbs so that it is thickly coated all over. Roll it in the beaten egg, then roll it again in more cracker crumbs to coat thickly. Center the sausage on a double thickness of cheesecloth. Wrap the cheesecloth lengthwise over the sausage to enclose it completely. Tie the ends securely with kitchen string. In the old days, the sausage would have been sewn into a kitchen cloth, but cheesecloth does just as well.

Place the sausage in a heavy, covered casserole large enough to hold it comfortable. Add the sliced onion and the bay leaf, and enough water to cover the sausage by about 2-inches. Bring to a boil, reduce the heat to a simmer, cover and cook for about an hour, or until the sausage is firm to the touch. Lift out of the casserole by the cheesecloth ends and allow to cool. Remove the cheesecloth and place the sausage on a large platter. The cracker crumbs and beaten egg will have formed an attractive outside coating. Cut into ½-inch slices to serve. Serves 6 to 8.

Carne Mechada

Cuba

Stuffed Meat

3-pound boliche*, or any
boneless beef roast
such as chuck or top
round
¼ pound chorizo
sausage, skinned and
chopped
2 slices bacon, chopped
2 ounces boiled ham,
chopped
1 hard-boiled egg,
chopped
2 ounces American cheese
cut in small cubes
12 pimiento-stuffed green
olives, halved
18 seedless raisins
4 pitted prunes, soaked
to soften, quartered
2 teaspoons large Spanish
capers, chopped

½ cup olive oil
1 cup dry sherry
1 onion, chopped
2 cloves garlic, chopped
1 green bell pepper,
seeded and chopped
1 carrot, scraped and
thinly sliced
¼ teaspoon ground
cumin
½ teaspoon orégano,
crumbled
1 bay leaf
Sprig parsley
Salt, freshly ground
pepper
1 cup Seville (bitter)
orange juice
2 cups beef stock

With a steel, or with a sharp narrow knife make six evenly spaced holes about the thickness of one's thumb in the roast, almost to the center of the meat. Divide the sausage, bacon, ham, egg, cheese, olives, raisins, prunes and capers into six equal heaps and stuff into the holes with the fingers, ending with the bacon.

In a heavy casserole big enough to hold the meat comfortably, heat 4 tablespoons of the oil and brown the stuffed meat on all sides. Remove the meat to a platter, discard the oil. Stir the sherry into the pot scraping the sides. Set this liquid aside. Rinse and dry the pot. In it heat the remaining 4 tablespoons of the oil. Sauté the onion, garlic, pepper and carrot until the onion is tender, but not browned. Add the meat, cumin, orégano, bay leaf, parsley, salt and pepper, orange juice, reserved sherry and the beef stock. Bring to a boil, reduce heat to a bare simmer. Cover and cook until the meat is tender, about 2 hours. Remove the meat to a warmed platter and slice.

Strain the sauce and push the solids through a sieve or reduce them to a purée in an electric blender. Stir this into the sauce and heat it through. It should be thickened lightly. Pour some of the sauce over the meat. Serve the remaining sauce separately. Serves 6.

* Boliche, or bola, is a Latin American cut of meat from the thigh. It is available in Latin American markets.

Carne Rellena   *Dominican Republic*
Stuffed Flank Steak

2½-pound flank steak	2 hard-boiled eggs, sliced
3 cloves garlic, crushed	¼ cup vegetable oil
1½ teaspoon salt	4 tablespoons tomato paste
⅛ teaspoon freshly ground pepper	1 tablespoon Worcestershire sauce
1 teaspoon orégano	1 tablespoon vinegar
4 ounces cooked ham	2½ cups beef stock
1 large carrot	1 bay leaf
1 fresh hot, red or green pepper, seeded and chopped	
1 large onion, finely chopped	

Spread the steak with a mixture of garlic, salt, pepper and orégano, stopping about ¼-inch from the edges of the steak. Cut the ham into thin strips and arrange in a layer on top of the garlic mixture. Scrape the carrot and cut into very thin slices with a vegetable peeler and arrange over the ham. Mix the hot pepper and onion together, spread on top of the carrot. Arrange the slices of egg down the center of the steak. Carefully roll the steak up. Fasten with toothpicks and tie firmly with string.

In a heavy covered casserole large enough to hold the steak comfortably, heat the oil. Brown the steak all over, then add the tomato paste, Worcestershire sauce, vinegar, the beef stock, and the bay leaf. Cover and cook at a gentle simmer for 2 to 2½ hours, or until the steak is tender, turning it once or twice during the cooking.

Lift out the casserole onto a warmed serving platter. Remove the toothpicks and string, cut into slices about an inch thick, and serve with the sauce poured over it. Check during the cooking, and if the sauce seems too thin, cook for the last hour partially covered. Serves 6.

Carry de Mouton *Martinique-Guadeloupe*

It could be argued that this is not really a curry since it contains so few of the curry spices. Whatever it is called it is a beautifully subtle dish.

2½ pounds lean lamb,
    cut into 1-inch cubes
4 tablespoons unsalted
    butter
1 onion, finely chopped
4 ounces ham, cut in dice
2 medium tomatoes,
    peeled and chopped
½ teaspoon thyme
1 bay leaf
3 cloves garlic, finely
    chopped

2 whole cloves
⅛ teaspoon nutmeg
⅛ teaspoon cinnamon
Salt, freshly ground
    pepper to taste
1 cup stock (chicken or
    lamb)
1 cup coconut milk
½ cup heavy cream
¼ cup lime, or lemon,
    juice

Heat the butter in a heavy covered casserole or baking pan. Add the onion and sauté until tender but not browned. Add the ham, tomatoes, thyme, bay leaf, garlic, cloves, nutmeg, cinnamon, salt and pepper. Stir and cook for 3 or 4 minutes. Add the lamb and cook for about 5 minutes longer, stirring from time to time. Add the stock, coconut milk and cream and cook, covered, at a gentle simmer for about 2 hours, or until the lamb is tender. Stir in the

lime or lemon juice and cook for a few minutes longer.
Serves 6.

Serve with Riz Créole or Pois et Riz.

Chou à Pomme
Avec la Viande Salée   *Northern Martinique*

Cabbage with Corned Beef

2 pounds corned brisket
    of beef
1 medium onion, stuck
    with a clove
2-pound green cabbage,
    finely shredded
1 cup finely chopped
    onions
½ cup chopped
    scallions using green
    and white parts

2 cloves garlic, minced
1 or 2 fresh hot red
    peppers, seeded and
    chopped, or use a hot
    pepper sauce to taste
Salt, freshly ground
    pepper
¼ cup olive oil

Soak the beef in cold water to cover for 30 minutes. Drain
and rinse. Cut the meat into 1-inch cubes and put on to
cook in fresh cold water with the onion, quartered. Cover
and simmer until the meat is tender, about 2 hours.

Cook the cabbage in boiling salted water, covered, until
tender, 5 to 8 minutes. Drain very thoroughly.

Drain the meat, reserving 1 cup of the stock. Make a
sauce with the stock, cup of chopped onions, scallions,
garlic, hot peppers or pepper sauce, salt, freshly ground
pepper and olive oil. Mix thoroughly, stir, heat through
and pour over the hot cabbage arranged in a serving dish.
Toss lightly. Arrange the beef cubes over the cabbage.
Serves 4.

May be accompanied by rice, or any starchy vegetable
such as breadfruit, potatoes, yams, etc.

Cocido de Riñones   *Puerto Rico*
Kidney Stew

8 lamb's kidneys
4 tablespoons olive oil
1 onion, finely chopped
1 clove garlic, chopped
3 medium tomatoes,
   peeled and chopped

1 fresh hot red or green
   pepper, seeded and
   chopped
Salt, freshly ground
   pepper to taste
Pinch of sugar
1 tablespoon cider or
   white vinegar

Remove skin and excess fat from kidneys. Cut lengthwise
in halves. Soak in salted water for 15 minutes, remove,
and pat dry with paper towels. Set aside.

Heat 2 tablespoons of the oil in a frying pan and sauté
the onion and garlic until the onion is tender but not
browned. Add the tomatoes, hot pepper, salt, pepper,
sugar and the vinegar. Stir well to mix, and cook over
medium heat for 5 minutes, or until the sauce is well
blended and fairly thick. Remove the pan from the heat.

Heat the remaining 2 tablespoons of oil in a heavy
frying pan large enough to hold the kidneys comfortably.
Sauté the kidneys over medium heat, turning frequently,
until they are done, about 5 minutes. Do not overcook,
as kidneys toughen very quickly. Turn the kidneys into
the sauce, and cook for a minute or two to heat the sauce
through. Serves 4.

The kidneys may be served on toast for a light meal.
Or as a main dish with rice, or a starchy vegetable and a
green vegetable or salad.

Colombo D'Agneau   *Northern Martinique*
Lamb Curry

*This curry, given me by Mme. Yveline de Lucy de Fos-
sarïeu of the* de Leyritz Plantation, *can be made with kid
as well as lamb. It is an old family recipe and perfectly*

*illustrates the Hindu influence in the north of Martinique;
the wine represents France, and the vegetables represent
the Americas. It is this ability to bring together foods and
cooking techniques from very widely scattered parts of
the world that is the real genius of Caribbean cooking.*

3 tablespoons peanut oil
3 pounds lean, boneless
  lamb, cut into 2-inch
  cubes
2 medium onions, finely
  chopped
2 cloves garlic, crushed
1 tablespoon tamarind
  pulp (see Glossary)
1 green mango, peeled
  and chopped
1½ tablespoons curry
  powder
2 cups dry white wine

1 pound potatoes, peeled
  and sliced
½ pound West Indian
  pumpkin (calabaza),
  peeled and sliced, or
  use Hubbard squash
1 christophene (chayote),
  peeled and sliced or
  use ½ pound
  zucchini, sliced
Salt
1 teaspoon lime juice
2 tablespoons dark rum,
  preferably Martinique
  rhum vieux

Heat the peanut oil in a large, heavy frying pan and sauté
the lamb until it is lightly browned all over. Transfer to a
casserole, earthenware* if possible. In the oil remaining
in the pan, sauté the onions until golden. Add the garlic,
tamarind pulp, mango, and curry powder. Cook, stirring
from time to time, for 3 to 4 minutes. Add to the casserole
with the wine. Cover and simmer gently for 1½ hours.
Add the potatoes, West Indian pumpkin, christophene,
and salt to taste. Cover and simmer for 30 minutes longer,
or until the lamb is tender and the vegetables done. Stir
in the lime juice and rum, and cook for 3 or 4 minutes
longer.

    The gravy should not be very abundant, but if the dish
seems to be drying out when the vegetables are added,
pour in a little water. Serves 6.

    Serve with Riz Créole, or with Pois et Riz (see Index),
and fried ripe plantains or bananas.

* NOTE: If using earthenware make sure it is heavy enough not to crack over
direct heat. Use one or more asbestos mats if necessary.

Curried Kid

Jamaica

The Jamaicans in a fine frenzy of honesty call this curried goat, which is enough to put anyone off what is an excellent dish. It is best to use kid. Lamb is sometimes substituted, but in my view this is one step too far from the original.

2 tablespoons vegetable
  shortening
3 pounds kid, cut into
  small serving pieces
2 large onions finely
  chopped
3 tablespoons curry
  powder

1 fresh hot red pepper,
  chopped
Bay leaf
½ teaspoon allspice
1 cup coconut milk
Beef or chicken stock
Salt, freshly ground
  pepper to taste
Juice ½ lime

Melt the shortening in a skillet and brown the meat all over. Remove meat to a covered heavy casserole. Sauté the onions in the fat remaining in the skillet until transparent. Add the curry powder and hot pepper and sauté, stirring, for a few minutes. Add to the casserole with the bay leaf, allspice, coconut milk, and enough stock to cover the meat. Season with salt and pepper, cover and simmer gently until meat is tender, about 2 hours. Just before serving, add the lime juice, and cook 2 or 3 minutes longer. Serves 6.

Conejo Tapado

Puerto Rico

Smothered Rabbit

2 2-pound rabbits, ready-
  to-cook and cut into
  serving pieces
1 average head garlic,
  peeled
1 large onion
2 cups tomatoes, peeled,
  seeded and chopped
1 tablespoon olive oil
3 tablespoons capers and
  1 tablespoon vinegar
  from capers

1 cup dry sherry
1 teaspoon orégano
Salt, freshly ground
  pepper to taste
12 new potatoes, scraped
  or peeled
12 pimiento-stuffed
  olives, quartered

Put the rabbit pieces in a heavy, covered casserole. Grind the garlic and the onion and add to the casserole with the tomatoes, oil, capers, caper vinegar, sherry, orégano, salt, and pepper. Cover and simmer gently for about 1½ hours. Add the potatoes and cook for a further 30 minutes.

Young rabbits will cook in about 2 hours; older ones take up to 3 hours, so allow for this when adding potatoes. Just before serving, add the olives. Simmer for a minute or two longer. Serves 6 to 8.

NOTE: This dish does not have a strong garlic flavour despite the fact that a whole head of garlic is used. Most of it disappears in the cooking.

Curried Rabbit

Leeward Islands

2½-pound rabbit,
ready-to-cook and cut
into serving pieces
2 tablespoons unsalted
butter
2 tablespoons peanut oil
2 onions, finely chopped
1 tablespoon curry
powder
3 tablespoons guava jelly

1 cup coconut milk
2 cups rabbit or chicken
stock, about
Salt, freshly ground
pepper to taste
1 to 3 tablespoons lime
juice
2 teaspoons arrowroot

Heat the butter and oil in a heavy frying pan and sauté
the rabbit pieces, a few at a time, until browned on all
sides. Transfer to a heavy, covered flame-proof casserole.
In the fat remaining in the pan, sauté the onions until
golden brown. Add the curry powder and cook for a minute or two, stirring. Add to the casserole, scraping up all
the brown bits from the pan. Add the guava jelly, coconut
milk and enough stock to cover the rabbit pieces, about
2 cups. Season to taste with salt and pepper. Cover and
simmer gently until the rabbit is tender, about 1½ hours.

Adjust the seasoning. Add 1 tablespoon of lime juice,
and taste. More lime juice may be needed according to
the sweetness of the guava jelly; add another tablespoon
or two if necessary. Mix the arrowroot with a little cold
water and stir into the casserole until the sauce has thickened lightly. Serves 4 to 6.

Serve with plain boiled rice, or plain boiled potatoes,
and mango chutney. If a hotter curry is preferred add a
chopped fresh hot red pepper with the cooking liquid.

Deep Dish Meat Pie

St. Thomas

MEAT FILLING:

1 pound lean ground beef, preferably chuck

1 medium onion, finely chopped

1 fresh hot red pepper, seeded and finely chopped, or 1 teaspoon hot dried red pepper, crumbled

1 teaspoon salt

Freshly ground pepper to taste

1 clove garlic, chopped

2 medium tomatoes, peeled and chopped

2 tablespoons unsalted butter

1 tablespoon distilled white vinegar

½ teaspoon thyme

1 tablespoon chopped parsley

1 tablespoon green bell pepper, seeded and chopped

1 tablespoon pimiento-stuffed green olives, chopped

1 tablespoon flour

½ teaspoon dry mustard

3 tablespoons dry sherry

Thoroughly mix together all the ingredients except the flour, mustard and sherry. Pack into a heavy 9-inch frying pan, cover, and cook over low heat for about half an hour. West Indians call this method "sweating"; actually the meat is steamed.

Mix the flour and mustard with a little water and stir into the meat mixture. Mix the meat thoroughly with its own pan liquid as it separates with this cooking method. Stir over low heat until slightly thickened. Add the sherry. Cool and set aside.

PIE CRUST:

2½ cups all-purpose flour

½ teaspoon salt

¾ cup lard, (12 tablespoons) chilled and cut into small bits

Cold water

Sift the flour and salt into a large bowl. With the fingertips rub the lard into the flour until the mixture is crumbly. Sprinkle it with enough cold water to form a stiffish dough, 4 to 6 tablespoons. Gather the dough into a ball and refrigerate for about 15 minutes. Divide the dough into two parts, one slightly larger than the other. Roll out the larger piece to a circle 13-inches in diameter and about ⅛th-inch thick. Drape the dough over the rolling pin and unroll it over a straight-sided 9-inch pie pan that is 1½-inches deep. Gently press the dough into the pan and allow it to overlap all round the outside edge. Trim the overlap to about half-an-inch all round. Spoon the filling into the lined pie pan. Moisten the edges of the crust with cold water.

Roll out the smaller ball of dough to a 10-inch circle, and using the rolling pin as before, fit the pastry over the filling in the pie pan. Turn up the edge of the under pastry and press the edges of top and bottom pastry together. Pinch with the fingers or press with the tines of a fork to make sure the edges are completely sealed. Cut three or four slits in the center of the top pastry to allow the steam to escape during baking.

Bake in a oven preheated to 450° for 10 minutes, then reduce the heat to 350° and continue baking for about 45 minutes longer, or until the crust is golden brown. Serve hot or cold directly from the pie dish. Serves 4 to 6.

Filete al Caldero   *Puerto Rico*
Beef Fillet Pot Roasted

Pot Roasted is a poor translation to explain the Puerto Rican caldero which is a large, heavy round, or oval cast iron or aluminum casserole used widely in this island. Enameled cast-iron is probably the best substitute, but the pot must be a heavy one.

3-pound fillet of beef,
  trimmed
½ cup olive oil, plus
  3 tablespoons
6 tablespoons vinegar
2 large cloves garlic,
  crushed

2 teaspoons salt
Freshly ground pepper
3 medium onions, thinly
  sliced
½ pound sliced
  mushrooms

Mix together the ½ cup of olive oil, vinegar, garlic, salt, a generous amount of freshly ground pepper, and one of the onions. Rub this into the fillet of beef and let it marinate overnight in the refrigerator. Take out the beef and pat dry with paper towels. Discard the marinade. Heat the 3 tablespoons of oil in the caldero and brown the beef all over. Add the remaining 2 onions and the mushrooms. Cover and cook over medium heat on top of the stove for 10 to 15 minutes for rare meat, 18 to 20 minutes for medium rare. Serve with rice and beans, and green peas. Serve the mushrooms and onions with the pan juices as a sauce. Serves 6.

Garlic Pork
Trinidad

Originally Portuguese, this dish reached Trinidad from Guyana where it is traditionally served at Christmas. It has also spread to some of the nearby Windward Islands. Haïtian Griots also bear a strong family resemblance to the dish. In both cases the crisp morsels are excellent served with a hot creole sauce, as an appetizer, or with drinks. With rice, fried plantains, breadfruit or any starchy root vegetable they make an attractive main course.

4 pounds boneless pork
  leg or shoulder
¼ pound garlic, about
  5 average heads
1 teaspoon fresh thyme,
  chopped

1 fresh hot pepper,
  seeded and chopped
2 teaspoons salt
Freshly ground pepper
Juice 1 large lime
2 cups white vinegar
Oil or fat for frying

Blanch garlic, peel and chop. Mix garlic, thyme, hot pepper, salt and several grinds of black pepper together. Wash the pork in lime juice and cut into small cubes, about 1-inch. Put into a container and mix thoroughly with the garlic mixture. Pour on the vinegar and refrigerate, covered, for 2 days. Drain. Pat dry and fry until tender in deep fat or oil. Serve hot. Serves 6 to 8 as a main course.

Daube de Porc
aux Bélangères   *Martinique*
Pork Stew with Eggplant

3-pound piece lean,
  boneless pork
3 tablespoons all-purpose
  flour
2 tablespoons peanut oil
2 tablespoons lard
½ teaspoon thyme
¼ teaspoon sage

6 corns melegueta pepper
  (see Glossary), or
  allspice
Salt, freshly ground
  pepper to taste
3 pounds eggplants,
  peeled and cut into
  1-inch cubes
1 cup water, about

Dredge the pork with flour. Heat the oil and lard in a heavy covered casserole and sauté the pork until it is golden all over. Add the thyme, sage, melegueta peppercorns, salt, freshly ground pepper and water. Cover and cook over low heat until the pork is almost tender, about 2 hours. Add the eggplant, cover, and cook for 15 minutes longer, or until the eggplant is done. Serves 6.

Goat Water

Montserrat

Kid Stew

3 pounds kid, cut into 1-
    inch cubes
2 large onions, finely
    chopped
2 cloves garlic, chopped
1 tablespoon tomato paste
3 cloves

1 teaspoon freshly ground
    pepper
Salt
2 tablespoons unsalted
    butter
2 tablespoons all-purpose
    flour

Put the kid, onions, garlic, tomato paste, cloves, pepper
and salt to taste into a large saucepan. Add enough water
to cover the meat, and cook, covered, at a gentle simmer
until the meat is tender, about 2 hours. Mix the butter
and flour together and add to the pot, stirring until the
stew is lightly thickened. Serves 6.

Serve with plain boiled white rice and boiled dasheen
leaves. Spinach is an adequate substitute for dasheen.

Griots de Porc

Haïti

Glazed Pork Pieces

3 pounds shoulder of
    pork, cut into 2-inch
    cubes
1 large onion, finely
    chopped
½ cup chopped
    shallots
½ teaspoon dried
    thyme
1 cup Seville (bitter)
    orange juice

1 fresh hot red or green
    pepper, chopped
2 cloves garlic, finely
    chopped (optional)
Salt, freshly ground
    pepper to taste
½ cup vegetable oil or
    lard

Place the pork in a heavy, covered casserole with the
onion, shallots, thyme, bitter orange juice, hot pepper,

garlic if liked, salt and pepper to taste and allow to stand for 1 hour at room temperature. Some cooks marinate the pork overnight in the refrigerator.

When ready to cook cover with water and simmer, covered, until the pork is tender, about an hour and a half. Drain thoroughly.

Rinse out the casserole, add the oil or lard and fry the pork pieces until they are brown and crusty on the outside. Serve with Sauce Ti-Malice, banane pesé (fried plantain slices), and fried sweet potatoes. Serves 6.

Guisado de Cabrito   *Puerto Rico*

Kid Stew

3 to 4-pound kid, cut into serving pieces

Juice of 1 Seville (bitter) orange, or ¼ cup orange and lemon juice in proportion of ⅔rds orange to ⅓rd lemon

2 cloves garlic, crushed

½ teaspoon orégano

1 teaspoon salt

½ teaspoon freshly ground pepper

2 tablespoons white vinegar

1 bay leaf

4 ounces ham, coarsely chopped

2-ounce jar pimiento-stuffed green olives, drained

1 tablespoon capers, preferably Spanish

2 medium tomatoes, peeled and chopped

3 pimientos, coarsely chopped

½ cup olive oil

1 cup dry, red wine

12 small, white onions, peeled

Put the kid pieces into a large, covered casserole. Pour the Seville orange juice over the meat turning the pieces to mix well. Leave for about 5 minutes, then drain. Mix the garlic, orégano, salt, pepper and vinegar, and rub into the meat. Leave at room temperature for 1 to 2 hours. Add all the other ingredients except the onions. Cover and cook at a gentle simmer until the kid is tender, about

2½ hours. Half an hour before serving, add the onions. Serves 6.

NOTE: If the kid is meaty, 3 pounds will be enough. If bony, 4 pounds will be needed.

Keshy Yena coe Carni   *Curaçao*
Stuffed Cheese with Beef Filling

4-pound Edam Cheese
½ cup unsalted butter
½ cup chopped onions
1½ pounds lean,
    ground beef
1 green bell pepper,
    seeded and coarsely
    chopped
1 fresh hot red or green
    pepper, seeded and
    chopped, or dash of
    Sambal Oelek or
    Tabasco
½ cup mushrooms,
    coarsely chopped
2 tablespoons brandy

2 tomatoes, peeled and
    coarsely chopped
2 hard-boiled eggs,
    coarsely chopped
¼ cup seedless raisins
¼ cup black olives,
    coarsely chopped
¼ cup finely chopped
    sweet gherkins
1 tablespoon tomato
    catsup
½ cup brown sauce
Salt, freshly ground
    pepper to taste

Heat the butter in a heavy frying pan and sauté the onions until golden brown. Add the beef and sauté lightly. Add the peppers and the mushrooms and sauté for 5 minutes longer, stirring frequently and taking care the mixture does not burn. Heat the brandy, pour over the mixture and ignite, stirring until the flame dies out. Add the rest of the ingredients, season to taste with salt and pepper and cook at a gentle simmer for 5 minutes stirring from time to time.

Meanwhile, remove the red wax covering from the cheese. Cut off the top, hollow out this lid and reserve. Scoop out the cheese leaving a shell about ½-inch thick. Cover the shell and lid with cold water and soak for an

hour. Then drain and wipe dry. Grate scooped-out cheese
and add 1 cup to the meat mixture. Save the rest of the
cheese for another use. Pack the meat mixture into the
cheese shell, replace the top, and put the filled cheese
into a greased 3-quart casserole. Bake uncovered in a
preheated 350° oven for 30 minutes. Do not overcook as
the cheese becomes tough, instead of soft and bubbly.
Slide the cheese out of the casserole onto a warmed serving dish, cut in wedges and serve immediately. Serves 6
to 8.

A popular way of cooking this dish is to peel off the
outer wax covering of the cheese and cut the cheese into
¼-inch slices. Use the slices to line a greased 3-quart
baking dish on bottom and sides, in an overlapping pattern. Pour in the meat mixture and cover with the remaining slices of cheese. Bake for 30 minutes in a preheated
350° oven. Small individual casseroles may also be used,
in which case reduce the cooking time to 15 to 20 minutes.

Kebabs   *Anguilla*

*Broiled, skewered beef with pineapple, tomatoes, peppers
and onions.*

½ cup unsweetened
   pineapple juice
¼ cup distilled white
   vinegar
2 tablespoons molasses
2 teaspoons salt
Freshly ground pepper to
   taste
2 pounds top sirloin of
   beef, cut into 12
   1½-inch cubes

12 small white onions
12 cherry tomatoes
2 medium sized green
   bell peppers, seeded
   and cut into
   1½-inch squares
12 1-inch cubes pineapple

Combine the pineapple juice, vinegar, molasses, salt and
several grinds of black pepper. Add the cubes of beef and
allow to stand in the marinade at room temperature for 1

hour. Drain, reserve marinade to use as a basting sauce.

Meanwhile drop the onions into boiling water and simmer for 5 minutes. Drain, and when cool slip off the skins.

Thread the meat, onions, tomatoes, green peppers and pineapple cubes alternately on four 12-to-14-inch skewers. Brush with marinade.

Using either a charcoal grill, or an oven broiler, both preheated, cook the kebabs 4 inches from the heat, turning every 3 minutes or so for about 10 minutes, or until the beef is cooked to the required degree of doneness. Baste with marinade each time the kebabs are turned. Serve with plain broiled white rice. Pour any remaining marinade over the kebabs. Serves 4.

Lambchi and Boonchi   *Aruba*

Skewered Lamb with Yard-long Beans

2 tablespoons grated onion	¼ cup peanut oil
1 tablespoon Spanish (hot) paprika	2 pounds lean lamb, cut into 16 1½-inch cubes
1 tablespoon curry powder	16 small white onions
1 tablespoon fresh ginger root, grated	8 slices bacon, halved
2 cloves garlic, crushed	2 green peppers, seeded and cut into 16 2-inch squares
1 teaspoon salt	16 1-inch cubes pineapple
¼ teaspoon freshly ground pepper	16 cherry tomatoes
½ cup lemon juice	4 young yard-long beans, parboiled

In a large bowl combine the onion, paprika, curry powder, ginger, garlic, salt, pepper, lemon juice and oil. Add the lamb cubes, mixing thoroughly. Marinate in the refrigerator overnight.

Drop the onions into boiling water and simmer for 5 minutes. Drain, and when cool slip off the skins. Wrap the bacon pieces round the pieces of pepper. Drain the marinated lamb and seasonings. Thread the meat, onions, pineapple, bacon and pepper squares, and the tomatoes alternately on four 12-to-14-inch skewers. Wrap the beans round the skewers, tying them in place at each end with string. Brush on all sides with the marinade.

Using either a charcoal grill, or an oven broiler, both preheated, cook the lambchi and boonchi 4 inches from the heat, turning every 3 minutes or so, for about 10 minutes, or until the lamb is done. Untie the boonchi and slide with the meat, vegetables and pineapple off the skewers on to heated plates. Serves 4.

Serve with the following sauce.

SAUCE:

2 tablespoons prepared mustard

2 tablespoons peanut butter

½ teaspoon ground turmeric

2 tablespoons soy sauce

2 tablespoons Worcestershire sauce

Hot pepper sauce (Tabasco) to taste

Combine all the ingredients and blend thoroughly.

NOTE: Boonchi, sometimes called yard-long beans, Chinese beans, or asparagus beans, are originally from the Asian tropics. The pods have been known to reach 4-feet in length yet only about ½-inch wide. When young they are soft and pliable. They can sometimes be found in Chinese markets.

Lengua Rellena   *Dominican Republic*

Stuffed Tongue

1 fresh beef tongue,
    4 to 5 pounds
2 cloves garlic, finely
    chopped
1 medium onion, finely
    chopped
2 ounces ham, finely
    chopped
1 carrot, scraped and
    finely chopped
1 teaspoon salt
¼ teaspoon freshly
    ground pepper
1 tablespoon Spanish
    capers, chopped

1 medium tomato, peeled
    and chopped
1 tablespoon seedless
    raisins, chopped
Freshly made bread
    crumbs
¼ cup olive oil
1 tablespoon vinegar
½ teaspoon orégano
¼ cup tomato paste
1 bay leaf
1 medium onion, coarsely
    chopped

Put the tongue into a large, heavy, covered casserole that will hold it comfortably. Cover with cold water, bring slowly to a boil, boil for 5 minutes, remove scum, reduce heat to a simmer, cover and cook for 2 hours. When cool enough to handle, remove from stock, skin, and trim the root end. Make a lengthwise incision down the front of the tongue, taking care not to sever the two halves. Reserve stock and rinse out casserole.

Meanwhile make a stuffing from the garlic, finely chopped onion, ham, carrot, salt, pepper, capers, tomato, raisins and enough bread crumbs to hold the mixture together. Stuff into the tongue and secure with toothpicks.

Heat the oil in the casserole and sauté the stuffed tongue on all sides. Turn right side up. Add enough of the reserved stock barely to cover, add the vinegar, orégano, tomato paste, bay leaf and onion. Simmer, partially covered, until the tongue is tender, about 1 hour.

If the sauce is very abundant and thin, remove tongue to a warmed serving platter and reduce the sauce over brisk heat until it is of medium thick consistency. Potatoes are often cooked with this dish. If liked, add 6 to 8 peeled potatoes during the last half hour of cooking. Serves 6 to 8.

Lapin aux Pruneaux   *Martinique*

Rabbit with Prunes

1 rabbit, about 2½
   pounds, ready-to-cook
   and cut into serving
   pieces
1 teaspoon thyme
2 cups dry red wine
4 ounces bacon, chopped
2 tablespoons olive oil
2 tablespoons all-purpose
   flour

Salt, freshly ground
   pepper to taste
3 onions, coarsely
   chopped
1 bay leaf
2 sprigs parsley
Celery stalk with leaves
8 ounces pitted prunes,
   soaked in 1 cup dry
   red wine
2 tablespoons dark rum

Marinate the rabbit for 24 hours in red wine and thyme. Heat the oil in a heavy covered casserole and try out the bacon. Season the flour with salt and pepper. Drain the rabbit, reserving the marinade. Pat the rabbit pieces dry with paper towels and dredge with the seasoned flour. Sauté the rabbit in the bacon fat and oil until lightly browned on both sides, a few pieces at a time. Set aside. In the fat remaining in the casserole, sauté the chopped onions until lightly browned.

Return the rabbit pieces to the casserole, add the bay leaf, parsley, celery, the reserved marinade and the prunes with the wine in which they have soaked. Bring to a boil, reduce the heat, cover and cook at a gentle simmer until the rabbit is tender, about 2 hours. Adjust the seasoning, stir in the rum and cook for 2 or 3 minutes longer. Serves 4 to 6.

Le Tassau de Boeuf   *Haïti*
Marinated Beef, Dried and Fried

*Various kinds of meat or poultry are cut into thin strips
and marinated for several hours in a mixture of Seville
(bitter) orange juice, lemon juice, vinegar, herbs, onions,
chives, shallots, salt and hot peppers. They are then
removed and dried, either in the sun, or a slow oven, and
finally fried in oil. Tasseau, which translates literally into
tassel, is often spelled Tasso as well as Tassau. It is served
with Bananes Pesées (Fried Plantain slices), and rice.
Seville (bitter) orange juice is used a great deal in Haïtian
cooking. When it is not available use equal quantities of
lemon and orange juice.*

1½ pounds flank
  steak, cut into
  ¼-inch slices
½ cup chopped
  shallots
2 cloves garlic, crushed
½ teaspoon thyme
1 medium onion, chopped
1 fresh hot green pepper,
  chopped
4 whole cloves
2 teaspoons salt

½ teaspoon freshly
  ground pepper
2 teaspoons sugar
  (optional)
¾ cup Seville (bitter)
  orange juice, or equal
  amounts orange and
  lemon juice
¾ cup lemon juice
Cane or white vinegar
3 tablespoons vegetable
  oil

Combine all the ingredients except the beef, vinegar and
vegetable oil. Stir to mix well, add the beef and enough
vinegar to cover. Marinate for 6 hours. Lift out, drain and
dry with paper towels. Place the marinated beef in a shallow baking dish, cover with cheesecloth and dry in the
sun for 2 hours, or (uncovered) in a 170° oven for 2½
hours.

Heat the vegetable oil in a large heavy frying pan and
sauté the meat over fairly brisk heat until lightly browned
on both sides.

Serve with Bananes Pesées (Fried Plantain slices) and

rice, or with boiled green bananas and rice.

Veal, turkey, kid and lamb may be cooked in the same way. Serves 4 to 6.

L'Épaule de Porc Fourre   *Guadeloupe*
Stuffed Shoulder of Pork

4-pound shoulder of pork
¾ cup dark rum
2½ cups dry bread
  crumbs
1 cup milk
½ teaspoon each sage
  and thyme
1 tablespoon chopped
  chives
½ small fresh hot
  pepper, seeded and
  chopped

1 bay leaf, crushed
1 tablespoon chopped
  parsley
2 large cloves garlic,
  chopped
Salt, freshly ground
  pepper
6 melegueta peppercorns
  (see Glossary) crushed
1 cup chicken stock

Have the butcher bone the shoulder of pork, or do it yourself. Score the skin, which should be left on, at intervals of about ⅛th-inch. Pour ½ cup of the rum over the meat and let it stand while the stuffing is prepared. Soak the bread crumbs in the milk then squeeze dry. Mix with the sage, thyme, chives, hot pepper, bay leaf, parsley, garlic, salt, and pepper to taste and the melegueta peppercorns. Drain the rum from the meat and pour it over the stuffing, mixing lightly. Stuff the shoulder and sew it up. Roast on a rack in a roasting pan in a 325° oven for 2 hours and 45 minutes or until a meat thermometer registers 180°. Remove the meat to a serving platter and keep warm.

Pour off the fat from the pan, add the remaining ¼ cup of rum into the pan, stir and scrape up all the brown bits. Pour in the chicken stock and simmer until reduced to 1 cup. Serve in a sauceboat separately. The skin of the shoulder should be crisp and crunchy. Serves 6.

Meat Patties

Jamaica

I used to buy these patties for a mid-morning snack during recess, when I attended Wolmer's School, in Kingston, Jamaica. The old woman who made them, and sold them to us from a big straw basket covered with a white cloth, had a generous hand with the hot peppers that give the patties their special flavor. She also used annatto which adds a subtle extra flavor. I have made the patties using other types of fresh hot peppers, but the result is not the same. However, hot crushed peppers, put up in vinegar and salt, from one or another of the Caribbean islands, are available in some Latin-American and Caribbean markets and Picka-pepper hot pepper sauce will also give the authentic flavor to the patties. The amount used is a matter of taste.

2 tablespoons vegetable oil
1 teaspoon annatto seeds
1 pound lean ground beef
1 medium onion, finely chopped
1 clove garlic, crushed
1 cup tomato, peeled, seeded and chopped
Salt, freshly ground pepper
1 whole fresh **red** pepper, minced, or 1 teaspoon crushed peppers in vinegar
½ teaspoon thyme
2 eggs, slightly beaten
1 egg white, beaten until foamy
Flaky pastry

Heat the oil in a large frying pan and add the annatto seeds. Cook for a minute or two, until the seeds have given up their color. Remove seeds with a slotted spoon and discard. Or use achiote oil if you have it ready made. Add the beef and cook it, breaking it up with a fork, until it begins to brown. Add the onion and garlic and cook until the onion is tender. Add the tomato, salt, pepper, hot pepper and thyme and cook, stirring, for 5 minutes longer. The mixture should be quite dry. Remove from the heat and stir in the 2 beaten eggs. Return to the heat and cook, stirring for 2 or 3 minutes longer. Cool to room temperature.

Roll out the pastry ⅛-inch thick and cut into 5-inch circles. Place ½-cup of the meat mixture on one side of each circle, fold over into a crescent. Seal the edges by pinching with the fingers or crimping with a fork. Brush with beaten egg white and prick the tops to let the steam escape.

Bake on an ungreased cooking sheet in a 425° oven for 20 to 30 minutes, or until lightly browned. Serve for lunch with a vegetable or a salad, or as a snack. Makes about 12 patties.

For cocktails put 1 teaspoon of the meat mixture on 2-inch pastry circles, bake 15 to 20 minutes.

A teaspoon of paprika may be used instead of the annatto seeds and 2 slices of bread, soaked in milk and squeezed dry, may be used instead of the 2 eggs.

FLAKY PASTRY:

2 cups all-purpose flour
½ teaspoon salt
3 ounces (6 tablespoons) unsalted butter
3 ounces (6 tablespoons) lard
Cold water

Sift the flour and salt into a basin. Divide the butter and lard into 4 equal parts. Rub 1 part each of lard and butter into the flour, and add enough cold water to make an elastic dough.

Roll out the dough onto a floured board into a strip about 8-inches wide. Cut 1 part each of the remaining butter and lard into small pieces and dot ⅔ of the pastry with it. Dredge lightly with flour.

Fold the section of pastry without fat over the middle one-third of the pastry strip. Then fold the first portion over to form a square. Press the open edges lightly together with a rolling pin to prevent the air escaping, and turn the pastry so that an open end faces you. Roll the pastry into a strip as before, and repeat the process until the remaining fat is used. Wrap the pastry in waxed paper and refrigerate for at least 1 hour before using.

Mondongo

Puerto Rico

Tripe Stew

3 pounds tripe
½ cup Seville (bitter)
    orange juice, or orange
    and lemon juice mixed
    in the proportion of
    ⅔ orange to ⅓
    lemon
2 ounces salt pork,
    chopped
1 teaspoon annatto
1 large onion finely
    chopped
4 ounces ham, coarsely
    chopped
2 large tomatoes, peeled
    and chopped
1 fresh hot green pepper,
    seeded and chopped

1 pimiento, chopped
2 or 3 sprigs fresh
    coriander, coarsely
    chopped
2 or 3 sprigs parsley,
    coarsely chopped
2 cups cooked chick peas
6 medium sized potatoes,
    peeled and halved
1 pound pumpkin, peeled
    and cut into
    1-inch cubes
Salt to taste

Put the tripe into a heavy, covered casserole. Pour the Seville orange juice over it and let it stand for 5 minutes or so. Cover with cold water, bring to a boil, reduce the heat, cover and simmer for 1½ hours. Drain, reserving stock, cool, cut into squares and return to the casserole.

In a heavy skillet try out the salt pork, add the annatto and cook until the seeds have given up all their color, a minute or two. Remove the seeds with a slotted spoon. Add the onion and sauté until it is tender. Add the ham, tomatoes, hot peppers, pimiento and coriander and cook for a few minutes longer. Add to the tripe. Add the chick peas, potatoes and pumpkin and enough of the reserved stock to cover, about 3 cups. Season to taste with salt, cover and cook at a gentle simmer until the tripe and potatoes are done, about half an hour. The pumpkin will disintegrate and thicken the sauce lightly. Serves 6.

Mondongo de Cerdo, Estilo Coloma

Dominican Republic

Pork Tripe, Coloma Style

3 pounds pork tripe
(available in pork
stores), or use
honeycomb tripe
1 tablespoon salad oil
1 onion, sliced
1 clove garlic, chopped
1 bell pepper, seeded and
chopped
1 hot green pepper,
chopped
1 cup canned Italian
plum tomatoes
Salt, freshly ground
pepper to taste

1 tablespoon capers and 1
tablespoon vinegar
from capers
1 tablespoon fresh
coriander chopped
¼ teaspoon dried
orégano
1 tablespoon
Worcestershire sauce
1 tablespoon tomato paste
½ cup dark, dry
Bacardi rum
Grated Parmesan cheese

Cook the tripe in salted water until tender, about 2 hours.
Drain and cut into squares. Transfer to a heavy casserole.
Heat the oil in a skillet and sauté the onion, garlic, bell
pepper, and hot pepper until the onion is transparent. Add
the tomatoes, salt, pepper, capers, caper vinegar, coriander, orégano, and Worcestershire sauce. Pour over the
tripe and simmer for 15 minutes. Add the tomato paste.
Add the rum and simmer for a few minutes longer. Serve
with grated cheese passed separately. Serves 6 to 8.

Olive's Seasoned-up Pot Roast

St. Kitts

3 pounds fresh brisket of beef
2 tablespoons malt vinegar
2 tablespoons soy sauce
1 teaspoon fresh thyme, coarsely chopped, or ½ teaspoon dried, crumbled
1 teaspoon fresh marjoram, coarsely chopped, or ½ teaspoon dried, crumbled
1 tablespoon coarsely chopped parsley, preferably flat Italian type
1 tablespoon coarsely chopped celery leaves

2 tablespoons chopped chives, or scallions, using green and white parts
1 teaspoon salt
¼ teaspoon freshly ground pepper
2 teaspoons brown sugar
2 tablespoons unsalted butter
1 carrot, scraped and quartered
¼ cup coarsely chopped shallots
1 whole fresh hot red or green pepper, stem left on
2 cups beef stock, or water
2 teaspoons arrowroot (optional)

Sprinkle the meat with the vinegar and soy sauce. Mix the thyme, marjoram, parsley, celery leaves, chives, salt and pepper together and rub into the meat. Leave at room temperature, uncovered, for 2 or 3 hours.

Scrape off and reserve the herbs together with any liquid. Pat the meat dry with paper towels and rub in the brown sugar.

Heat the butter in a heavy, covered casserole and brown the meat on all sides, adding carrot and shallots to lightly brown at the same time. Add the whole pepper, the reserved herbs, marinade liquid, and the beef stock or water. Cover and cook at a bare simmer until the meat is tender, about 2½ hours, turning the meat once or twice during the cooking. Remove and discard the pepper before serving.

Potatoes, tannias, more carrots, or any other root vegetables may be added during the last half hour of cooking. If a thicker gravy is preferred, mix the arrowroot with 1 tablespoon of cold water, stir into the casserole and cook, stirring, until the gravy is lightly thickened. Serves 6 to 8.

Nicole Scott's Grillots   *Haïti*

Baked Pork Cubes

1 cup vinegar
1 large onion, very thinly sliced
1 red or green bell pepper, seeded and chopped
2 cloves garlic, chopped
Salt, freshly ground pepper

2 tablespoons chopped parsley
3 or 4 fresh hot red peppers, seeded and chopped
5-pound shoulder of pork, cut into 2-inch cubes

Combine the vinegar, onion, sweet pepper, garlic, salt, freshly ground pepper, parsley and hot peppers in a large bowl and mix well. Add the pork cubes and marinate overnight in the refrigerator, turning from time to time.

Pour the contents of the bowl into a shallow baking pan and bake in a 400° oven. From time to time pour off and reserve any juices that accumulate in the baking tin. They will be used as a sauce to serve with the grillots. The pork is ready when the pieces are crusty, about 1½ hours. Serves 8 to 10.

To serve, heat the pan juices and pour into a sauceboat. Have Nicole Scott's Ti-Malice sauce in another sauceboat (see Recipe index). Serve with platters of Banane Pesé (Fried Plantain slices), and fried sweet potatoes, preferably white sweet potatoes (see Index).

Otro Mondongo
Another Tripe Stew

Puerto Rico

3 pounds tripe
Juice 1 Seville (bitter)
    orange or ¼ cup
    orange and lime juice
    mixed in proportions of
    ⅔ orange to ⅓
    lime
4 ounces salt pork, cubed
4 ounces boiled ham,
    chopped coarsely
3 or 4 sprigs fresh green
    coriander, finely
    chopped
⅛ teaspoon ground
    saffron

¼ cup ground almonds
1 tablespoon Spanish
    capers
2-ounce jar pimiento-
    stuffed green olives
1 pound each cassava
    root, sweet potato,
    dasheen (taro root) and
    yam, peeled and sliced
2 green plantains
Salt, freshly ground
    pepper

Put the tripe and the bitter orange juice into a large saucepan with enough water to cover and simmer gently until
the tripe is tender, about 2½ hours. Drain, reserving stock,
and cut into squares.

Try out the salt pork in a heavy frying pan and sauté
the pieces of tripe. Return them to the saucepan. In the
fat remaining in the pan, sauté the ham until lightly
browned. Add to the tripe. Add the coriander, saffron,
almonds, capers, green olives, cassava, sweet potato,
dasheen and yams to the tripe with enough of the reserve
stock to cover. Season to taste with salt and pepper, cover
and cook for half an hour longer, or until the vegetables
are done. Meanwhile put the plantains on to cook in their
skins in plain water and simmer for half an hour. Cool,
peel, slice and add to the tripe, cooking just long enough
to heat through. Serve in large, rimmed soup plates giving
each person a slice of each of the vegetables. Serves 6.

Accompany the tripe with a hot pepper sauce.

Oxtail Stew   *St. Kitts and Leeward Islands*

1 oxtail, about 3 pounds,
  cut into
  2-inch pieces
4 tablespoons unsalted
  butter
½ cup chopped
  shallots
½ pound carrots,
  scraped and sliced
2 cups beef stock, about
1 teaspoon annatto,
  ground

⅛ teaspoon cinnamon
⅛ teaspoon nutmeg
Salt, freshly ground
  pepper to taste
2 teaspoons caramel
  colouring
2 tablespoons all-purpose
  flour
1 cup golden rum
1 tablespoon lime juice

Heat the butter in a heavy covered casserole. Sauté the oxtail pieces together with the shallots and carrots until the oxtail is lightly browned all over. Add enough beef stock barely to cover. Add the annatto, cinnamon, nutmeg, salt, pepper and caramel. Cover and simmer gently for 2½ hours.

Remove from the heat, skim off excess fat, reserving 1 tablespoon to mix with the flour. Mix the flour and fat together and add to the stew, stirring over low heat until the liquid is lightly thickened. Stir in the rum, partially cover, and cook over low heat for another 15 minutes, or until the oxtail is tender. Stir in the lime juice. Serves 6 to 8.

Serve with boiled potatoes or any starchy root vegetable.

Pasteles   *Puerto Rico*
Steamed Meat Patties

Pasteles are very popular in Puerto Rico, especially during the Christmas season. They resemble the tamales of Mexico and the hallacas of Venezuela.

FILLING:

1 pound lean, boneless pork loin, coarsely chopped

½ pound lean, boneless ham, coarsely chopped

1 medium onion, finely chopped

1 clove garlic, minced

1 green bell pepper, seeded and finely chopped

2 pimientos, finely chopped

1 tablespoon fresh green coriander, finely chopped

1 teaspoon dried orégano

2 tablespoons capers

18 small pitted green olives

½ cup seedless raisins

2 tomatoes, peeled and chopped

1 cup cooked chick peas

½ cup slivered almonds (optional)

¼ cup achiote lard (see Index)

½ cup chicken stock, or water

½ teaspoon hot pepper sauce (optional)

Mix all the ingredients together and set aside until ready to fill the pasteles.

Some cooks simmer the mixture for 30 minutes, others cook it for 1 hour. Still others prefer it left raw feeling the flavor is better if the mixture cooks in the dough. It is a matter of choice.

DOUGH:

3 green plantains, or same weight in green bananas, (about 3 pounds), or a mixture of both

1½ pounds yautía (taro), white or yellow

½ cup achiote lard (see Index)

Salt

Milk or stock

Peel the plantains and yautías and grate on the coarse side of a grater. Reduce to a smooth paste in an electric blender with the achiote lard, salt to taste, and enough milk or stock to make a spreadable paste. The plantains and *yau-*

tías can also be reduced to a paste, after grating, in a large mortar.

Traditionally pasteles are wrapped in plantain leaves, but these are not easy to get. Kitchen parchment is an adequate substitute. Have ready 18 pieces of kitchen parchment cut into 10- by 8-inch rectangles. Grease lightly with butter or oil. Spread a thin layer, 4- by 6-inches, of the masa on to each piece, patting with the fingers to make the layer smooth and fairly thin.

Place 3 tablespoons of the filling a little to one side of the center of the masa. Fold the parchment in half so that the filling is covered by the dough. Fold the parchment back towards the center. Fold the ends toward the middle to make a neat package. Repeat the process with the remaining sheets of parchment.

Tie the pasteles in pairs with the folded sides inside, and tie securely with kitchen string. Have ready a large pot filled with boiling water. Lower the pasteles into it and bring back to a boil. Reduce the heat and simmer for 1 hour, turning once during the cooking period.

Drain, remove the strings and serve the pasteles in their wrappings on warmed plates. Makes 18 pasteles.

Pastel de Mapueyes   *Dominican Republic*
Yam Pie

Mapuey is a middle-sized white yam of the Dioscorea family, not to be confused with the sweet potato which is so often incorrectly called a yam. This particular yam is a great favorite in the Dominican Republic. Ask for it by name in Caribbean markets and where it is not available use any high quality white yam.

1½ pounds mapuey or other middle-sized white yam
1 tablespoon lemon juice
Salt
6 tablespoons unsalted butter
½ cup milk
3 eggs
4 tablespoons vegetable oil
2 pounds pork, ground
½ pound ham, ground
1 onion, finely chopped
2 cloves garlic, finely chopped
½ teaspoon orégano
3 tablespoons tomato paste
1 cup water
1 teaspoon Worcestershire sauce
1 tablespoon white vinegar
1 teaspoon salt
2 teaspoons capers
12 pimiento-stuffed green olives, halved

Peel and slice the mapueyes and put on to cook in a large saucepan with water to cover, lemon juice and salt. Cover and simmer until the yam is tender, about 30 minutes. Drain, and mash with the butter, milk and 2 of the eggs, lightly beaten. Set aside.

Heat the oil in a large frying pan and sauté the pork, ham, onion, garlic and orégano until the meat has lost all its color. Add the tomato paste, water, Worcestershire sauce, vinegar, and salt, and cook, uncovered, for 30 minutes. Add the capers and olives, and remove from the heat.

Butter a fireproof soufflé dish or mold and put in half of the yam purée, spreading the purée up the sides of the mold. Put in the filling, then cover with the rest of the purée. Beat the remaining egg and brush the top of the pie with it. Bake in a 350° oven until heated through, about 30 minutes. Serves 6.

Patas de Cerdo Guisada   *Puerto Rico*

8 fresh pig's feet
2 cups Sofrito
½ pound chorizo
   sausage, sliced
2 cups cooked chick peas
1 tablespoon fresh
   coriander, chopped

½ pound potatoes,
   peeled and cut into
   1-inch slices
½ pound West Indian
   pumpkin, or Hubbard
   squash peeled and cut
   into 1-inch cubes
Salt

Put the pig's feet into a large kettle or casserole with enough cold water to cover by about 1-inch, bring to a boil, cover, reduce the heat and simmer until they are almost tender, about 3 hours. Drain, reserve liquid, and return the pig's feet to the casserole. Add the Sofrito, sausage, chick peas, coriander, potatoes and pumpkin. Add as much of the reserved liquid as necessary to cook the potatoes and pumpkin, and simmer gently, covered, until the potatoes are done, about 30 minutes. Taste for seasoning, and add a little salt, if necessary. Serves 4.

For a meatier dish, used 4 fresh pork hocks instead of the pig's feet.

Pastel de Mondongo   *Dominican Republic*
Tripe Soufflé

1 pound tripe
4 tablespoons freshly
   grated Parmesan
   cheese
1 cup freshly made bread
   crumbs

Salt, white pepper
2 tablespoons unsalted
   butter, melted
4 eggs

Cut the tripe into squares and place in a heavy saucepan with water to cover by about 1 inch. Cook until tender, about 2½ hours, partially covered so that when the tripe is cooked there is very little liquid left. Be careful not to let the tripe burn. Transfer the tripe and liquid to a blender and reduce to a purée on high speed.

Pour the tripe into a mixing bowl. Add the cheese and bread crumbs. Season to taste with salt and pepper. Add the butter. Beat the eggs until light and fold into the mixture. Pour into a 6-cup soufflé dish or baking dish and bake in a 400° oven until set, about 20 minutes. Serves 3 to 4.

Pepperpot   *Trinidad, Barbados, St. Kitts*

This meat stew is a very ancient Amerindian dish from Guyana that has spread throughout the English-speaking Caribbean islands. I have had it in Trinidad, and in St. Kitts, and it is popular in Barbados.

The ingredient which gives the dish its distinctive character is cassareep, which the Guyanese pronounce cassarip. It is made by grating raw cassava and squeezing out the juice, which is then boiled down. When it begins to turn brown, it is flavoured with salt, brown sugar, cinnamon and cloves and the boiling continued until the cassareep has the consistency of a thick, dark brown syrup. Some cooks add a little gravy-browning to get the rich colour needed. Commercially bottled cassareep can be bought in some West Indian markets.

Cassareep keeps indefinitely, and the "trash", the squeezed dry grated raw cassava can be used to make cassava bread, or biscuits. Cooked and drained, it can be adapted for the cassava in the Cuban dish, Brazo Gitano, a baked cassava roll with a corned beef filling.

All sorts of stories are told about cassareep. It is said to be a meat tenderizer, and/or a preservative, and since meats can be added to the pot daily there are stories of pepperpots kept going from generation to generation.

It should not be confused with Jamaican pepperpot, which is a soup.

1 pound oxtail, cut into
  joints
1 calf's foot, quartered
2 pounds lean pork or
  beef, cut into 2-inch
  cubes
1 stewing chicken, cut
  into serving pieces

½ pound salt beef
½ cup cassareep
2 or 3 hot peppers, tied
  in cheesecloth
Salt

Put all the ingredients into a large casserole or soup kettle
with enough cold water to cover, bring to a boil, lower
the heat and simmer gently until the meats and the chicken
are tender and the sauce quite thick. Remove the hot
peppers before serving. Serves 8 to 10. Serve with boiled
rice.

Picadillo *Cuba*

Beef Hash

¼ cup annatto oil
1 large onion, finely
  chopped
1 large green bell pepper,
  seeded and finely
  chopped
1 clove garlic, finely
  chopped
1 fresh hot red or green
  pepper, seeded and
  chopped
2 pounds ground round
  steak

2 large tomatoes, peeled
  and chopped, about
  2 cups
½ teaspoon ground
  cumin
Salt
Freshly ground pepper
½ cup seedless raisins
¼ cup pimiento-stuffed
  green olives, chopped
1 tablespoon capers

Heat the oil in a large frying pan and cook the onion, bell
pepper, garlic and hot pepper until the onion is tender but
not browned. Add the meat and cook, stirring and breaking it up until it has lost its color. Add the tomatoes,
cumin, salt and pepper to taste. Add the raisins, mix thoroughly and simmer gently, uncovered, until cooked about

20 minutes. Add the olives and capers, and cook for a few minutes longer. Serve with plain boiled white rice, black beans and fried ripe plantains. Serves 6.

If liked, this hash may be made with 1½ pounds ground beef and ½ pound ground pork.

Pernil al Horno a la Criolla   *Puerto Rico*
Roast Leg of Lamb, Creole Style

4-pound leg of lamb	1 tablespoon olive oil
2 cloves garlic	1 tablespoon all-purpose
2 teaspoons orégano	flour
1 teaspoon salt	1 cup lamb or chicken
1 teaspoon freshly ground	stock
black pepper	

Remove the tough, fiber-like covering from the leg. Score the fat in a criss-cross pattern. Crush the garlic and mix it with the orégano, salt, pepper and olive oil. Rub into the meat, cover and refrigerate for 24 hours.

Before cooking let the meat come to room temperature. Drain off any liquid that has collected and pour it over the meat as a marinade. Put the lamb on a rack in a roasting pan and roast in an oven preheated to 350° for 1¼ hours for underdone meat when the juices will run rosy if meat is pricked with a fork, to 1½ hours for well-done meat. Transfer the lamb to a platter.

Spoon off excess fat from the roast pan, leaving about 1 tablespoon. Over low heat stir in the flour, scraping up all the brown bits. Cook for a minute or two, add the stock, bring to a boil, lower heat and simmer for a few minutes. Adjust seasoning, add any juices that may have run out of the meat, and pour into a sauceboat. Serves 6 to 8.

Picadillo de Carne Cocida   *Cuba*
Beef Hash

This traditional dish is served with plain white rice, black beans, fried ripe plantains and Cuban-style fried eggs.

2 to 2½ pounds boiled beef, preferably brisket, coarsely chopped

2 tablespoons vegetable oil

2 tablespoons unsalted butter

2 green bell peppers, seeded and chopped

1 large onion, finely chopped

1 clove garlic, chopped

4 large tomatoes, peeled, seeded and chopped

1 bay leaf

¼ teaspoon ground cloves

Salt, freshly ground pepper to taste

1 tablespoon white distilled vinegar

Heat the butter and oil in a large frying pan and add the green peppers, onion and garlic and cook until the onion is lightly browned. Add the tomatoes, bay leaf, cloves, salt and pepper and cook gently for about 10 minutes. Add the vinegar and the boiled beef and cook until the meat is heated through. Serves 6.

HUEVOS ESTILO CUBANO:

Deep-fried eggs, Cuban Style

Vegetable oil for deep frying

6 eggs

Pour the oil to a depth of about 1½ inches into a heavy frying pan large enough to hold at least 3 eggs at a time. Heat the oil until the surface ripples gently (175° on a deep-frying thermometer).

Be careful not to overheat the oil as this will make the whites puff and brown. They should remain smooth, almost like an egg poached in water. Break the eggs into saucers and slide into the frying pan. Gently lift the whites over the yolk with a tablespoon. Deep fry the eggs for 2 or 3 minutes. The yolks should be soft. Lift out with a slotted spatula and drain on paper towels. Serve immediately as an accompaniment to the picadillo.

Pierna de Cerdo al Horno
Dominican Republic

Roast Leg of Pork

5 to 6-pound leg of pork
4 cloves garlic, crushed
1 teaspoon orégano
2 teaspoons salt
1 teaspoon freshly ground pepper
¼ cup lime, or lemon, juice
3 tablespoons vegetable oil
1 fresh hot pepper, seeded and mashed
2 cups dry white wine
2 teaspoons arrowroot, or potato starch
½ cup sliced green olives

Prick the pork leg deeply all over with a two-tined fork. Mix together the garlic, orégano, salt, pepper, lime juice and 1 tablespoon of the oil. Rub into the leg. Place the leg in a Dutch oven or heavy casserole large enough to hold it comfortably, cover and refrigerate overnight, turning once or twice, or leave at room temperature for 3 or 4 hours. Bring chilled leg to room temperature before cooking.

Using a rubber spatula, scrape the marinade from the pork and reserve together with any marinade remaining in the casserole. Rinse and dry the casserole. Pat the leg dry with paper towels. Heat the remaining 2 tablespoons of oil in the casserole and brown the leg all over. Add the hot pepper, the wine and the reserved marinade and cook, covered in a 325° oven for 3½ hours or until done. A meat thermometer should register 180°.

Remove the leg to a serving platter and keep warm.

Dissolve the arrowroot in cold water and stir into the juices in the casserole. Add the olives. Cook over medium heat, stirring, until thickened lightly. Serve separately. If there is not sufficient liquid in the casserole, add either white wine or chicken stock as needed. Serve with rice or any starchy vegetable. Serves 6 to 8.

Port Royal Lamb Shanks   *Jamaica*

6 small lamb shanks, trimmed
Salt, freshly ground pepper
4 tablespoons unsalted butter
Bay leaf
1 tablespoon vinegar
Juice of 6 oranges
Grated peel of 2 oranges
½ teaspoon Angostura bitters
½ teaspoon Pickapeppa hot pepper sauce
Chicken stock, if necessary
2 egg yolks

Rub the lamb shanks with salt and plenty of pepper. Heat the butter in a heavy, covered casserole, add lamb and brown all over. Add the bay leaf, vinegar, orange juice and grated peel, bitters, hot pepper sauce, and a little stock if necessary to barely cover the lamb. Cover and cook over low heat until the lamb is tender, about 1½ hours.

Remove the lamb shanks to a serving dish and keep warm. Remove excess fat from the pan liquid and boil to reduce to about 2 cups. Beat the egg yolks lightly and beat in 2 or 3 tablespoons of the hot liquid. Gradually add the egg mixture to the casserole, beating constantly. Do not allow the mixture to boil. When the sauce is thickened, pour over lamb shanks. Serves 6.

Piononos

Puerto Rico

Stuffed Plantains

The name of this dish is an unsolved mystery. Pio means pious and nono means ninth in Spanish, so that the nearest translation would seem to be Pious the Ninth. Perhaps the idea behind the name is that only a Pope could equal the dish in goodness. I once saw it translated as pious nuns, a dreadful error as nuns in Spanish are monjas, not nonos.

3 ripe plantains, each cut into 4 lengthwise slices	**Lard or oil for frying**

FOR STUFFING:

3 tablespoons annatto oil or lard (see Index)	**2 ounces boiled ham, finely chopped**
1 pound lean ground beef	**½ teaspoon orégano**
1 medium onion, finely chopped	**Salt, freshly ground pepper to taste**
1 clove garlic, minced	**1 tablespoon capers, chopped**
½ green bell pepper, seeded and finely chopped	**2 tablespoons pimiento-stuffed green olives, chopped**
2 medium tomatoes, peeled, seeded and chopped	**3 eggs, well beaten**
	Oil for deep frying

Heat the lard or oil in a heavy frying pan and sauté the plantain pieces on both sides until they are golden. Remove carefully to a platter. As soon as they are cool enough to handle, shape each slice into a circle and secure with a toothpick. Set aside.

To make the filling, heat the annatto oil in a heavy frying pan and sauté the beef until it is browned and all the particles separate. Add the onion, garlic and hot and sweet peppers and sauté until tender. Add the tomatoes, ham, orégano, salt and pepper, and cook, stirring until the mixture is well blended and thick. Stir in the capers and olives. Remove from the heat. Fill each plantain ring with the meat stuffing, dip in the beaten egg, and deep fry in hot oil or lard on both sides. Serves 6.

Pork may be used instead of beef, if liked.

Port Antonio Beefsteak
Jamaica

6 steaks, broiled to the desired degree of doneness. Rib steaks are excellent for this dish. Have 1½ to 2 inch steaks. Broil under a gas flame at 350° about 3-inches from the heat for 4-5 minutes on the first side and about 5-6 minutes on the other side for a rare steak.

6 tablespoons golden Jamaican rum
2 tablespoons of shallots, finely chopped
Salt, freshly ground pepper to taste
4 ounces (8 tablespoons) unsalted butter
1 tablespoon lime juice
2 tablespoons chopped parsley

Put the rum and shallots into a small saucepan, add salt and plenty of pepper, and simmer until the volume is reduced by half. Cool to warm, stir in the butter, lime juice and parsley, and blend well. Pack into 6 butter pots, or any small mold, and refrigerate. When steaks are done, place a pat of the rum butter on each and serve immediately. Serves 6.

Pulpeta
Cuba

Meat Sausage

It is impossible to translate pulpeta literally since it means a small slice of stuffed meat. It might more accurately have been called pulpetón, a large slice of stuffed meat. Whatever its name, it is excellent hot for dinner, or cold for lunch, or picnics.

1½ pounds lean ground beef	Milk
¼ pound lean boneless ham, ground	2 eggs
¼ pound lean pork, ground	Salt, freshly ground pepper
1 medium onion, finely chopped	¼ teaspoon hot pepper sauce (optional)
2 cloves garlic, chopped	3 hard-boiled eggs, shelled
3 tablespoons parlsey, finely chopped	1 medium onion, sliced
1 cup soft bread crumbs	1 bay leaf
	¼ cup dry sherry

Combine the beef, ham, pork, onion, garlic and parsley in a large bowl. Soak the bread crumbs in a little milk and squeeze dry. Add to the meat. Add the eggs, unbeaten, salt and pepper to taste and the hot pepper sauce if liked. Mix thoroughly until the mixture is smooth and light. Shape half the meat into a rectangle about 12-inches long and 4-inches wide. Lay the hard-boiled eggs lengthwise down the center. Cover with the remaining meat mixture to form a cylinder. Wrap in a cloth, or in a double thickness of cheesecloth, keeping the sausage shape and tie the ends firmly with string.

Fill a heavy casserole, large enough to hold the sausage comfortably, about halfway with water, bring to a boil, add the onion, bay leaf and sherry and the sausage. Cover, and cook at a gentle simmer for 1½ to 2 hours, or until the sausage feels firm to the touch. Unwrap and arrange on a warm serving platter, and cut into 1-inch slices. If liked, the sausage may be served with a fresh tomato sauce poured over it, or with tomato sauce served separately. If served cold, garnish the platter with sliced tomatoes, lettuce, parsley sprigs, green olives and radishes. Serves 6 to 8.

Pudding and Souse   *Barbados*

This is popular in Barbados as an informal Saturday night meal. It also makes a good lunch, or appetizer. The pud-

ding is black pudding or blood pudding, a large sausage made from pig's blood encased in an intestine. It can be bought ready-made and can be heated in the oven, broiled, or fried in lard or butter. However, the black puddings of Barbados differ from most others by having sweet potatoes, West Indian pumpkin and hot peppers in their ingredients. It is sometime possible to find these sausages in West Indian markets. With a little ingenuity one can make one's own, in which case it might be well to note the Bajan superstition that no one must talk in the kitchen while the puddings are cooking, as they will burst.

BLACK PUDDING:

3 pounds sweet potatoes
2 pounds West Indian pumpkin (calabaza), or use Hubbard squash
1 cup finely chopped shallots
1 tablespoon each thyme and marjoram
1 tablespoon fresh hot pepper, seeded and minced
1 teaspoon ground cloves
Salt
Pig's blood

Have ready some pig's intestines, cleaned and ready to stuff, either prepared at home, or bought from a butcher. Peel and finely grate the sweet potatoes and pumpkin into a large bowl. Add the shallots, herbs, hot pepper, and cloves. Season to taste with salt. Add enough pig's blood to give a fairly soft consistency. Fill the skins with the mixture, but do not pack tightly. Tie into lengths, or leave whole, tying at both ends with string.

Have ready a large pot of boiling salted water. As the puddings may burst if they rest on the bottom of the pot, place a trivet for the puddings to rest on. Poach them gently for about 20 minutes, or until no juice runs out when they are pricked. About halfway through the cooking, the puddings will rise to the surface. Prick in 2 or 3 places with a large needle to expel air and prevent bursting. Drain and serve immediately, or cool and heat later. Serves 8 to 10 according to appetite.

NOTE: The sausages are sometimes made without the pumpkin, in which case use 5 pounds of sweet potato.

SOUSE:

Young pig's head	4 pig's feet

FOR THE PICKLE:

1½ cups lime juice	1 tablespoon salt
2 or 3 fresh hot red peppers, sliced	Water

FOR THE GARNISH:

1 medium cucumber, peeled and thinly sliced	1 green bell pepper, seeded and sliced
1 medium onion, chopped	Watercress, if liked
1 red bell pepper, seeded and sliced	

FOR THE SAUCE:

⅓ cup lime juice	1 fresh hot green pepper, seeded and chopped
1 teaspoon salt	1 cup stock reserved from cooking pig's head
1 medium cucumber, peeled and thinly sliced, or coarsely chopped	

Wash the pig's head and feet. Place in a large saucepan with cold, salted water to cover. Bring to a boil, lower the heat and cook, covered, at a gentle simmer until the meat is tender, 2 hours or longer, depending on the age of the pig. Drain, reserving 1 cup of stock for the sauce, and plunge into cold water. Cut the pig's feet in half. Cut the meat from the head. Skin and slice the tongue. Put all the meats into a large bowl with a pickle made from the lime juice, hot peppers, salt, and enough water to cover. Allow to steep overnight in refrigerator. Drain, and arrange on a platter with the garnish.

If preferred, make a sauce by mixing the lime juice, salt, cucumber, hot pepper and cup of stock. Omit the garnish and serve the meats with the sauce in a separate bowl.

Many islands, among them St. Kitts, serve souse without the blood sausage. In the Spanish-speaking islands the sausage is called morcilla.

Rabbit and Groundnut Stew

Leeward Islands

2½-pound rabbit, ready-to-cook and cut into serving pieces
2 ounces salt pork, cut into cubes
1 onion, chopped
1 clove garlic, chopped
2 cups chicken stock, or water
1 bay leaf
¼ teaspoon thyme
¼ teaspoon marjoram
Sprig parsley
Salt, freshly ground pepper to taste
½ cup chopped peanuts
2 fresh hot peppers, preferably red, seeded or Tabasco to taste
¼ teaspoon nutmeg

In a heavy, covered casserole try out the salt pork. Sauté the rabbit pieces until browned all over. Add the onion and garlic and sauté lightly. Add the stock or water, bay leaf, thyme, marjoram, parsley, salt and pepper to taste. Cover and cook at a gentle simmer until the rabbit is almost tender, about 1 hour, depending on the age of the rabbit.

Place the peanuts, the hot peppers and the nutmeg in an electric blender with 1 cup of the rabbit stock and blend until smooth. Pour into a saucepan with 1 cup more of the stock, and simmer gently for 15 minutes. Taste for seasoning. Add the rabbit pieces and simmer on very low heat just long enough to heat the meat through. Serve with plain rice, or any root vegetable, and a hot pepper sauce on the side. Serves 4 to 6.

Rabbit in Batter

Leeward Islands

2½-pound rabbit,
    ready-to-cook and cut
    into serving pieces
2 ounces salt pork, cut
    into cubes
1 onion, halved and each
    half stuck with a clove
1 carrot, scraped and
    quartered

1 bay leaf
⅛ teaspoon ground
    nutmeg
1 fresh hot red or green
    pepper, whole with
    stem on
2 cups chicken or rabbit
    stock
Salt, freshly ground
    pepper to taste

Try out the salt pork in a heavy, covered casserole. Brown the rabbit pieces lightly in the pork fat. Add the onion, carrot, bay leaf, nutmeg, whole pepper, stock and salt and pepper to taste. Cover and cook at a gentle simmer for 1 hour. Let meat cool in stock. Take out the rabbit pieces and remove the bones, leaving the meat in fairly big chunks. Butter a shallow (2-inch deep) baking dish, large enough to hold the rabbit pieces comfortably in a single layer, about 8 by 10 inches, and arrange the rabbit. Put 1 cup of rabbit stock in a small saucepan and reduce to 3 tablespoons. Pour over the rabbit. Meanwhile, make the batter.

BATTER:

1½ cups all-purpose
    flour
1 teaspoon salt

3 egg yolks
1¾ cups milk

Sift the flour and salt together into a mixing bowl. Stir the egg yolks into the flour. Add half the milk, stirring and beating until a smooth paste is formed. Add the rest of the milk, beating well. Let the batter rest for half an hour then pour over the rabbit. Bake on the center shelf of an oven preheated to 400° for 30 to 35 minutes, or until the pudding has risen and is crisp and brown. Serves 6.

Rabbit Stew

Leeward Islands

2½-pound rabbit,
  ready-to-cook and cut
  into serving pieces
¼ cup all-purpose
  flour
Salt, freshly ground
  pepper to taste
2 tablespoons peanut oil
2 tablespoons unsalted
  butter
1 onion, chopped
2 sprigs parsley

1 sprig celery with leaves
½ teaspoon thyme
1 bay leaf
4 tablespoons tomato
  catsup
2 cups chicken stock
4 tablespoons lime juice
1 teaspoon caramel
  coloring
1 orange, thinly sliced

Toss the rabbit pieces in flour seasoned with salt and
pepper. Heat the oil and butter in a heavy frying pan and
sauté the rabbit pieces a few at a time until browned all
over. Transfer to a heavy, covered casserole.

In the fat remaining in the frying pan, sauté the onion
until lightly browned. Add to the casserole. Tie the parsley, celery, thyme and bay leaf in a square of cheesecloth
and add to the casserole together with the tomato catsup,
chicken stock and lime juice. Bring to a boil, lower the
heat, cover, and simmer gently until tender, about 1½
hours. Stir in the caramel coloring and cook for a few
minutes longer. Remove and discard the *bouquet garni*.
Serve garnished with orange slices. Serves 6.

Riñones con Jerez

Puerto Rico

Kidneys with Sherry

8 lamb's kidneys
4 tablespoons clarified
  butter
1 large onion, finely
  chopped
1 teaspoon salt

¼ teaspoon freshly
  ground pepper
4 tablespoons all-purpose
  flour
½ cup dry sherry

Remove skin and excess fat from kidneys. Cut lengthwise in halves. Soak in salted water for 15 minutes. Remove from water and pat dry with paper towels. Set aside.

Heat the butter in a frying pan and sauté the onion until tender and lightly browned. Remove with a slotted spoon and keep it warm. Mix the salt, pepper and flour. Toss the kidneys in this mixture.

If necessary add a little more butter to the frying pan, and sauté the kidneys, over a medium to high heat, turning frequently until they are done, about 5 minutes. Do not overcook as kidneys toughen very quickly. Return the onion to the pan, add the sherry, stir, cook for a minute or so and serve on buttered toast. Serves 4.

This makes an excellent breakfast, luncheon or late supper dish.

Riñones Guisados   *Dominican Republic*

Kidney Stew

8 lamb's kidneys	1 tablespoon fresh green
¼ cup peanut oil	coriander, chopped, or
1 large onion, coarsely	flat leaved parsley
chopped	1 teaspoon orégano
1 green bell pepper,	1 tablespoon tomato paste
seeded and chopped	½ cup Seville (bitter)
3 medium tomatoes,	orange juice
peeled, seeded and	½ cup chicken stock
chopped	Salt, freshly ground
	pepper to taste

Remove skin and excess fat from the kidneys. Cut lengthwise into halves. Soak in salted water for 15 minutes. Remove from water and pat dry with paper towels.

Meanwhile prepare the sauce. Heat 2 tablespoons of the oil in a frying pan and sauté the onion and bell pepper until both are tender, but not browned. Add the tomatoes, coriander or parsley, orégano, tomato paste, orange juice, chicken stock, salt and pepper. Stir to mix thoroughly, pour into a small saucepan, bring to a simmer, cover and cook until the kidneys are ready. Rinse out and dry the frying pan.

Heat the remaining 2 tablespoons of oil in the frying pan and over medium to high heat sauté the kidneys, turning often, until they are done, about 5 minutes. Do not overcook as kidneys toughen very quickly. Turn the kidneys into the sauce and serve immediately. Serves 4.

The kidneys may be served on toast for breakfast or lunch, or with plain boiled white rice, or a starchy root vegetable and a green vegetable or salad, for a main meal.

If Seville orange juice is not available use 2 parts orange juice mixed with 1 part lemon juice and a drop or so of oil squeezed from the orange peel.

Roast Pork Calypso   *Jamaica*

5 to 6-pound loin of pork
½ teaspoon freshly
  ground black pepper
1 teaspoon salt
1 teaspoon ground ginger
½ teaspoon ground
  cloves

2 cloves garlic, crushed
2 bay leaves, crumbled
1 cup dark, dry
  Jamaican rum
2½ cups chicken stock
½ cup brown sugar
⅓ cup lime juice
2 teaspoons arrowroot

Have the butcher saw through the chine bone (the backbone or spine) of the pork loin. Score fatty side in a diamond pattern. Mix the pepper, salt, ginger, cloves and garlic and rub well into the scored surface. Lay crumbled bay leaves on top.

Put roast on a rack in a roasting pan with ½ cup rum and ½ cup of the stock. Roast in a preheated 325° oven, allowing 30 minutes to the pound. Halfway through cooking baste with a sauce made by combining the brown sugar, lime juice and remaining ½ cup rum. Spoon it over the pork 3 or 4 times. Add more stock to the pan during cooking if necessary.

When the roast is done, remove bay leaves, set meat

on a platter, and keep warm. Spoon off excess fat, measure liquid, add any remaining basting sauce, and bring the quantity up to 2 cups by adding remaining stock. Bring to a boil. Mix the arrowroot with a little water, add to the pan, stirring constantly until the gravy has thickened. Adjust seasoning, pour into a sauceboat and serve with the roast. Serves 8 to 10.

Roast Suckling Pig   *All Islands*

This is a great favorite in all the islands, especially at Christmas time. In the past the pigs were roasted on a spit over a wood fire, a method that is still popular and nowadays is made easier by modern barbecueing equipment. However, many suckling pigs today are cooked in the oven. The method of roasting the pig does not vary materially from island to island, but stuffings do, and so do accompanying sauces, a selection of which are given here.

10 to 12 pound oven-ready suckling pig	**¼ cup vegetable oil, or melted butter**
Salt	**Stuffing**

Wash the cleaned and prepared pig in cold water and wipe dry. Sprinkle inside and outside with salt. Fill the cavity loosely with the stuffing and close the opening with skewers and kitchen string, or sew together. Draw the legs back and tie with string. Stuff the mouth with a piece of crumpled aluminum foil to keep it open during cooking.

Brush pig with oil or butter, place on a rack in a large, shallow roasting pan. Cover pig loosely with foil and roast in a 325° oven for 2½ hours, basting 2 or 3 times. Remove the foil, and cook for 30 minutes longer, basting frequently.

To test for doneness, prick the thigh with a fork, or the tip of a small knife. The juices will run clear if the pig is done. Cook for a little longer if necessary.

Transfer the pig to a heated platter. Remove the foil

from the mouth and replace it with an orange, an apple, or a baked potato. Allow the pig to rest for 10 to 15 minutes at room temperature before carving. Serves 10 to 12.

In Barbados and Trinidad, the pig is rubbed inside before stuffing, with Seasoning Mixture, (see Index), a typical Bajan seasoning, also used for fish.

In the Spanish-speaking islands, the pig is seasoned inside and out, with an adobo that is left on all night. While cooking, the pig is basted with the adobo and its own juice and fat. It is more often than not left unstuffed. Though stuffings, when used, tend to be elaborate. (For Adobo see Index.)

In Martinique, Guadeloupe, and Haiti the pig may be rinsed out with a cupful of good, dark rum, which is saved and added to the stuffing. Lemon juice is used to baste the pig until the last half hour of cooking when it is basted with olive oil mixed with a little vinegar.

STUFFING (JAMAICA NO. 1):

6 cups bread crumbs
Milk
2 cloves garlic, minced
½ cup chopped pitted green olives
1 cup cooked green peas, slightly crushed

2 tablespoons coarsely chopped capers
½ teaspoon allspice
1 teaspoon thyme
Salt, freshly ground pepper

Moisten the bread crumbs with a little milk and add all the remaining ingredients. Season to taste with salt and pepper. Makes about 7 cups.

This stuffing is very similar to one used in Barbados. For the Bajan version sauté 2 medium onions, finely chopped, and the garlic cloves as above, in 3 tablespoons of sweet butter, and add to the stuffing.

For a stuffing more typical of Trinidad, add 2 medium onions finely chopped, 4 tablespoons sweet butter, ½ cup seedless raisins, 2 medium tomatoes, peeled and chopped, and 1 teaspoon of finely chopped fresh hot red pepper.

Omit the allspice and green peas. Mix all the ingredients together as in the Jamaican stuffing.

STUFFING (JAMAICA NO. 2):

4 tablespoons unsalted
  butter
1 large onion, finely
  chopped
1 clove garlic, chopped
6 cups bread crumbs
1 cup seedless raisins,
  coarsely chopped
1 tablespoon fresh hot
  red peppers, chopped

1 tablespoon ground
  ginger
½ teaspoon grated
  lime rind
¼ cup Pickapeppa
  sauce
Salt

Heat the butter in a frying pan and sauté the onion and garlic until the onion is tender, but not browned. Transfer to a large bowl. Add all the rest of the ingredients, except the Pickapeppa sauce and the salt, and toss lightly to mix well. Add the Pickapeppa sauce and toss again. Taste for seasoning and add salt if necessary. Makes about 7 cups.

STUFFING (DOMINICAN REPUBLIC):

3 tablespoons unsalted
  butter
½ pound pork
  sausages
2 medium onions, finely
  chopped
1 clove garlic, chopped
Liver of suckling pig

6 cups bread crumbs
2 tablespoons chopped
  parsley
1 egg, well-beaten
¼ cup milk
Salt, freshly ground
  pepper
½ cup brandy

Heat the butter in a frying pan and sauté the sausages until lightly browned all over. Remove from the pan, cool, slice and place in a large bowl.

In the fat remaining in the pan, sauté the onions and garlic until the onions are tender but not browned. Lift out with a slotted spoon and add to the sausages. Sauté the liver over fairly brisk heat until it is browned on both sides, but still pink inside. Cool, chop coarsely and add to the bowl with the bread crumbs, parsley, egg, milk, and salt and pepper to taste. Toss lightly with a fork to mix, add the brandy and toss again. Makes 7 cups or slightly more.

STUFFING (GUADELOUPE):

1 cup dark rum
Pig's heart, liver, kidneys, lungs, etc. washed and cleaned
4 cups bread crumbs
¼ teaspoon fresh, hot, red pepper, chopped
1 head garlic, peeled and chopped
1 teaspoon sage

1 bay leaf, crumbled
½ teaspoon melegueta peppercorns (see Glossary) ground
1 teaspoon thyme
3 tablespoons chopped chives
Salt, freshly ground pepper

Rinse out the suckling pig with the rum. Reserve the rum that runs out of the animal's body. Chop the heart and other organs, using whatever you wish, and place in a large bowl. Add the bread crumbs mixed with the milk, hot pepper, garlic, sage, bay leaf, melegueta pepper, thyme, chives and salt and pepper to taste. Pour the rum over the contents of the bowl and toss lightly with a fork to mix well. Makes about 5 cups.

In the English-speaking islands the sauces popularly served with suckling pig are Mango, Papaya "Applesauce", and Creole sauce.

The French-speaking islands have their own version of sauce *créole*, and in the Spanish-speaking islands Mojo and Ajilimójili are perhaps the most popular sauces.

They can all be found in the chapter on sauces.

STUFFING (MARTINIQUE):

1 pound chopped scallions	¼ cup vegetable oil
2 fresh hot green peppers, chopped	2 large onions, chopped
1 bunch parsley, chopped	Pig's heart, liver, kidneys, lungs, etc. washed, cleaned and chopped
3 cloves garlic, chopped	
¼ cup *rhum vieux*, or use a dark rum such as Myer's	White wine
	Oil and lime juice

Combine the scallions, peppers, parsley and garlic in a large bowl. Add the rum. Heat the oil in a large frying pan and lightly sauté the onions and the pig's heart, liver, kidneys, lungs, etc. Add to the mixture in the bowl. Moisten with a little white wine. Toss lightly to mix and stuff into the suckling pig.

Rub the skin of the pig with oil and lime juice and place on a rack in a large baking pan. Roast for 3 hours in a 400° oven. Serves 10 to 12.

This very interesting stuffing is from the kitchen of the *de Leyritz Plantation Inn* at Basse Pointe in Martinique and was given me by Mme. Yveline de Lucy de Fossarieu after I had eaten and admired a portion of the dish.

St. Jago Pork Chops   *Jamaica*

6 pork loin chops, each weighing about ½ pound	3 tablespoons soy sauce
	½ cup tomato catsup
1 tablespoon vegetable oil	1 cup chicken stock
1 onion, finely chopped	1 teaspoon freshly ground pepper
1 or 2 teaspoons light rum	2 cups cooked rice

Trim any excess fat from the chops. Heat the oil in a frying pan large enough to hold the chops comfortably and sauté them on both sides until lightly browned. Remove from the pan and set aside.

In the fat remaining in the pan sauté the onion until lightly browned. Set aside the onion. Pour off and discard the fat. Deglaze the pan with the rum. Add the soy sauce, catsup, chicken stock and pepper, and bring to a boil, stirring to mix thoroughly. Add the onion and arrange the chops close together but not overlapping.

Cover, and simmer gently until the chops are tender, about 1 hour. Top each chop with the cooked rice, about 4 tablespoons for each chop. Pour a little of the sauce over the rice, and cook, uncovered, for 15 minutes longer. If preferred omit this step and serve with plain white rice, or bake, covered, in a 350° oven for 1 hour. Serves 6.

Salpicón Estilo Camagüey   *Cuba*

Meat Salad, Camagüey style

1½ pounds cold boiled
  beef, chopped
2 cups fresh pineapple,
  diced
3 oranges, peeled,
  sectioned

and membrane
  removed
Lettuce leaves or
  watercress for garnish

DRESSING:

1 cup olive oil
⅓ cup white wine
  vinegar
1 teaspoon Dijon mustard

Pinch of salt
Salt, freshly ground
  pepper to taste

In a salad bowl combine the beef, pineapple and orange sections. Mix together the oil, vinegar, mustard, sugar, salt and pepper, whisking to blend well. Pour over the beef and fruit and toss lightly. Garnish with lettuce or watercress. Serves 6.

Roast beef may also be used for this dish. Soup meat is also traditionally used.

Salpicón   *Cuba*
Meat Salad

1½ cups cold roast
  beef, chopped
1½ cups cold roast
  chicken, chopped
3 cups boiled potatoes,
  cubed
1 large green bell pepper,
  peeled*, seeded and
  chopped

1 cup chopped lettuce
¼ cup finely chopped
  onion
1 tablespoon capers
½ cup sliced pimiento-
  stuffed green olives
2 pimientos, chopped

DRESSING:

1 cup olive oil
⅓ cup white vinegar
Salt, freshly ground
  pepper to taste

Lettuce leaves or
  watercress for garnish

In a salad bowl combine all the ingredients. Mix together
the oil, vinegar, salt and pepper whisking to blend well.
Pour over the salad, and toss lightly.

Garnish with lettuce leaves or watercress. Serves 6.

Roast veal or pork may be used, if liked in place of
beef and chicken.

*To peel the bell pepper, impale on a kitchen fork and hold over a gas
flame or electric heat turning constantly. The thin, tough skin covering the
pepper will blister and blacken. Wrap the pepper in a damp kitchen towel,
and leave for about 15 minutes, when the skin will peel off easily.

Ropa Vieja
Old Clothes

Cuba

This is a traditional Spanish dish that migrated early to the Caribbean, and remains popular in the Spanish-speaking islands, as indeed it does throughout Latin America. This Cuban version is a very good one.

2½-pound flank steak
1 carrot, scraped and sliced
1 turnip, peeled and cubed
1 leek, chopped
2 tablespoons olive oil
1 large onion, finely chopped
1 clove garlic, chopped
1 green bell pepper, seeded and chopped
1 fresh hot red or green pepper, seeded and chopped

2 large tomatoes, peeled and chopped, about 2 cups
1 bay leaf
⅛ teaspoon ground cinnamon
⅛ teaspoon ground cloves
Salt, freshly ground pepper
2 canned pimientos, chopped
1 tablespoon capers (optional)

Put the beef with the carrot, turnip and leek on to cook in sufficient water to cover, and simmer gently until it is tender, about 1½ hours, in a covered pot. Allow it to cool sufficiently to handle then shred it until it resembles its name, old clothes which are in rags. Reserve the stock.

Heat the oil in a large, heavy frying pan and sauté the onion, garlic, bell pepper and hot pepper until the onion is tender but not browned. Add the tomatoes, bay leaf spices, salt and pepper and cook until the sauce is thick and well blended. Add 2 cups of the stock in which the steak was cooked, the shredded steak and the pimientos and simmer for about 5 minutes longer. Add the capers if liked. The sauce, which should be abundant, may be thickened with bread crumbs if liked. Serve garnished with triangles of fried bread. Serves 6.

Sancoche

This Trinidadian plantation meal certainly started life as Sancocho, like its South American and Caribbean relations, but time has altered its spelling.

4 ounces salt pork, diced
½ pound corned beef,
  cut into 2-inch cubes
2 pounds lean, boneless
  beef, cut into 2-inch
  cubes
2 large onions, coarsely
  chopped
3 quarts beef stock
1 cup dried yellow split
  peas
½ pound each yam,
  dasheen (taro root),
  and cassava root,
  peeled and cut into
  slices 1-inch thick

1 pound sweet potatoes,
  peeled and cut into
  1-inch slices
1 pound potatoes, peeled
  and cut into 1-inch
  slices
1 whole fresh very hot
  red or green pepper,
  intact with stem on
1 cup coconut cream
Salt, freshly ground
  pepper to taste
Corn Meal Dumplings
2 green plantains

In a heavy, covered casserole try out the salt pork. Lightly sauté the corned beef and fresh beef, and the onions in the fat from the salt pork. They should not be heavily browned. Add the stock and the split peas, cover and simmer gently for 1 hour. Add the yam, dasheen, cassava, sweet potatoes and potatoes with the whole pepper and the coconut cream. Cover and continue to simmer gently for 15 minutes. Season to taste with salt and pepper. Add the dumplings and cook partially covered for 20 minutes longer. In the meantime cook the green plantains, with their skins on, for half an hour in water to cover. As soon as they are cool enough to handle, peel, and cut into 1-inch slices. Add to the casserole just long enough to heat through. Serves 6 to 8.

CORN MEAL DUMPLINGS:

½ cup yellow corn meal	1 teaspoon salt
½ cup all-purpose flour	Pinch of nutmeg
1 teaspoon double-acting baking powder	3 tablespoons unsalted butter

Sift the corn meal, flour, baking powder, salt and nutmeg into a large bowl. Rub in the butter with the fingertips and add just cold water, about 3 tablespoons, to make a soft dough. Divide the dough into 12 equal portions, form gently into balls and drop 1 at a time into the sancoche. Continue cooking as described.

Wilma's Pork and Spinach   *St. Lucia*

1½ pounds lean pork, cut into 1-inch cubes	1 teaspoon ground ginger
1 onion, halved	2 cups chicken stock, or water, about
Salt, freshly ground pepper	1½ pounds spinach

Put the pork, onion, salt and pepper to taste, the ginger and enough stock or water to cover the pork, into a heavy saucepan or casserole. Cover, and simmer until the pork is tender, about 1½ hours. Lift out the pork and reserve. Strain the stock, return it to the saucepan and reduce it over brisk heat to ½ cup. Adjust the seasoning and add a little more ginger if necessary.

Wash the spinach, drain thoroughly and chop coarsely. Add to the saucepan with the pork. Cover, and simmer until the spinach is done, about 5 minutes. Serve with rice. Serves 4.

Sancocho de Chivo
Dominican Republic

Kid Stew

4 pounds kid, cut into
serving pieces

4 tablespoons Seville
(bitter) orange juice

8 cloves garlic, crushed

1 leek, whole, well
washed

3 or 4 sprigs each of
parsley and fresh
coriander

2 fresh hot red or green
peppers, seeded and
chopped, or Tabasco to
taste

1 bay leaf

1 teaspoon orégano

2 medium onions,
coarsely chopped

3½ quarts water

1 pound each white and
yellow yautía, peeled
and cut into 1-inch
slices

1 pound each large white
yam and cush-cush
yam, peeled and cut
into 1-inch slices

1 pound sweet potatoes,
preferably white,
peeled and cut into
1-inch slices

1½ pounds West
Indian pumpkin
(calabaza), peeled and
cubed, or use Hubbard
squash

Salt, freshly ground
pepper to taste

2 tablespoons distilled
white vinegar

4 green plantains

Pour the Seville orange juice over the kid, leave for 15 minutes, drain. Put the kid pieces into a soup kettle or heavy casserole big enough to hold all the ingredients. Add the garlic, leek, parsley, coriander, hot peppers, bay leaf, orégano, onions, and water. Bring to a boil for 5 minutes. Skim, lower heat, and cook at a gentle simmer for 2 hours.

Remove the kid pieces and strain and reserve the liquid. Rinse out the kettle and return the meat and broth together with the yautías, yams, potatoes, pumpkin, and salt and pepper to taste. Cover, and continue to cook at a gentle simmer until both kid and vegetables are done, about 30 to 45 minutes. The pumpkin will disintegrate and thicken the sauce lightly. Just before serving add the vinegar and cook 1 or 2 minutes longer.

Meanwhile, put the plantains on to cook, in their skins, in water to cover. Boil for half an hour. Cool, peel and cut into 1-inch slices. Add to the kettle just long enough to heat them through. Serves 10 to 12.

Three pounds of lean, boneless lamb may be used instead of the kid, in which case reduce the first cooking time from 2 to 1½ hours.

Sancocho de Carne de Cerdo
Dominican Republic

Pork Stew

3 pounds pork loin, cut
 in 2-inch chunks
Salt, freshly ground
 pepper to taste
2 onions, chopped fine
1 leek, chopped
4 cloves garlic, chopped
1 tablespoon each
 chopped parsley and
 fresh coriander
Bay leaf
1 hot pepper, chopped
1 tablespoon vinegar
3 tablespoons Seville
 (bitter) orange juice, or
 2 tablespoons orange
 and 1 tablespoon lime
 juice

2 green plantains, peeled
 and sliced
3 tablespoons lime, or
 lemon, juice
1 pound longaniza
 sausage, or Italian
 sweet sausage
1 tablespoon salad oil
1 pound each yuca,
 yautía, pumpkin, sweet
 potatoes, and yam,
 peeled and sliced
3 ears sweet corn, each
 cut into 3 pieces

Season the pork with salt and pepper. Put into a heavy, covered 4-quart casserole with the onions, leek, garlic, parsley, coriander, bay leaf, hot pepper, vinegar, and bitter orange juice. Add enough water to barely cover. Simmer over low heat.

Meanwhile soak the plantains in the lime or lemon juice for 10 minutes. Drain, and add to the casserole.

Fry the sausage lightly in the salad oil, drain, cool, cut in slices and add to the casserole with the yuca, yautía, pumpkin, sweet potatoes, yam, and sweet corn. Bring to a boil, cover, and simmer very gently until all the ingredients are tender. The pumpkin will disintegrate and thicken the sauce. Serves 6 to 8.

Sancocho de Mondongo *Dominican Republic*

Tripe Stew

3 pounds tripe	2 tablespoons white
½ cup peanut oil	vinegar
2 large onions, chopped	1 teaspoon orégano
½ cup tomato paste	Salt
1 pound tomatoes,	Tabasco to taste
peeled, seeded and	2 green plantains
chopped	2 cups cooked chick peas
4 cloves garlic, crushed	2 ripe plantains, peeled
½ pound chorizo	and cut in 1-inch slices
sausages, cut in	1 pound potatoes, peeled
½-inch slices	and sliced
1 tablespoon fresh	1 small cabbage,
coriander, chopped	quartered
1 tablespoon parsley,	1 pound sweet potatoes,
chopped	peeled and sliced
1 large green bell pepper,	2 pounds pumpkin,
seeded and chopped	peeled and sliced
2 tablespoons Seville	
(bitter) orange juice	

Put the tripe on to cook in a large saucepan with water to cover and simmer, covered, until tender. Drain, reserving liquid. Cut tripe into 1½-inch strips and set aside.

Heat the oil in a large kettle, or heavy casserole and add the onions. Sauté until lightly browned. Add the tomato paste, 1 cup of the reserved tripe liquid, the tomatoes, garlic, chorizo sausages, coriander, parsley, bell pepper, orange juice, vinegar, orégano, salt and Tabasco to taste. Add the tripe, cover, and cook gently for 10 minutes. Meanwhile put the green plantains, unpeeled, into a large saucepan, cover with cold water, bring to a boil and simmer for 30 minutes. Drain, cool, peel and cut into 1-inch slices. Add to the casserole with all the remaining ingredients and the rest of the tripe liquid. Add a little more liquid, water or stock, if necessary to cover. Cover and simmer gently until all the ingredients are tender and the soup is fairly thick. The pumpkin will disintegrate and thicken the soup. Before serving cut the cabbage quarters crosswise to make 8 or more servings. Serve in large rimmed soup plates. Serves 8 to 10.

Sancocho de Gandules *Dominican Republic*
Pigeon Pea Stew

¼ cup peanut oil

2 ounces salt pork, cut into ¼-inch cubes

2 pounds longaniza sausage, cut into ½-inch slices

2 medium tomatoes, peeled and coarsely chopped

4 cups fresh or canned pigeon peas

2 pounds West Indian pumpkin (Calabaza) peeled and cubed, or use Hubbard squash

1 leek, chopped

1 teaspoon each of parsley and fresh coriander, chopped

½ teaspoon orégano

½ pound yautía, peeled and cut into 1-inch slices

1 pound cush-cush yams, peeled and cut into 1-inch slices

½ pound cassava root, peeled and cut into ½-inch slices

2 tablespoons cider vinegar

1 tablespoon Seville (bitter) orange juice

Salt to taste

Tabasco sauce to taste

Heat the oil in a heavy frying pan and try out the salt pork. Add the sausage and sauté lightly. Add the tomatoes and cook for a few minutes until the mixture is well blended. Transfer to a heavy, covered casserole with the fresh pigeon peas, pumpkin, leek, parsley, coriander, orégano, yautía, yams, cassava, vinegar, and orange juice. Add 2½ quarts of water. Season to taste with salt, cover and simmer gently until the vegetables are done. Season to taste with Tabasco. Serves 8 to 10.

If using canned pigeon peas, refresh them in cold water and add to the casserole half-way through the cooking.

Sancocho de Rabo de Vaca
Dominican Republic

Oxtail Stew

3 pounds oxtail, cut up
4 cloves garlic, mashed
2 medium onions
1 green bell pepper, seeded and chopped
1 teaspoon each parsley and coriander, chopped
3 grains melegueta pepper
1 teaspoon orégano
2 tablespoons cider vinegar
2 tablespoons Seville (bitter) orange juice
3 quarts beef stock, or half stock, half water

1 pound each white and yellow yautía, peeled and cut into 1-inch slices
1 pound cush-cush yams, peeled and cut into 1-inch slices
1 pound West Indian pumpkin, (calabaza) peeled and cubed, or use Hubbard squash
1 pound cassava root, peeled and cut into ½-inch slices
2 ripe plantains, peeled and cut into 1-inch slices
Salt to taste
Tabasco sauce to taste

Put the oxtail into a soup kettle or heavy casserole big enough to hold all the ingredients. Add the garlic, onions,

bell pepper, parsley, coriander, melegueta pepper, orégano, vinegar, Seville orange juice and stock. Cover, and
simmer gently for 2 hours. Add the yautía, yams, pumpkin, cassava, plantains, salt and Tabasco to taste, cover
and simmer for 1 hour longer, or until the oxtail and the
vegetables are done. Serves 6 to 8.

Seasoned-up Pork Stew   *St. Kitts*

3 pounds boneless pork,
  cut into 2-inch cubes
2 tablespoons distilled
  white vinegar
1 tablespoon
  Worcestershire sauce
2 sprigs coarsely chopped
  parsley, preferably flat
  Italian type
1 teaspoon fresh sage,
  coarsely chopped, or
  ½ teaspoon dried,
  crumbled
1 tablespoon celery
  leaves, chopped
2 tablespoons chopped
  chives, or scallions,
  using green and white
  parts

2 cloves garlic, crushed
1 onion, grated
¼ teaspoon fresh
  ground pepper
Salt to taste
1 tablespoon golden rum
2 teaspoons brown sugar
2 tablespoons unsalted
  butter
2 cups chicken, or pork,
  stock
1 tablespoon tomato
  catsup
2 teaspoons arrowroot

Mix together the vinegar, Worcestershire sauce, parsley,
sage, celery leaves, chives, garlic, onion, pepper, salt,
and rum in a large bowl. Add the meat and mix thoroughly.
Leave, loosely covered, at room temperature for 3 to 4
hours, turning from time to time so that all the pieces of
meat are able to absorb the flavors of the marinade.

    Scrape off the marinade and if liked, purée it in an
electric blender with some of the stock, or strain, discarding the solids. Sprinkle the pork pieces with the brown
sugar. In a heavy, covered casserole heat the butter and

sauté the pork lightly. Add the marinade and enough stock to cover. Stir in the tomato catsup. Cover and cook at a gentle simmer until the pork is tender, 1½ to 2 hours. Taste for seasoning. Mix the arrowroot with a little cold water and stir into the stew. Cook, stirring until the gravy is lightly thickened. Serve with any root vegetable or with rice. Serves 6.

Stobá di Concomber   *Curaçao*
Kid and Cucumber Stew

The cucumbers used in Curaçao are the small round tropical variety sometimes called apple, or lemon, cucumbers. If they are not available, use ordinary cucumbers, peeling them if they have been waxed. Do not peel the apple cucumbers.

1 pound corned beef
2 tablespoons vegetable oil
4 tablespoons unsalted butter
3 pounds lean, boneless kid, or lamb, cut in 3-inch cubes
3 medium onions, finely chopped
3 cloves garlic, chopped
2 shallots, chopped
¼ cup celery, finely chopped
1 medium green bell pepper, seeded and chopped
1 or 2 fresh hot red or green peppers, seeded and chopped

2 medium tomatoes, peeled and chopped
2 tablespoons lime juice
1 tablespoon white vinegar
Salt, freshly ground pepper
1 teaspoon ground cumin
1 teaspoon ground nutmeg
2 pounds cucumbers, coarsely chopped
8 small potatoes, peeled and cubed
1 tablespoon capers
10 pitted green olives

Put the corned beef into a heavy saucepan, cover with cold water, bring to a boil, reduce heat and simmer, covered for 45 minutes. Set aside.

Heat the oil and butter in a heavy casserole and lightly brown the kid (or lamb). Add the onions, garlic, shallots, celery, peppers, and tomatoes and cook until the onion is tender. Drain the corned beef, cut it into 1-inch cubes and add to the casserole with the lime juice, vinegar, salt and pepper to taste, cumin, nutmeg and 1 cup of water. Cover, and cook at a gentle simmer until the kid is tender, about 1½ hours. Check from time to time to see if there is enough liquid, adding hot water if necessary. Add the cucumbers, potatoes, capers and olives and cook for about 15 minutes longer, or until the potatoes are done. Serves 6.

Vaca Frita
Cuba

Fried Cow

2½ pound flank steak	1 onion, chopped
1 carrot, scraped and sliced	Bay leaf
1 turnip, peeled and cubed	¼ cup olive oil

Put the steak on to cook in water to cover with the carrot, turnip and onion. Cover and simmer gently until it is tender, about 1½ hours. Remove the meat from the stock when it is cool enough to handle. Pound it thoroughly. Heat the oil in a large frying pan and fry the meat on both sides. Drain the oil from the pan and serve the meat masked by the Tomato Sauce. Serves 6.

Refrigerate the stock for use in other dishes.

TOMATO SAUCE:

Salsa de Tomato

¼ cup olive oil
2 large tomatoes, peeled
and chopped, about
2 cups
2 cloves garlic, peeled
and chopped
1 fresh hot red pepper,
seeded and chopped, or
½ teaspoon cayenne

4 whole canned pimientos
and the liquid from the
can
½ cup tomato purée
½ teaspoon orégano
¼ teaspoon freshly
ground pepper
½ teaspoon sugar
Salt to taste

To make the sauce, heat the olive oil in a large frying pan.
Add the tomatoes, garlic, and fresh hot pepper and cook,
stirring over medium heat until the mixture is well blended.
Add all the rest of the ingredients, lower the heat and
cook gently, stirring from time to time, until the sauce is
thick. Makes about 2½ cups.

Poultry

Almond Chicken   *Trinidad*

This dish has a very strong Asian influence, not uncommon in Trinidad. The technique of stir-frying is not difficult. Food is fried quickly at a high temperature while being stirred constantly. A little liquid is added and the cooking quickly finished.

3 boned chicken breasts, thinly sliced
¼ cup peanut oil
½ cup chopped onion
3 scallions, chopped, using green and white parts
1 cup cucumber, peeled and coarsely chopped
1 cup carrots, scraped and coarsely chopped

8-ounce can water chestnuts, drained and sliced
1 cup mushrooms, sliced
8-ounce can bamboo shoots, drained and chopped
2 teaspoons salt
3 tablespoons soy sauce
¾ cup whole blanched almonds
Butter or oil

Heat the oil in a heavy frying pan or wok and stir-fry the chicken over brisk heat for 3 minutes. Add the onion,

scallions, cucumber, carrots, water chestnuts, mushrooms, bamboo shoots and salt and cook stirring constantly over brisk heat, for about 5 minutes longer. Pour
soy sauce over the mixture and cook without stirring for
1 minute more. Meanwhile, sauté the almonds in a little butter or oil until golden brown. Pile the chicken-
vegetable mixture into a warmed serving dish and top with
the almonds. Serve with rice. Serves 4 to 6.

Asopao de Pollo   *Puerto Rico*
Chicken and Rice Stew

½ teaspoon orégano
2 cloves garlic, crushed
1 teaspoon salt
2½ to 3-pound
    chicken, cut into 6 to 8
    serving pieces
3 tablespoons lard, or
    vegetable oil
1 medium onion, finely
    chopped
1 green bell pepper,
    seeded and chopped
2 ounces ham, coarsely
    chopped
2 medium tomatoes,
    peeled and chopped

2 cups long-grain rice
Freshly ground pepper
6 cups chicken stock
1 cup cooked green peas
1 tablespoon capers,
    preferably Spanish
¼ cup small pimiento-
    stuffed green olives
½ cup freshly grated
    Parmesan cheese
2 pimientos, cut into
    strips
Asparagus tips for
    garnish

Mix the orégano, garlic and salt together and rub into the
chicken pieces. Heat the lard or oil in a heavy casserole,
and sauté the chicken, a few pieces at a time, until lightly
golden. Set chicken aside. Add the onion and green pepper to the casserole and cook, stirring, until the onion is
tender but not browned. Add the ham, then the tomatoes
and cook for a few minutes longer, until the mixture is
well blended. Return the chicken pieces to the casserole,
cover and cook over low heat for 30 minutes, or until the
chicken is tender. Remove the chicken pieces to a plate

and when they are cool enough to handle, remove the bones and cut the meat into 2-inch squares. Set aside. Add the rice, freshly ground pepper and chicken stock to the casserole, cover, and cook over low heat until the rice is tender, about 20 minutes. Add the peas, capers, olives, cheese and chicken. Garnish with the pimiento strips, cover and simmer just long enough to heat the chicken through. The rice should not be dry but soupy, which is what asopao means. Garnish with asparagus tips. Serves 6.

Arroz con Pollo

Cuba, Puerto Rico,
Dominican Republic

Chicken with Rice

This traditional Spanish dish is popular not only in the Spanish-speaking islands of the Caribbean, but throughout Latin America. The Caribbean version is slightly different from the parent recipe, but differs little from island to island. Sometimes French-cut green beans replace the traditional green peas.

3 to 3½-pound
    chicken, cut into
    serving pieces
2 cloves garlic
½ teaspoon orégano
2 teaspoons salt
¼ teaspoon freshly
    ground pepper
2 tablespoons red wine
    vinegar
3 tablespoons olive oil
1 onion, chopped
1 green bell pepper,
    seeded and chopped
1 cup tomatoes, peeled,
    seeded and chopped
1 bay leaf

4 ounces ham, chopped
    coarsely
1 tablespoon fresh
    coriander, or parsley,
    chopped
4 cups chicken stock,
    about
2 cups rice
1 tablespoon achiote oil
    (see Index)
1 tablespoon capers
¼ cup pitted green
    olives, sliced
¼ cup dry sherry
1 cup cooked green peas
2 pimientos, sliced

Mix together the garlic, orégano, salt, pepper and vinegar and rub into the chicken pieces. Let them stand for about an hour. Heat the oil in a frying pan and sauté the drained chicken pieces until golden. Transfer to an earthenware* casserole. Add any remaining marinade. In the oil remaining in the pan sauté the onion and bell pepper until the onion is lightly browned. Add the contents of the pan to the casserole with the tomatoes, bay leaf, ham, coriander, and 2 cups of the chicken stock. Cover and simmer for 30 minutes. At the end of this time, lift out the chicken pieces and other solids and set aside. Measure the liquid and add enough chicken stock to make the quantity up to 4 cups. Pour into a saucepan and bring to a boil.

Wash the rice thoroughly, drain and pour into the casserole. Pour in the boiling stock and the achiote oil and stir. Add the capers and olives and chicken pieces, and other solids. Cover and cook over low heat until the liquid has been absorbed and the rice is tender. Remove the bay leaf. Sprinkle the rice with the sherry and garnish with the peas and pimiento strips and cook just long enough to heat through. Serve directly from the casserole. Serves 6.

*When using earthenware make sure it is heavy enough not to crack over direct heat. Use one or more asbestos mats if necessary.

Annie's Tropical Chicken   *Jamaica*

¼ cup peanut oil
3½ to 4-pound
  chicken, cut into
  serving pieces
1 onion, finely chopped
2 cloves garlic, chopped
1 pound fresh pineapple,
  chopped *or*
1 pound unsweetened
  pineapple chunks
  canned in own juice
6 ounces water chestnuts,
  sliced
1 fresh hot red pepper,
  seeded and chopped

3 medium tomatoes,
  peeled and chopped, or
  2 cups canned Italian
  plum tomatoes,
  drained
Salt, freshly ground
  pepper to taste
Chicken stock, if
  necessary
½ pound snow peas
1 tablespoon chopped
  chives or scallion tops

Heat the oil in a heavy frying pan and sauté the chicken pieces until golden on both sides. Transfer chicken to a heavy covered casserole. In the oil remaining in the frying pan sauté the onion and garlic until the onion is tender but not browned. Add to the chicken, together with the pineapple and any juice, or the canned pineapple and juice, the water chestnuts, hot pepper, tomatoes, salt and pepper, cover and simmer gently until the chicken is tender, about 45 minutes. Add a little chicken stock if necessary. During the last ten minutes add the snow peas and the chives. Serves 6.

Chicharrones de Pollo   *Dominican Republic*

Cracklings of Chicken

This is very hard to translate as chicharrones are pork cracklings. The word is used here to indicate that the chicken is cut into small pieces, a technique that betrays the Chinese influence in this dish which clearly belongs in the great family of stir-fry foods.

2 2-pound fryers, each
    cut into 16 pieces
¼ cup heavy soy sauce
¼ cup golden rum,
    preferably Dominican
    or Jamaican type
¼ cup lime juice

1 cup all-purpose flour
Salt, freshly ground
    pepper to taste
½ teaspoon Spanish
    (hot) paprika (optional)
2 cups peanut oil, about
1 lemon, thinly sliced

In a large bowl mix together the soy sauce, rum, and lime juice. Add the chicken pieces and mix well. Marinate for 2 hours at room temperature. Season the flour with salt and pepper and the Spanish paprika, if liked. Remove the chicken pieces from the marinade, pat dry on paper towels, and roll in the seasoned flour.

Heat the oil in a large, heavy frying pan and fry the chicken pieces, a few at a time, on both sides until tender, about 6 minutes. Keep warm while frying the remaining pieces. Garnish with slices of lemon and serve with rice. Serves 6.

Chicken Calypso   *Dominica*

5 tablespoons olive oil
3½ to 4-pound
    chicken, cut into
    serving pieces
2 cups rice
1 medium onion, finely
    chopped
1 clove garlic, chopped
1 green bell pepper,
    seeded and chopped
1 small hot green pepper,
    seeded and chopped

½ pound mushrooms,
    sliced
½ teaspoon saffron
2 to 3-inch piece of lime
    peel
¼ teaspoon Angostura
    bitters
4 cups chicken stock
1 tablespoon lime juice
Salt, freshly ground
    pepper
¼ cup light rum

Heat 3 tablespoons of the olive oil in a skillet and sauté the chicken pieces until browned all over. Remove to a heavy casserole. Add the rice, onion, garlic, bell pepper, and hot pepper to the oil remaining in the skillet, and sauté, stirring, until the oil is absorbed, being careful not to let the rice scorch. Add to the chicken in the casserole. Add the remaining 2 tablespoons of oil to the skillet and sauté the mushrooms over fairly high heat for 5 minutes. Add to the casserole with the saffron, lime peel, lime juice, bitters, chicken stock, and salt and pepper to taste. Cover and simmer gently until rice and chicken are tender and the liquid is absorbed, about ½ hour. Add the rum and cook, uncovered, for 5 minutes longer. Serves 6.

Chicken Casserole   *Trinidad*

6 tablespoon clarified butter	3 medium potatoes, peeled and diced
3½ to 4-pound chicken, cut into serving pieces	3 medium tomatoes, peeled and sliced
2 medium onions, chopped	Chicken stock, about 2 cups
3 medium carrots, scraped and sliced	Salt, freshly ground pepper
3 small white turnips, peeled and diced	1 teaspoon sugar
	1 tablespoon Angostura bitters

Heat the butter in a large frying pan and sauté the chicken pieces on both sides until golden brown. Set the chicken aside. In the butter remaining in the pan, sauté the onions, carrots, turnips, and potatoes until all the butter is absorbed. Turn the vegetables into an ovenproof casserole, add the tomatoes, then arrange the chicken pieces on top. Add enough stock to barely cover the chicken, season to taste with salt and pepper and add the sugar and Angostura bitters. Cover the casserole with aluminum foil or waxed paper and its own lid. Cook in a 350° oven for about 1 hour, or until chicken and vegetables are done. Serves 6.

Chicken in Orange Sauce   *Trinidad*

½ cup all-purpose
    flour
2 teaspoons salt
½ teaspoon freshly
    ground pepper
3½ to 4-pound
    chicken, cut into
    serving pieces
¼ cup peanut oil
2 cups orange juice
2 tablespoons dark brown
    sugar
2 tablespoons white
    vinegar

1 teaspoon freshly ground
    nutmeg
1 teaspoon fresh basil,
    chopped or ½
    teaspoon dried
2 cloves garlic, finely
    chopped
3 oranges peeled,
    sectioned and
    membrane removed

Combine the flour, salt and pepper and dredge the chicken
pieces heavily with the mixture. Heat the oil in a frying
pan and sauté the chicken pieces until golden on both
sides. As they are done, transfer them to a heavy, covered
casserole. Pour off and discard any oil remaining in the
frying pan, but scrape the brown bits into the casserole,
deglazing the pan with a little of the orange juice if necessary.

Add all the ingredients, except the orange sections, to
the casserole, cover and simmer gently until the chicken
is almost done, about 45 minutes. Add the orange sections
and cook for 5 minutes longer. The flour in which the
chicken was dredged will have thickened the sauce lightly.
Serves 6. Serve with plain boiled white rice, or a starchy
root vegetable and either a green vegetable or a salad.

Chicken Pilau   *St. Vincent*

3½ to 4-pound
   chicken, cut into
   serving pieces
Salt, freshly ground
   pepper to taste
2 tablespoons
   Worcestershire sauce
3 tablespoons cooking oil
Stock or water

½ cup water
1 onion, finely chopped
1 clove garlic, chopped
2 cups rice
½ teaspoon cinnamon
¼ cup seedless raisins
¼ cup roasted peanuts

Season chicken pieces with salt, pepper, and Worcester-shire sauce. Heat the oil in a large, heavy, covered skillet, and sauté the chicken pieces until golden. Add stock or water to cover and simmer, covered until half-done, about 30 minutes. Remove from heat, drain stock from pan and reserve it. Heat the butter in another skillet and sauté the onion and garlic until golden brown. Add the rice and sauté until all the butter is absorbed. Add the cinnamon and the raisins. Transfer to the skillet with the chicken and add the reserved stock. Add enough extra stock or water to make the quantity up to 4 cups. Cover, and cook until the rice is tender and all the liquid is absorbed. Sprinkle with roasted peanuts. Serves 6.

Chicken Pelau

Trinidad

3½ to 4-pound chicken, cut into serving pieces
1 pound pork, cut into 1-inch cubes
Salt, freshly ground black pepper
1 fresh hot green pepper, seeded and minced
1 onion, peeled and finely chopped
3 or 4 blades of chive, chopped
1 sprig thyme, crumbled

1 medium tomato, peeled and chopped
2 teaspoons brown sugar
3 tablespoons oil
2 cups long-grained rice, well washed
1 tablespoon butter
12 almonds, blanched and chopped
12 small pimiento-stuffed, green olives, halved

Season the chicken pieces and the pork with salt, pepper, fresh hot pepper, onion, chives, thyme, tomato and sugar, and allow to stand for several hours or overnight in the refrigerator. Scrape off and reserve seasonings. Heat the oil in a large, covered frying pan and sauté the chicken and pork until golden brown. Add the reserved seasonings, pour in enough water to barely cover the meats, cover the pan and simmer gently until half done, about 30 minutes. Remove the meats from the frying pan, strain the stock, measure it and bring the quantity up with extra stock or water to make 4 cups. Return the meats to the frying pan, add the stock and stir in the rice, cover, and cook at a simmer, until the rice is tender and all the liquid is absorbed, about 20 minutes. Add the butter, nuts and olives. Serves 6 to 8.

Chicken Fricassée   *Jamaica*

3½ to 4-pound
    chicken, cut into
    serving pieces
4 cloves garlic, crushed
1 teaspoon rose paprika
1 teaspoon ground ginger
1 teaspoon salt
½ teaspoon freshly
    ground pepper
4 tablespoons chicken fat,
    about

2 large onions (1-pound),
    coarsely chopped
3 medium tomatoes,
    peeled and coarsely
    chopped
1 hot fresh pepper, red if
    possible
Chicken stock, if
    necessary

Rub the chicken pieces with the garlic, paprika, ginger, salt and pepper mixed together. Refrigerate in a covered container overnight. Scrape off and reserve the seasonings. Pat the chicken pieces dry with paper towels. Heat the chicken fat in a heavy frying pan and sauté the chicken pieces until golden on both sides. Transfer to a heavy covered casserole. In the chicken fat remaining in the frying pan, adding a little more if necessary, sauté the onions until golden. Add the onions to the casserole with the tomatoes, the reserved seasonings, and the hot pepper, left whole and with the stem still on. Cover, and simmer gently until the chicken is tender, adding a little chicken stock if there is not sufficient liquid. The sauce should not be watery. Before serving, remove and discard the hot pepper. Serves 6.

Chicken Pie with
Sweet Potato Crust   *Barbados*

The boniato sweet potato, which has a brown or pink skin and white flesh, should be used in this dish. The yellow-fleshed sweet potato, often called a Louisiana yam, is far too sweet and its texture too moist for this pie crust.

3 cups cubed cooked
  chicken
6 small white boiled
  onions
1 cup cooked diced
  carrots
1 cup cooked green peas
1 tablespoon chopped
  parsley
Salt, freshly ground
  pepper

3 tablespoons all-purpose
  flour
3 tablespoons butter
1 cup chicken stock
1 cup milk
2 tablespoons sherry
  (optional)
Sweet Potato Crust

Combine the chicken, onions, carrots, peas, parsley, and salt and pepper to taste and place in a soufflé or baking dish. Mix the flour and butter together. Heat the chicken stock and milk in a small saucepan and add the flour mixture. Cook, stirring, until thickened. Add sherry if liked, and pour over the chicken. Top with the crust. Bake in a 350° oven until golden brown, about 45 minutes. Serves 4 to 6.

SWEET POTATO CRUST:

1 cup all-purpose flour
1 teaspoon salt
1 teaspoon baking
  powder

1 cup cold, mashed white
  sweet potato
4 ounces (8 tablespoons)
  unsalted butter

Sift the flour, salt and baking powder together into a bowl. Add the sweet potato and mix well. Rub in the butter to make a smooth mixture. Add a little water if necessary. Gather the dough into a ball and transfer to a floured board. Roll out lightly to fit the top of the soufflé or baking dish. Place on top of the chicken mixture inside the dish as with a biscuit topping.

Fricasé de Pollo   *Puerto Rico*

Chicken Fricassé

2 cloves garlic, crushed
1 teaspoon orégano
Salt, freshly ground
  pepper
1 tablespoon red wine
  vinegar
2 tablespoons achiote oil
  (see Index)
3½-pound chicken, cut
  into serving pieces
4 ounces ham, coarsely
  chopped
Bay leaf

1 onion, thinly sliced
1 fresh hot pepper, left
  whole
1 cup tomatoes, peeled,
  seeded and chopped
2 cups chicken stock
1 pound potatoes, peeled
  and sliced
½ cup pitted green
  olives, sliced
1 tablespoon capers
2 pimientos, coarsely
  chopped

Mix together the garlic, orégano, salt to taste, a generous
amount of pepper, the vinegar and achiote oil, and rub
into the chicken pieces. Place in a covered bowl and
refrigerate for about 4 hours. At the end of that time
transfer the chicken pieces and the marinade to a heavy
casserole and add the ham, bay leaf, onion, hot pepper,
tomatoes and chicken stock. Cover and simmer gently for
half an hour. Add the potatoes and continue cooking until
potatoes and chicken are both done, about 15 to 20 minutes. Remove and discard the hot pepper and bay leaf.
Add the olives, capers and pimientos and cook for a few
minutes to heat through. Serves 6.

Empanada de Pollo   *Cuba*

Chicken Pie

*This is an old Cuban dish from Oriente province. The
recipe was given me by my friend Nieves Rendueles who
was given it by her mother-in-law. It has been handed
down through the generations, and goes back to early*

colonial times when the family received land grants from the Spanish crown. The pastry is particularly interesting.

PARA EL RELLENO:

For the Filling

2 2½-pound fryers, cut into serving pieces	1 teaspoon Spanish (hot) paprika
Lemon juice	Bay leaf
Salt, freshly ground pepper	2 tablespoons chopped, pitted green olives
3 tablespoons olive oil	2 teaspoons capers
3 medium onions, finely chopped	2 canned pimientos, chopped
1 pound tomatoes*, peeled and chopped	2 hard boiled eggs, sliced

Pat the chicken pieces dry, rub with lemon juice and season to taste with salt and pepper. Heat the oil in a large, heavy frying pan and sauté the chicken pieces until golden. Lift out and set aside. Add the onions and green peppers to the frying pan and sauté until the onion is tender but not browned. Add the tomatoes, paprika, and bay leaf. Season to taste with salt and pepper, stir to mix well, cover and simmer gently for 15 minutes. Return the chicken pieces to the pan, cover and simmer for about 30 minutes, or until the chicken can be boned easily. Do not overcook the chicken. Allow to cool, bone the chicken, and cut the meat into bite-sized pieces. At this point check if the sauce is at all watery and if necessary reduce it over brisk heat for a few minutes. It should be quite thick. Remove and discard the bay leaf. Add the olives, capers, pimientos and chicken and mix gently. Set aside.

Remove the pastry from the refrigerator and roll out the larger ball to fit a 2 to 2½-inch deep by 7 by 12-inch rectangular pyrex, or other baking dish. Line the pie dish allowing the pastry to overlap the edges. Fill with the chicken and sauce mixture. Arrange the egg slices on top. Roll out the smaller ball of pastry to cover the dish. Trim, then moisten the edges of the lower crust with water, cover with the top crust, and seal well. Pinch with the fingers to make a decorative border, or mark with a fork. Cut three or four slits in the top to allow the steam to escape during cooking. Bake in a 350° oven for 45 minutes, or until the crust is golden. Serve hot or cold. Serves 8 to 10.

*It is important to use very ripe, flavorful tomatoes. If good fresh ones are not available, use the best available canned ones.

PASTEL PARA LA EMPANADA:

Pastry for the Pie Crust

4 cups all-purpose flour
1 teaspoon baking
  powder
1 tablespoon sugar
4 ounces (8 tablespoons)
  lard, chilled and cut
  into ½-inch pieces

2 ounces (4 tablespoons)
  unsalted butter, chilled
  and cut into ½-inch
  pieces
2 egg yolks and 1 whole
  egg
4 tablespoons dry white
  wine

Sift the flour, baking powder and sugar into a large bowl. Rub the fat into the flour with the tips of the fingers until the mixture resembles coarse meal. Beat the egg yolks and the egg lightly with 2 tablespoons of the wine and blend into the fat-flour mixture. Knead quickly into a ball. If the dough crumbles, sprinkle up to 2 tablespoons more wine over it until it holds together. Shape into 2 balls, one slightly larger than the other, wrap in wax paper and refrigerate until ready to use.

VARIATION: Puerto Rico has a chicken pie, Pastelón de Pollo, that bears a strong family resemblance to the Cuban version. It is baked with a double crust in a straight-sided 9-inch pie pan using the same pastry as Deep Dish Meat Pie, St. Thomas (see Index), and serves 4 to 6. The filling is made with a 2-pound chicken seasoned with salt, freshly ground pepper, 2 cloves of crushed garlic and ½ teaspoon of orégano, then marinated in ¾ cup each Seville (bitter) orange juice and olive oil for 2 hours. It is simmered in a heavy saucepan with a bay leaf, and a cup each of sofrito (see Index) and chicken stock. Olives and capers are added as in the Cuban version (½ cup chopped olives, 1 tablespoon capers), but the pimientos and eggs are omitted. Instead ½ cup potatoes cut into ½ inch cubes, ½ cup fresh or frozen green peas, and ¼ cup raisins are added 15 minutes before the chicken is done. The chicken is boned and the pie assembled in the same way as for Empanada de Pollo. It is baked for 10 minutes in a 450° oven, then at 350° for 45 minutes longer, or until the pie crust is golden brown. It is served hot, directly from the pie dish.

Gallina en Pepitoria   *Puerto Rico*

Chicken in Almond Sauce

3½-pound chicken, cut
    into serving pieces
Flour
¼ cup olive oil
1 medium onion, finely
    chopped
1 clove garlic, chopped
½ cup tomato, peeled,
    seeded and chopped
1 or 2 sprigs parsley
2-inch piece stick
    cinnamon
4 whole cloves
2 cups chicken stock
½ cup (2 ounces)
    blanched almonds
Salt
¼ teaspoon white
    pepper
2 teaspoons lime, or
    lemon, juice
2 eggs

Dredge the chicken pieces with flour, shaking to remove the excess. Heat the oil in a frying pan and sauté the onion and garlic in the frying pan and add to the chicken together with the tomato, parsley, cinnamon, cloves and chicken stock. Pulverize the almonds in an electric blender at high speed and add to the casserole. Season with salt, if necessary, and white pepper. Cover and simmer gently until the chicken is tender, about 45 minutes.

Remove the chicken pieces to a serving platter and

keep warm. Skim off any grease from the sauce and reduce the sauce to 2 cups over brisk heat. Adjust seasoning, and strain the sauce through a fine sieve. Place over low heat. Beat the eggs with the lime juice. Pour ½ cup of the sauce on to the eggs, beating it in with a wire whisk. Then pour the egg mixture into the sauce, beating constantly over low heat until the sauce has thickened. Do not let the sauce boil as it will curdle. Pour over the chicken. Serve with plain white rice. Serves 6.

Fowl Down-in-Rice   *Barbados*

This is an Arroz con Pollo (Chicken with Rice) that has wandered into English-speaking territory and changed its character somewhat en route. It is quite astonishingly good.

3½ to 4-pound chicken, cut into serving pieces
4 tablespoons lime, or lemon, juice
1 teaspoon salt
2 cups chicken stock
2 cups rice
Bay leaf
2 or 3 sprigs parsley

½ teaspoon thyme
Salt, freshly ground pepper to taste
2 medium onions, thinly sliced
2 medium tomatoes, sliced
3 tablespoons butter
1 teaspoon dry mustard

Season the chicken pieces with the salt and 2 tablespoons of the lime or lemon juice and allow to stand at room temperature for 1 hour. Transfer to a heavy casserole, earthenware* if possible. Drain and discard the marinade. Add the chicken stock, bring to a simmer and cook, covered, for 40 minutes. Lift out the chicken from the casserole and set aside. Measure the liquid and add enough water to bring it up to 4 cups. Wash the rice, drain and add to the casserole with the bay leaf, parsley, thyme and salt and pepper to taste. Bring to a boil, add the chicken pieces, reduce the heat, cover, and simmer until the chicken and rice are tender and all the liquid is absorbed, about 20 minutes.

Meanwhile make the sauce. Combine the onions, tomatoes, butter, mustard, and salt and pepper to taste in a small saucepan. Bring to a boil, cover and simmer for 5 minutes. If serving directly from the casserole, pour the sauce over the chicken or make a bed of the rice on a warmed platter, arrange the chicken pieces on top, and cover with the sauce. Serves 6 to 8.

*If using earthenware make sure it is heavy enough not to crack over direct heat. Use one or more asbestos mats if necessary.

Fricassée de Poulet au Coco   *Martinique*
Chicken in Coconut Milk

3 tablespoons vegetable oil	Salt, freshly ground pepper
3-pound chicken, quartered	Sprig parsley
	Sprig thyme
1 large onion, finely chopped	1 fresh hot red pepper (optional)
1 clove garlic, chopped	2 cups coconut milk
½ pound mushrooms, sliced	

Heat the oil in a heavy, flameproof casserole and add the chicken pieces. Cook over medium heat until they have stiffened and are very lightly golden on both sides, about 5 minutes. They should not brown. Remove and set aside. Add the onion, garlic and mushrooms and sauté until the onion is tender, but not browned. Return the chicken pieces to the casserole. Season to taste with salt and pepper. Tie the parsley, thyme and pepper in a square of cheesecloth and add. Pour in the coconut milk. Simmer gently, covered, until the chicken is tender, about 1 hour. Remove the bouquet garni. Serve with Riz Créole. Serves 4.

VARIATION: This is sometimes served as a sauté, (Sauté de Poulet au Coco, Sautéed Chicken with Coconut Milk Sauce). For this, heat 3 tablespoons each of oil and unsalted butter in a heavy casserole and sauté the chicken pieces over medium heat until they are golden on both sides, about 8 minutes. Season with salt and pepper, cover and cook over low heat until the chicken is tender, about half an hour. Remove the chicken pieces to a serving platter and keep warm. Add the onion, mushrooms and garlic to the casserole and sauté over fairly brisk heat until the onion is tender. Add 1 cup of rich coconut milk, 1 tablespoon finely chopped parsley, ¾ teaspoon of thyme and, if liked, ½ a fresh hot pepper seeded and chopped. Cook, stirring from time to time, over low heat, until the sauce is well blended and heated through. Pour over the chicken. Serves 4.

Keshy Yena Coe Galinja   *Curaçao*

Cheese with Chicken Stuffing

4-pound Edam cheese
2 tablespoons vegetable
  oil
2 tablespoons butter
3½ to 4-pound
  chicken, cut into
  serving pieces
2 cups chicken stock,
  about
2 medium onions, finely
  chopped
2 green bell peppers,
  seeded and coarsely
  chopped

1 fresh hot green pepper,
  seeded and chopped
1 large tomato, peeled,
  seeded and chopped
1 tablespoon seedless
  raisins
Salt, freshly ground
  pepper
2 or 3 chopped gherkins
1 cup tomato purée
½ cup freshly made
  bread crumbs

Peel the red wax covering from the cheese, cut a 1-inch slice from the top, hollow out the slice and reserve. Scoop out the cheese leaving a shell about ½-inch thick. Cover the shell and top slice with cold water and soak for an hour. Store the scooped out cheese for another use.

Heat the oil and butter in a frying pan and sauté the chicken pieces lightly. Transfer the chicken to a saucepan, add enough stock to cover and cook gently, covered, until the chicken is done, about 45 minutes. Cool, take out of the stock, remove the skin and bones and cut the meat into bite-size pieces. Set aside.

Meanwhile, in the fat remaining in the frying pan, sauté the onions and peppers until the onions are tender. Add the tomato and raisins and cook for about 5 minutes. Season to taste with salt and pepper, add the gherkins, tomato purée and breadcrumbs, cook for a minute or two, mixing well. Add the chicken.

Remove the cheese from the water and pat dry. Stuff with the chicken mixture. Replace top of cheese. Put stuffed cheese into a greased 3-quart oven-proof casserole. Bake uncovered in a preheated 350° oven for 30 minutes. Do not overcook as the cheese becomes tough, instead of soft and bubbly. Slide the cheese out of the casserole onto a warmed serving dish. Cut into wedges and serve immediately. Serves 6 to 8.

A popular way of cooking this dish is to peel off the outer wax covering of the cheese, then cut it into ¼-inch slices. Line a greased 3-quart oven-proof casserole on bottom and sides with the cheese slices overlapping. Pour in the chicken mixture and cover with the remaining slices of cheese. Bake for 30 minutes in a 350° oven. Small individual casseroles may also be used, in which case reduce the baking time to 15 to 20 minutes.

Curri de Pollo con Salsa de Ciruelas Pasas

Cuba

Chicken Curry with Prune Sauce

3½ to 4-pound chicken, cut into serving pieces
3 cloves garlic, crushed
½ teaspoon orégano
¼ teaspoon cumin
1 teaspoon salt
¼ teaspoon freshly ground pepper
1 tablespoon mild curry powder

4 ounces (8 tablespoons) unsalted butter
½ pound mushrooms
2 cups unsweetened prune juice
Chicken stock, if necessary
2 teaspoons arrowroot (optional)

Mix the garlic, orégano, cumin, salt, pepper and curry powder together and rub into the chicken pieces. Refrigerate overnight. Heat half the butter in a heavy frying pan and lightly sauté the chicken pieces. Transfer the contents of the pan to a heavy, covered casserole. Rinse out the pan and heat the rest of the butter. Sauté the mushrooms (whole if small, sliced if large) over fairly high heat until they are lightly browned, 4 or 5 minutes. Add to the casserole. Pour the prune juice over the chicken pieces and add chicken stock, if necessary, to cover. Cover the casserole and cook the chicken at a gentle simmer until tender, about 45 minutes to 1 hour. Cook partially covered for the last 15 minutes to reduce the sauce. If the sauce is too thin, mix the arrowroot with a tablespoon of cold water, stir into the sauce and cook until lightly thickened. The sauce should not be very thick. Serve with Arroz con Ajo (garlic rice). Serves 6.

Le Colombo
Martinique-Guadeloupe

The Colombo, which is a type of curry, was introduced into Martinique and Guadeloupe around the middle of the last century by migrant Hindu workers, mostly from Bengal. They brought with them the ingredients for a sort of curry powder which is made from mustard seeds, toasted rice, garlic, hot peppers, coriander, saffron, and black pepper. The spices and herbs are ground, then fried in oil. Tamarind pulp is always added to the curries, which may be made from chicken, pork, kid, lamb, fish or shellfish. Tropical vegetables, onions and garlic complete the dish, which has become a great favorite for holidays. Pork is traditionally used for the Christmas Colombo in Martinique. The cooking liquid more often than not is white wine, perhaps combined with stock, and a little *rhum vieux* or dry Madeira. Coconut milk is sometimes used, though not for fish or shellfish curries. Curry powder is often used nowadays instead of the original poudre de colombo though many islanders still make their curry powder from old recipes. I have included here a curry powder recipe from St. Kitts, as well as the poudre de colombo. Recipes for the Colombos tend to be flexible, depending on the talents and inclinations of the cook.

In Martinique the curries are considered northern dishes, as the Hindus settled mainly in Basse Pointe and Macouba in the north of the island. If two different kitchens seems an extravagance in an island only 50 miles by 19 miles it must be remembered that distance is relative, and Martinique is mountainous, so that before the invention of the internal combustion engine, a trip from south to north was indeed a journey.

In Trinidad, Indians, again mostly Bengalis, make up about a third of the population. There is a whole world of Indian cooking on this island, differing subtly from the original, and embracing both Moslem and Hindu.

Curry Powder

St. Kitts

1 ounce coriander seeds
2 ounces cumin seeds
1 tablespoon poppy seeds
1 tablespoons cloves
1 tablespoon mustard
   seeds, preferably
   brown

1 ounce peppercorns
2 ounces ground turmeric
1 ounce ground ginger,
   preferably Jamaican

Toast the coriander, cumin, poppy and mustard seeds in a heavy iron frying pan until the mustard seeds begin to jump about. Grind in a mortar or in an electric blender, and mix with the turmeric and ginger. Put through a fine sieve and store in a glass jar. Makes about 8 ounces. As a general rule use 1 tablespoon of curry powder for each 2 pounds of meat or poultry, rather less for fish and shell-fish.

Poudre de Colombo

⅛ teaspoon turmeric
1 teaspoon ground
   coriander
1 teaspoon ground
   mustard seeds

3 cloves garlic, crushed
2 fresh hot red peppers,
   seeded and mashed

Combine all the ingredients and mix to a paste. Use as directed for Colombo de Poulet (Chicken Curry). This amount is enough for a curry made from chicken, pork, kid, lamb, fish or shellfish to serve 6 to 8.

Colombo de Poulet   *Martinique-Guadeloupe*

Chicken Curry

3½-pound chicken, cut
 into serving pieces
4 tablespoons peanut or
 coconut oil
2 medium onions, finely
 chopped
2 cloves garlic, crushed
1 or 2 tablespoons curry
 powder, or 1 recipe
 Poudre de Colombo
1 tablespoon tamarind
 pulp (see Glossary)
1 green mango, peeled
 and coarsely chopped
½ pound West Indian
 pumpkin, peeled and
 sliced, or use Hubbard
 squash
½ pound green
 papaya, peeled and
 sliced (optional)

½ pound eggplant,
 peeled and sliced
1 christophene (chayote),
 peeled and sliced
1 pound dasheen (taro),
 peeled and sliced, or
 use white tropical yam
1 cup dry white wine, or
 coconut milk, if liked
1 cup chicken stock
1 or more fresh, hot
 peppers, seeded and
 chopped
1 teaspoon lime juice
Salt
2 tablespoons dry
 Madeira, or *rhum
 vieux*

Heat the oil in a heavy frying pan and sauté the chicken
pieces lightly on both sides. Transfer to a heavy casserole,
earthenware* if possible. In the oil remaining in the pan,
sauté the onions until golden. Add the garlic and curry
powder or Poudre de Colombo and cook, stirring from
time to time, for 3 or 4 minutes. Transfer to the casserole.
Add all the remaining ingredients, except the lime juice.
Cover and simmer gently until the chicken is tender and
the vegetables done. Add salt to taste, and stir in the lime
juice. Just before serving stir in the Madeira or *rhum
vieux*. Serve with Riz Créole. Serves 6 to 8.

As a rule the Colombo is extremely spicy and hot. For
non-Caribbean people, or those not accustomed to this
sort of dish, the amount of fresh hot pepper could be
reduced.

*If using earthenware make sure it is heavy enough not to crack over direct heat. Use one or more asbestos mats if necessary.

Le Caneton Aux Ananas   *Guadeloupe*

Duckling with Pineapple

4½-pound ready-to-
  cook duckling
Salt, freshly ground
  pepper
2 tablespoons unsalted
  butter
¾ cup dark rum
1 cup unsweetened
  pineapple juice, fresh if
  possible

1 cup stock made from
  neck, giblets and liver
  of duckling
2 cups chopped fresh, or
  unsweetened canned,
  pineapple
2 teaspoons arrowroot

Pull any loose fat from the cavity of the duckling, and prick all over the fatty parts with a fork. Season with salt and pepper. Heat the butter in a heavy casserole large enough to hold the duckling comfortably. Brown the bird all over, lift out, and discard all the fat. Return the duckling to the casserole with ½ cup of the rum and ½ cup pineapple juice. Cover and cook in a 325° oven for 1 to 1½ hours.* Remove the duckling to a serving platter and keep it warm. Discard all the fat that has accumulated in the casserole. Add the remaining ¼ cup of rum, stir and scrape up all the brown bits. Pour into a saucepan. Add the rest of the pineapple juice and the giblet stock, cook over brisk heat until reduced to 2 cups. Adjust the seasoning, add the chopped pineapple and cook for 5 minutes longer, over very low heat. Mix the arrowroot with ¼ cup cold water and stir into the sauce. Cook just long enough to thicken lightly. Serve separately to accompany the duckling. Serves 4.

*The duckling is cooked when its juices run pale pink for medium rare, clear yellow for well done. One hour cooks the duckling to the medium rare stage.

Le Caneton au Rhum   *Guadeloupe*

Duckling with Rum

5 to 6-pound ready-to-
    cook duckling
2 tablespoons unsalted
    butter
Salt, freshly ground
    pepper
1 medium onion, finely
    chopped
1 cup stock made from
    neck, giblets, liver of
    duckling

1 clove garlic, chopped
1 sprig parsley
¼ teaspoon each sage,
    thyme, marjoram
1 bay leaf
1 leaf Bois d'Inde (see
    Glossary) or
3 grains melegueta
    pepper (see Glossary)
½ cup dark rum

Pull any loose fat from the cavity of the duck and prick
all over the fatty parts with a fork. Heat the butter in a
heavy casserole large enough to hold the duck comfortably and lightly brown the bird all over. Discard all but
2 tablespoons of the fat. Season the bird with salt and
pepper. Add the onion and garlic to the casserole and
sauté until the onion is tender. Return the bird to the
casserole with the herbs tied in a square of cheesecloth.
Add the giblet stock, cover and simmer gently until the
duckling is tender, about 1½ hours. Discard the *bouquet
garni* and remove any fat that has accumulated. Warm
the rum, pour it over the duck and flame it. Serve on a
bed of Riz Créole, with the sauce separately. Serves 6.

To make the stock put the neck, giblets, liver and lower
wing tips to cook with 3 cups of water. Simmer, partially
covered, for 1½ hours or until the liquid is reduced to
1 cup. Season to taste with salt and pepper.

Pato con Aceitunas   *Dominican Republic*
Duckling with Olives

4-pound ready-to-cook
  duckling
Salt, freshly ground
  pepper to taste
2 tablespoons vegetable
  oil
1 large onion, finely
  chopped
1 bay leaf
¼ teaspoon thyme
1 clove

Sprig parsley
1 cup dry white wine
1 tablespoon capers
¼ cup small, pimiento-
  stuffed green olives,
  halved crosswise
1 tablespoon arrowroot
1 cup stock made from
  neck, liver, and giblets
  of duckling

Pull away any loose fat from the cavity of the duckling and prick all over the fatty parts with a fork to aid in releasing the subcutaneous fat. Dry thoroughly. Season with salt and pepper and truss. Heat the oil in a heavy oval casserole large enough to hold the duckling comfortably. Brown the duckling on all sides, pour out and discard the fat.

Place the duckling breast side up in the casserole with the onion, garlic, bay leaf, thyme, clove, parsley and white wine. Cover and set in the middle of an oven preheated for 325° and cook until tender, about 1 hour and 15 minutes for medium rare, 15 minutes longer for well done. For a large bird (5½ to 6 pounds) allow 1 hour and 25 to 40 minutes.

Remove the duckling to a warmed serving platter. Remove trussing strings and cut into serving pieces. Degrease the sauce in the casserole and strain it. Pour into a small saucepan, add the olives, capers, and stock and simmer to heat the olives through. Mix the arrowroot with a little water, add to the sauce and cook until it is lightly thickened. Adjust the seasoning and pour into a sauceboat. Serve with lentil purée or rice and a green vegetable. Serves 4.

Pato con Piña   *Dominican Republic*

Duck with Pineapple

5½-pound ready-to-cook duck

STUFFING:

2 cups white bread in
½-inch cubes
8 tablespoons unsalted
butter
½ cup finely chopped
blanched almonds
1 cup finely chopped
onions
2 teaspoons finely
chopped garlic
Liver of duckling
½ pound lean,
boneless ham

chopped into
¼-inch dice
½ cup tomatoes,
peeled, seeded and
chopped
¼ cup finely chopped
parsley
¼ cup pimiento-stuffed
green olives, chopped
¼ cup seedless raisins
1 tablespoon capers
Salt, freshly ground
pepper to taste

PINEAPPLE GARNISH:

2 tablespoons butter
2 cups coarsely chopped
fresh pineapple, or
unsweetened pineapple
canned in its own juice

½ cup dry white wine
¼ cup pineapple juice
½ cup chicken stock
1 teaspoon arrowroot,
mixed with 2
tablespoons water

TO MAKE THE STUFFING:

Heat 4 tablespoons of the butter in a heavy frying pan
and sauté the bread cubes until crisp and golden brown.
Remove with a slotted spoon. Add the rest of the butter
and sauté the almonds for 2 or 3 minutes until golden,
then add onions and garlic and sauté stirring, until the
onions are tender but not brown. Add the duck liver and
cook until it is lightly browned but still pink inside. Remove
the liver, chop finely and reserve. Add the ham and toma-

toes to the frying pan and cook until most of the liquid
has evaporated, stirring from time to time. Remove from
the heat, add the liver, parsley, olives, raisins, capers,
bread cubes, salt and pepper to taste, and toss to mix.

Stuff the duck, with this mixture. Truss and prick all
over with a fork to release the fat. Place on a rack in a
baking pan and roast in an oven preheated to 450° for 20
minutes. At the end of this time remove any fat that has
accumulated. Reduce oven to 250° and roast for 2½ hours,
removing fat as it accumulates. When the duck is cooked
remove it to a warmed platter and allow it to rest. Meanwhile make the pineapple garnish. Pat the pineapple pieces
dry. Pour off all the fat from the baking pan, add the butter
and sauté the pineapple until lightly brown. Lift out and
arrange around the duck on the platter. Pour wine, pineapple juice and stock into the pan, scraping up all the
brown bits. Add the arrowroot and cook, stirring, until
the sauce is lightly thickened. Pour over the pineapple,
or serve separately if preferred. Serves 4 to 6.

Pastel de Maiz   *Cuba*

Corn Pie

16 ears sweet corn, or 4 cups frozen sweet corn kernels, thoroughly defrosted	Salt to taste
	1 tablespoon sugar
	4 egg yolks
8 tablespoons unsalted butter	

Cut the kernels from the ears of corn, and place in an
electric blender and purée. There will be about 4 cups.
In a heavy saucepan heat the butter, add the corn, salt
and sugar and cook, stirring from time to time until the
mixture thickens, about 20 minutes. Cool slightly, then
beat in the egg yolks. Set aside.

FILLING FOR PIE:

2½-pound chicken
2 tablespoons vegetable
  oil
1 onion, finely chopped
2 pounds tomatoes,
  peeled, seeded and
  chopped
Salt, freshly ground
  pepper to taste
1 tablespoon seedless
  raisins

1 tablespoon chopped
  pimiento-stuffed olives
1 tablespoon capers
12 pitted prunes,
  plumped in hot water,
  then drained
2 hard-boiled eggs, sliced

Poach the chicken in water to cover for about 45 minutes, or until tender. Cool, remove skin and bones. Cut chicken meat into bite-size pieces. Set aside.

Heat the oil in a heavy frying pan and sauté the onion until tender but not brown. Add the tomatoes and cook until the mixture is thick. Season to taste with salt and pepper. Add to the chicken, raisins, olives, capers and prunes, and mix together lightly.

Line a 2-quart soufflé dish with ⅔ of the corn mixture, patting it up the sides of the dish with the fingers. Pour in the chicken mixture, top with the eggs and cover with the remaining corn mixture. Bake in an oven preheated to 350° until done, about 45 minutes. Serves 6.

Lean boneless pork, cut into 1-inch cubes and simmered until tender, may be used instead of the chicken.

Pollo a la Pepitoria   *Cuba*

Chicken Fricassée with Onions

This is another recipe given me by my friend Nieves Rendueles. It comes from Cuba's Oriente province, and like the recipe for Empanada de Pollo (Chicken Pie) has been handed down from early colonial times in the Rendueles family. It reminds me of Poulet Antiboise in Elizabeth

David's A Book of Mediterranean Food, *which I have cooked many times with great pleasure. The two dishes, which may have a common origin, come to table very different. The name cannot be translated literally since* pepitoria *means a medley of things and "Chicken with a Medley of Things" sounds odd, and is not very enlightening.*

1 3½-4 pound chicken,
   cut into serving pieces
3 tablespoons all-purpose
   flour
Salt, freshly ground
   pepper
4 tablespoons olive, or
   vegetable oil, about

2 pounds Spanish, or
   Bermuda onions (3-4),
   very finely sliced
Bay leaf
½ cup dry white wine
2 eggs, well beaten

Pat the chicken pieces dry. Season the flour with salt and pepper and place in a plastic or paper bag. Shake the chicken pieces, one at a time, in the bag, take out and shake again to remove any excess flour. Heat 2 tablespoons of the oil in a large, heavy, frying pan and sauté the chicken pieces until they are golden on both sides. Transfer to a heavy casserole. If the oil in the pan is discolored, discard it, and wash and dry the pan. Heat the remaining 2 tablespoons of oil in the pan, or if the oil is not discolored, add enough oil to bring the amount to 2 tablespoons. Add the onions and mix well. Add a teaspoon of salt which helps release the juice in the onions, and stir. Add the bay leaf and the wine, and cook for 2 or 3 minutes. Pour over the chicken in the casserole and mix gently, using a rubber spatula. Cover and simmer for about 45 minutes, or until the chicken is tender. Shake the pot two or three times during the first 20 minutes of cooking to make sure the chicken does not scorch on the bottom. The onions will release their juice, creating a sauce, as they cook down.

    Lift out the chicken pieces on to a serving dish and keep warm. The onions should have melted into a purée. If necessary cook them for a few minutes longer. Take out and discard the bay leaf. Beat a cupful of the hot sauce into the eggs, a tablespoon at a time, then pour the mixture into the casserole and cook, stirring constantly over very low heat, until the sauce has thickened. Do not let the sauce come to a boil as it will curdle. Pour a little of the sauce over the chicken pieces and serve the rest separately in a sauceboat. Serve with plain white rice. Serves 6 to 8.

Pollo Asado a la Criolla   *Puerto Rico*
Roast Chicken Creole Style

2½-pound chicken
Salt, freshly ground
  pepper
½ cup Seville (bitter)
  orange juice
½ cup dry sherry
4 tablespoons unsalted
  butter

1 tablespoon vegetable oil
1 medium onion, finely
  chopped
2 cloves garlic, chopped
Bay leaf

Season the chicken inside and out with salt and pepper and place in a heavy casserole. Add the orange juice and sherry, cover and refrigerate overnight, turning 2 or 3 times. Drain chicken, and reserve marinade. Rinse out and dry the casserole and pat the chicken dry with paper towels. Heat the butter and oil in the casserole and sauté the chicken until golden all over. Add the onion, garlic, bay leaf and the reserved marinade. Cover and cook in a 350° oven for 1¼ hours, or until tender, basting 2 or 3 times during the cooking. Transfer to a heated serving platter. Pour the sauce into a sauce boat. Serve with white rice, or any starchy vegetable, and a green vegetable. Serves 4.

Pollo con Lentejas y Piña

Dominican Republic

Chicken with Lentils and Pineapple

2 tablespoons vegetable
  oil
2½-pound fryer, cut
  into serving pieces
1 onion, finely chopped
1 clove garlic, chopped
1 medium-sized fresh
  pineapple, or a
  1-pound 4-ounce can of
  pineapple chunks,
  unsweetened in own
  juice

½ teaspoon orégano
1 fresh hot pepper,
  seeded and chopped
Salt, freshly ground
  pepper
2 cups brown lentils
2 cups pineapple juice
2 cups chicken stock

Heat the oil in a frying pan and sauté the chicken pieces lightly on both sides. Transfer to a heavy casserole. In the oil remaining in the frying pan, adding a little more if necessary, sauté the onion and garlic until the onion is tender but not browned. Transfer to the casserole together with the pineapple, peeled and cut into 1-inch cubes if fresh, if canned drained and the juice reserved. Add the orégano, the hot pepper, and salt and pepper to taste.

If using unprocessed lentils these should be picked over and soaked in cold water for several hours before cooking. They should then be cooked half an hour in plain water, drained and added to the casserole with the pineapple juice and chicken stock. Simmer, covered for 45 minutes. If using the quick cooking type, add the juice and stock to the casserole, cover and simmer for 20 minutes, then add the lentils and cook for 25 minutes longer as they tend to get mushy if overcooked. By the time the lentils and chicken are both tender, the liquid should be absorbed. Serve from the casserole. Serves 4.

Pollo con Uvas
Dominican Republic

Chicken with Grapes

2½-pound chicken, quartered
3 large cloves garlic, crushed
Salt, freshly ground pepper
3 tablespoons unsalted butter
1 large onion, finely chopped
1 bay leaf

½ cup dry white wine
½ cup dry red wine
1 cup chicken stock
4 ounces pitted prunes, halved
½ cup pimiento-stuffed green olives
1 pound seedless white grapes
2 teaspoons arrowroot, or potato starch

Season the chicken pieces with the garlic, and salt and pepper to taste. Allow to stand for about half an hour. Heat the butter in a heavy casserole and sauté the chicken pieces, 2 at a time, until lightly golden on both sides, and set aside. Add the onion to the butter remaining in the casserole and sauté until tender but not browned. Return the chicken pieces to the casserole. Add the bay leaf, both wines, the chicken stock and the prunes. Cover and simmer gently for half an hour. Cut the olives in halves crosswise and add to the casserole with the grapes. Cover and cook for 15 minutes longer, or until the chicken is tender. Lift out the chicken onto a serving platter and keep it warm. Dissolve the arrowroot in cold water and stir into the casserole. Cook, stirring, until the sauce is lightly thickened. Pour the sauce over the chicken pieces and serve with rice or a starchy vegetable. Serves 4.

Pollo con Piña a la Antigua   *Cuba*
Chicken with Pineapple in the Old Style

Juice and grated rind
 1 large lime
3½ to 4-pound
 chicken, cut into
 serving pieces
Salt, freshly ground
 pepper to taste
¼ cup olive oil
1 medium onion, chopped
1 clove garlic, chopped
2 very ripe tomatoes,
 peeled and coarsely
 chopped

3 tablespoons seedless
 raisins
1 fresh hot pepper,
 preferably, red, seeded
 and chopped
¼ teaspoon orégano
1 bay leaf
1 cup rich chicken stock,
 about
2 cups coarsely chopped
 fresh pineapple and
 juice
4 tablespoons golden rum

Rub the lime juice and rind into the chicken pieces, season with salt and pepper, and let stand for half an hour. Heat the oil in a frying pan and sauté the chicken pieces until just colored. Transfer them to a heavy casserole large enough to hold them comfortably, in layers. In the oil remaining in the pan sauté the onion and garlic until the onion is tender but not browned, add the tomatoes, raisins, hot pepper, orégano and bay leaf and cook, stirring occasionally for 5 minutes or so to blend the flavours. Pour over the chicken in the casserole and add enough chicken stock barely to cover. Partially cover the casserole and cook over low heat until the chicken is tender, about 45 minutes.

Put the pineapple and any juice in a small saucepan and cook until reduced to half. Add the rum, mix thoroughly and cook for a minute or two. Pour over the chicken and cook 5 minutes longer. Serves 6.

Pollo Tropical
Dominican Republic

Chicken Tropical Style

3½-pound chicken, cut into serving pieces
Flour
¼ cup peanut oil
1 medium onion, finely chopped
1 clove garlic, chopped
2 tablespoons light rum
2 tablespoons cucumber pickles
1 or 2 pickled hot peppers, chopped
2-inch piece stick cinnamon
⅛ teaspoon anise
Salt, freshly ground pepper
1 cup unsweetened pineapple juice
1 cup chicken stock
2 cups pineapple pieces
2 large, slightly under-ripe bananas, cut into 2-inch slices
½ pound seedless white grapes
1 avocado, peeled and sliced

Dredge the chicken pieces lightly with flour. Heat the oil in a frying pan and sauté the chicken until golden. Transfer to a heavy casserole. Sauté the onion and garlic in the frying pan and add the chicken. Pour off and discard any oil remaining in the pan and deglaze it with the rum, scraping to get up all the brown bits. Pour this into the casserole. Add the cucumber pickles, hot peppers, stick cinnamon, anise, salt and pepper to taste, the pineapple juice, and chicken stock. Cover, and simmer gently for half an hour or until the chicken is almost done. Add the pineapple pieces, bananas and grapes and continue to cook, partially covered, for 15 minutes longer.

Remove the cinnamon stick. Arrange the chicken on a warmed platter with the fruit and some of the sauce. Garnish the platter with a ring of avocado slices and serve the remaining sauce separately. Accompany the dish with plain white rice. Serves 6.

Pollo en Escabeche
Dominican Republic and Spanish-speaking islands

Pickled Chicken

3½-pound chicken, cut
  into serving pieces
Salt, freshly ground
  pepper
3 medium onions, thinly
  sliced
6 large cloves garlic

1 fresh hot green pepper,
  left whole
Bay leaf
1 teaspoon orégano
1 cup olive oil
½ cup white wine
  vinegar

Season the chicken pieces with salt and pepper, and place in a heavy casserole with the onions and garlic. Tie the hot pepper, bay leaf and orégano in a small square of cheesecloth and add to the casserole. Pour the oil and vinegar over the chicken, cover and simmer gently for 30 minutes. If the onions are very watery, continue cooking, with the casserole partially covered, to reduce the sauce, for 15 minutes longer, or until the chicken is tender. Otherwise continue cooking with the casserole covered as before. Remove and discard the cheesecloth covered as before. Serve with plain white rice, or any plainly cooked starchy vegetable. This is equally good served cold. Refrigerate and serve with the jellied sauce, lettuce, sliced tomato, radishes, avocado, and olives. Serves 6.

Pollo en Salsa de Almendras y Avellanas   *Dominican Republic*

Chicken in Almond and Hazelnut Sauce

3½-pound chicken, cut into serving pieces
Flour
Salt, freshly ground pepper
¼ cup olive oil
1 medium onion, finely chopped
1 whole head garlic, blanched and peeled
1 cup tomatoes, peeled, seeded and chopped
Grated rind ½ lime, or lemon
½ cup blanched almonds
½ cup hazelnuts
2 slices white bread toasted
2 cups chicken stock
1 whole fresh or canned hot pepper
Liver of the chicken
2 tablespoons dry sherry

Dip the chicken pieces into flour seasoned with salt and pepper. Shake to remove the excess. Heat the oil in a frying pan and sauté the chicken pieces until golden on both sides. Transfer to a heavy casserole. In the oil remaining in the pan sauté the onion and garlic cloves until the onion is tender but not browned, taking care not to let the garlic burn. Add to the casserole with the tomatoes and grated lime peel.

Pulverize the almonds in an electric blender at high speed. Spread the hazelnuts on a cookie sheet and toast in a 350° oven for 15 minutes. Then drop them into a bowl of boiling water, drain immediately and rub off the skins in a kitchen towel. Break the toast into small pieces and pulverize in the blender. Pulverize the hazelnuts in the blender at high speed. Add the nuts and toast crumbs to the casserole with the chicken stock and the hot pepper, stir to mix, cover and simmer gently until the chicken is tender, about 45 minutes. Shake or stir the casserole mixture from time to time during the cooking to prevent the sauce catching.

Transfer the chicken pieces to a serving platter and keep it warm. Remove the hot pepper. Skim off any grease from the sauce and strain the sauce through a fine sieve. Return it to the casserole. Push the raw chicken liver through a sieve and stir into the sauce. Add the sherry and cook for a minute or two longer. Pour over the chicken pieces and serve with plain white rice, or any plainly boiled root vegetable. Serves 6.

Pollo Frito a la Criolla *Cuba*
Fried Chicken Creole Style

3 to 3½-pound chicken, cut into serving pieces
2 teaspoons salt
½ teaspoon freshly ground pepper

2 large cloves garlic, crushed
¼ cup Seville (bitter) orange juice
Flour
½ cup vegetable oil or lard

Mix the salt, pepper and garlic together and rub well into the chicken pieces. Put them into a large bowl, and pour the bitter orange juice over them. Refrigerate for about 4 hours, turning 2 or 3 times. Remove chicken from the marinade and pat dry with paper towels. Reserve the marinade. Dredge chicken with flour, shaking the pieces to remove any excess.

Heat the oil in a heavy frying pan large enough to hold all the chicken pieces comfortably. Sauté the chicken on both sides until golden brown, reduce the heat, sprinkle chicken with the marinade, cover and continue cooking until the chicken is tender, about 30 minutes. Uncover, increase the heat to crisp and brown the chicken, turning the pieces once. There will be no liquid left in the pan. Serves 4 to 6.

If Seville (bitter) orange juice is not available, mix lime juice and orange juice in the proportion of 1 part lime juice to 3 parts orange juice and use as a substitute. It will not have the subtly different flavour of Seville orange juice, but is an acceptable substitute.

Poulet à la Créole   Haïti
Chicken Creole Style

Though this very simple, very good chicken dish is labeled Créole, its influences are clearly Asian, perhaps brought by the French from India, or perhaps it is Burmese influence making its way into the Caribbean via what was French Indo-China.

3½ to 4-pound
  chicken, cut into
  serving pieces
6 tablespoons peanut oil
4 large onions, finely
  chopped
2 teaspoons curry powder
¼ teaspoon powdered
  saffron

2 very hot fresh peppers,
  preferably red, seeded
  and finely chopped
Salt, freshly ground
  pepper to taste
2 cups coconut milk

Heat the oil in a heavy frying pan and sauté the chicken pieces until golden on both sides. Transfer to a heavy, covered casserole. In the oil remaining in the pan sauté the onions until tender but not browned, add the curry powder, saffron, and hot pepper and cook for 3 or 4 minutes longer. Add to the chicken. Season to taste with salt and pepper, add the coconut milk, cover and cook at a gentle simmer until the chicken is tender, about 45 minutes. Serve with rice. Serves 6.

Poulet Farci   *Haïti*
Stuffed Chicken

3 tablespoons vegetable shortening	1 teaspoon brown sugar
1½ cups freshly made coarse bread crumbs	¼ teaspoon grated nutmeg
Salt, freshly ground pepper to taste	6 tablespoons dark dry rum
¼ teaspoon cayenne pepper	3½ to 4-pound chicken
Juice and grated rind of 1 large lime	3 or 4 bananas peeled and chopped
	4 tablespoons butter
	1 cup chicken stock

Heat the shortening and fry the bread crumbs until golden. Drain. Season the breadcrumbs with salt, pepper and cayenne. Add the lime juice (reserve a few drops) and rind, sugar, nutmeg and 2 tablespoons of rum, mixing to a stiff paste. Stuff this paste into the chicken breast cavity, lifting skin over breast to do so. Season the bananas with salt, pepper, a few drops of lime and a sprinkle of rum. Stuff the cavity of the bird with the bananas and insert a crumpled piece of aluminum foil into the tail end to prevent the banana oozing out during the cooking. Truss the bird, set it on a rack in a roasting pan. Roast in a preheated 350° oven for 1 hour and 20 minutes, basting with butter every 15 minutes.

Remove trussing strings and set bird on a serving platter. Keep it warm. Add the stock to the juices in the pan together with 1 tablespoon of rum. Set over high heat, stirring and scraping up all the brown bits. Cook until the gravy is slightly reduced. Adjust seasoning, and pour gravy into a sauceboat. Just before serving heat the remaining rum, pour over the bird, and set aflame. Serves 6.

Pavo Relleno

Puerto Rico

Stuffed Turkey

3 tablespoons salt
3 cloves garlic, crushed
¼ teaspoon freshly
  ground pepper
3 tablespoons olive oil

1 tablespoon cider
  vinegar
8 to 9-pound ready-to-
  cook turkey

Mix salt, garlic, pepper, oil and vinegar together and rub the bird thoroughly, inside and out. Cover loosely with foil and refrigerate for at least 8 hours, or overnight.

STUFFING:

½ pound firm white
  bread
1 cup chicken stock
4 tablespoons butter
½ cup blanched
  almonds, coarsely
  chopped
2 tablespoons vegetable
  oil
1 medium onion, finely
  chopped

1 pound lean boneless
  pork, ground
¾ pound lean,
  boneless ham, coarsely
  chopped
½ cup dry sherry
1 teaspoon finely
  crumbled bay leaf
Salt, freshly ground
  pepper to taste
4 ounces (8 tablespoons)
  unsalted butter, melted

Cut the crusts off the bread and tear it into ½-inch pieces. Place bread in a large bowl and pour the chicken stock over it. Mix well and set aside.

Heat the 4 tablespoons of butter in a heavy frying pan and sauté the almonds, stirring constantly, until they are golden. Lift out with a slotted spoon and add to the bread.

Add the vegetable oil to the butter remaining in the frying pan, and sauté the onion until it is tender but not browned. Add the ground pork, mashing with a fork to break up any lumps. Cook until the meat has lost all trace of pink. Add the contents of the frying pan to the bread mixture together with the ham, sherry, bay leaf, salt and pepper, and mix gently but thoroughly.

Stuff the turkey with the mixture, close the vent with foil or with metal skewers, then truss the bird. Brush all over with about 2 tablespoons of the melted butter then place on a rack in a roasting pan and roast in a preheated 350° oven, uncovered, basting frequently, and allowing 25 minutes to the pound. To test for doneness, pierce the thigh joint with a fork. If the juice runs clear the bird is done. If it runs red roast for 5 minutes longer and test again. Do not overcook turkey as this makes the meat dry and flavorless. Serves 8 to 10.

Poulet à L'Orange   *Haïti*

Chicken in Orange Juice

2½ to 3-pound chicken, cut into serving pieces
1 cup Seville (bitter) orange juice
¼ cup olive oil
1 medium onion, thinly sliced
2 tablespoons chopped shallots
Sprig parsley
¼ teaspoon thyme
1 hot fresh red or green pepper, seeded and chopped
Salt, freshly ground pepper to taste
8 cloves garlic, chopped

Put the chicken pieces and the orange juice in a covered container and marinate overnight in the refrigerator. Remove the chicken pieces from the marinade and pat dry on paper towels. Reserve the marinade. Heat the oil in a heavy covered casserole and sauté the chicken pieces until lightly golden on both sides. Add the onion and shallots and sauté lightly. Add the parsley, thyme, hot pepper, salt and pepper, the garlic and reserved marinade. Bring to a boil, lower the heat and cook at a gentle simmer until the chicken is tender, about half an hour. Serves 4 to 6.

Pelau

St. Lucia

Chicken and Rice Stew

All the pilaus and pelaus in the Caribbean have a common origin, having been introduced by Moslems from India. This one is simple, but very pleasant.

3 tablespoons unsalted butter
3½ to 4-pound chicken, cut into serving pieces
2 medium onions, finely chopped
1 clove garlic, chopped
Sprig thyme, or ½ teaspoon dried thyme
2 or 3 sprigs parsley
Bay leaf
1 sprig celery with leaves

1 small fresh hot red pepper, or 1 hot dried pepper
1 pound tomatoes peeled and chopped, or use 2 cups canned tomatoes
Salt, freshly ground pepper to taste
Chicken stock
2 cups rice
10-ounce package frozen green peas, thawed

Heat the butter in a heavy, covered frying pan large enough to hold the chicken pieces comfortably. Sauté the chicken pieces until golden brown. Remove from the pan and set aside.

In the same pan sauté the onions and garlic until tender but not browned. Return the chicken pieces to the pan. Tie the thyme, parsley, bay leaf, celery and hot pepper in a small square of cheesecloth, and add to the pan with the tomatoes, and salt and pepper to taste. Add enough chicken stock barely to cover. Simmer gently, covered, for 30 minutes. Remove the chicken pieces from the pan. Strain the stock and discard the cheesecloth bag. Bring the quantity of stock up to 4 cups. Return the chicken pieces to the pan, add the stock, stir in the rice, cover and cook for 15 minutes. Add the peas, cover and continue cooking for about 10 minutes longer, or until the rice is tender and all the liquid is absorbed. Serves 6 to 8.

Pavo Guisado   *Dominican Republic*

Turkey Stew

8 to 8½-pound turkey,
   cut into serving pieces
4 cloves garlic, crushed
Salt, freshly ground
   pepper
2 tablespoons red wine
   vinegar
½ cup vegetable oil
½ cup tomato purée
2 cups chicken or turkey
   stock

1 cup dry red wine
1 green bell pepper,
   seeded and chopped
24 pitted green olives
4 tablespoons capers
1 pound potatoes, peeled
   and sliced
10-ounce package frozen
   peas, thawed

Season the turkey pieces with a mixture of the garlic, salt
and pepper to taste, and the vinegar. Leave for 1 hour.
Heat the oil in a heavy casserole or Dutch oven large
enough to hold the turkey and sauté the pieces 2 or 3 at
a time until lightly browned. Add any of the marinade
that remains. Add the tomato purée, stock, wine and pepper, cover and cook for 1 hour. Add the olives, capers
and potatoes and cook for half an hour longer, or until
both the potatoes and turkey are tender. Add the peas
and cook 5 to 7 minutes longer. Serves 8 to 10.

Sancocho de Pollo   *Dominican Republic*

Chicken and Vegetable Stew

5-pound chicken, cut into serving pieces

3 tablespoons Seville (bitter) orange juice

1 pound cassava root, peeled and cut into 1-inch slices

4 quarts chicken stock, or half stock, half water

3 green plantains

¼ cup lime juice

1½ pounds West Indian pumpkin (calabaza) peeled and cubed, or use Hubbard squash

4 cloves garlic, crushed

1 large onion, finely chopped

1 teaspoon orégano

2 fresh hot red or green peppers, seeded and chopped, or Tabasco to taste

3 grains melegueta pepper

2 or 3 sprigs each of parsley and fresh coriander

1 pound potatoes, peeled, and cut into 1-inch slices

1 pound yam, peeled and cut into 1-inch slices

1 pound sweet potatoes, preferably white, peeled and cut into 1-inch slices

1 pound each of white and yellow yautía, peeled and cut into 1-inch slices

3 ears sweet corn, cut into 1-inch slices

Salt, freshly ground pepper to taste

1 small cabbage, cut into 6 wedges

2 tablespoons cider vinegar

Wash the chicken in the orange juice and put into a soup kettle or heavy casserole big enough to hold all the ingredients. Add the cassava root and the chicken stock, bring to a boil, reduce the heat to a bare simmer and cook, covered for 1 hour.

Peel the plantains using a paring knife as the skin will not come off readily, and cut into 1-inch slices. Pour the lime juice over the plantain pieces and set aside.

Add all the other ingredients, except the vinegar and

the cabbage, to the kettle. The pumpkin will disintegrate, thickening the sauce lightly. Drain the plantains, and add. Simmer for half an hour longer. Add the cabbage and cook 5 to 10 minutes longer, or until the cabbage is done. Add the vinegar and cook for a minute or two longer.

Taste for seasoning and check that all the ingredients are done. Add the vinegar and cook for a minute or two longer.

Taste for seasoning and check that all the ingredients are done. When serving cut the cabbage wedges crosswise in halves. Serve in large, rimmed soup plates with a hot pepper sauce on the side. Serves 10 to 12.

Poulet aux Pruneaux   *Martinique*

Chicken with Prunes

4-pound roasting chicken
1½ cups pitted prunes,
   halved
2 cups seedless raisins
1 cup Martinique *rhum
   vieux*, or use a dark
   rum such as Myer's

4 ounces sausage meat
2 large apples, peeled,
   cored and chopped
1 medium onion, finely
   chopped
Salt, freshly ground
   pepper
2 tablespoons butter,
   melted

Allow the chicken to come to room temperature. Combine the prunes and raisins in a bowl, add the rum and allow to stand for 2 hours. Then add the sausage meat, apples, onion, and salt and pepper to taste, mixing well. Stuff the chicken with the prune mixture and truss. Place in a baking pan with any remaining stuffing wrapped in aluminum foil. Roast in a 350° oven, basting with the butter every 15 minutes. Roast 1½ hours, or until the juices run clear when the chicken is pierced with a fork in the thickest part of the leg. Remove the trussing string, transfer chicken to a hot platter. Serve with the extra stuffing, and Riz Créole. Serves 4 to 6.

Vegetables and Salads

Alu Talkari

Trinidad

Potato Curry

4 tablespoons coconut, or
  vegetable, oil
1 tablespoon fenugreek
  (optional)
2 cloves garlic, finely
  chopped
2 tablespoons massala
  (curry powder or
  paste)

2 pounds potatoes, peeled
  and sliced
1 small green mango,
  peeled and sliced
  (optional)
Salt
1 cup water

Heat the oil in a heavy frying pan or saucepan and add
the fenugreek, if liked, and the garlic cloves. Cook over
medium heat, stirring with a wooden spoon, until the garlic
is dark brown. Lift out, and discard the fenugreek and
garlic. Add the massala to the pan and cook, stirring, for
3 or 4 minutes. Add the potatoes, the green mango slices,
if liked, salt to taste and the water. Cover and cook at a

simmer until the potatoes are tender. If necessary, add a little water during the cooking, but the finished dish should be quite dry. This is very good as a stuffing for Roti (see Index), one of which makes a light lunch, supper or snack. Serves 4.

Ackee Soufflé   *Jamaica*

3 tablespoons unsalted butter	1 teaspoon Worcestershire sauce
3 tablespoons all-purpose flour	4 egg yolks
1 cup milk	1 cup canned ackees, mashed to a purée
½ teaspoon salt	5 egg whites, stiffly beaten
¼ teaspoon white pepper	

Melt the butter in a heavy saucepan and stir in the flour. Cook stirring constantly with a wooden spoon for a minute or two, without letting the flour brown. Heat the milk and add all at once to the flour mixture. Cook, stirring until thick and smooth. Add the salt, pepper, and Worcestershire sauce. Remove from the heat and allow to cool a little.

Stir in the egg yolks one by one. Stir in the ackee purée. Stir in about a quarter of the egg whites, then fold in the rest, gently but thoroughly. Pour into a buttered 6-cup soufflé dish mold. Bake in a 375° oven for about 30 minutes or until the soufflé is firm. Serves 4.

Acrats D'Aubergine   *Martinique-Guadeloupe*

Eggplant Fritters

1½ pounds eggplant	⅛ teaspoon cayenne
1 egg, well-beaten	1 cup all-purpose flour
2 tablespoons milk	1 teaspoon double-acting baking powder
Salt, freshly ground pepper	Oil for deep frying

Peel the eggplant and cut into 1-inch cubes. Cook in boiling salted water until tender, about 15 minutes. Drain thoroughly and mash into a smooth purée. Add the egg, milk, salt, pepper and cayenne, mixing well. Sift baking powder with the flour and beat in the flour tablespoon by tablespoon into the eggplant mixture until it is smooth and light. Deep-fry by tablespoons in oil heated to 375° on a frying thermometer until golden brown. Serve hot as an accompaniment to drinks, or as a vegetable with meat, fish or poultry. Makes about 18 fritters.

Acrats de Chou Palmiste

Martinique-Guadeloupe

Palm Heart Fritters

14-ounce can palm hearts, drained and coarsely chopped
1 cup all-purpose flour
1 teaspoon double-acting baking powder
1 teaspoon salt
2 eggs, lightly beaten
1 medium onion, finely chopped
1 clove garlic, minced

2 fresh hot red or green peppers, seeded and chopped
1 tablespoon parsley, chopped
½ teaspoon thyme, crumbled
Salt, freshly ground pepper to taste
¼ cup milk, if necessary
Oil for deep frying

Sift together into a large bowl, the flour, baking powder and salt. Stir in the eggs, onion, garlic, peppers, parsley, thyme, salt, pepper and the palm hearts, folding the ingredients lightly together to form a stiffish dough. Add the milk, if necessary. Allow the batter to stand for about 1 hour, then deep-fry by tablespoons in oil heated to 350° to 375° (on a frying thermometer), until golden brown. Drain on paper towels, keep warm and serve as a first course, or as an accompaniment to drinks. Makes about 24 fritters. Serves 6.

Arroz Blanco   *Dominican Republic*

White Rice

2 cups long-grain rice   1 teaspoon salt
Juice 1 large lime   ¼ cup peanut oil
3 cups water

Wash the rice thoroughly. Drain, cover with cold water, add the lime juice and allow to stand for 2 or 3 minutes. Drain. Pour the water into a heavy saucepan with a tight-fitting lid, add the salt, bring to a boil and pour in the rice. Stir, bring back to a boil, cover, lower the heat and cook for 10 minutes. Stir the oil into the rice, cover and cook on the lowest possible heat until the rice is tender. Serves 6.

Arroz con Ajo   *Cuba*

Garlic Rice

4 tablespoons unsalted   4 cups chicken stock
  butter   Salt, white pepper to
2 cloves garlic, crushed   taste
2 cups long-grain rice

Heat the butter in a heavy saucepan, add the garlic, stir, add the rice, and cook, stirring constantly, until the butter has been absorbed. Take care not to let the rice brown. Add the stock, season to taste, cover, bring to a boil then reduce the heat as low as possible and cook until the rice is tender and all the liquid absorbed, 20 to 30 minutes. Serves 6.

Arroz con Frijoles   *Dominican Republic*

Rice with Beans

3½ cups coconut milk
(see Index)
2 ounces boiled ham,
coarsely chopped
1 fresh hot pepper,
seeded and chopped
3 cloves garlic, minced
2 ounces bacon, coarsely
chopped

2 medium tomatoes,
peeled, seeded and
chopped
1 tablespoon fresh
coriander, chopped
Salt to taste
2 cups long-grain rice
1 cup cooked red kidney
beans

Pour ½ cup of coconut milk into a heavy saucepan with
a tight-fitting lid. Add the ham, bacon, hot pepper, garlic,
tomatoes, coriander and salt to taste. Cook, stirring, over
low heat for 3 or 4 minutes or until the mixture is well
blended. Stir in the rice, the beans and the 3 cups of
coconut milk. Stir gently, then cover and cook over low
heat until the rice is tender and the liquid absorbed. Serves
6 to 8 as a side dish, or 4 if served with a salad, as a main
course.

Asparagus Pudding   *U.S. Virgin Islands*

*This recipe is of Danish origin and is a good example of
the pluralist nature of Caribbean cooking. Both foods and
cooking methods illustrate the history of the islands.*

8 tablespoons unsalted
butter, plus butter for
mold
½ cup all-purpose
flour
Salt, white pepper
½ cup liquid from
canned asparagus

½ cup milk
1 teaspoon onion juice
8 eggs
1-pound 3-ounce can
asparagus, cut into
½-inch pieces

Thickly butter a covered quart mold. In a heavy saucepan melt the butter over low heat, stir in the flour and cook, stirring for 2 minutes without letting the flour color. Add salt, pepper, asparagus liquid, milk, and onion juice. Stir over low heat to make a smooth, thick sauce. Off the heat beat in the eggs, one by one. Carefully fold in the asparagus. Pour into the mold. Cover the mold and set it in a large pan with hot water coming about halfway up the mold. Cover the pan and steam on top of the stove for about 30 minutes, or until firm. Add a little boiling water to the pan during cooking, if necessary. Serve with Lemon Butter Sauce, or Curry Sauce, (see Index). Serves 6.

Fresh or frozen asparagus may be used for this dish. If using frozen asparagus thoroughly defrost 2 10-ounce packages, and cut into ½-inch pieces. If using fresh asparagus, cut the tough ends off 1½ pounds asparagus, peel and cook in boiling salted water for 12 to 15 minutes. Drain thoroughly and cut into ½-inch pieces. Use 1 cup milk to make up the liquid.

Aubergine à la Tomate   *Martinique*

Eggplant with Tomatoes

2 ounces bacon, chopped
1 tablespoon vegetable oil
   or butter
1 onion, finely chopped
2 cloves garlic, chopped
1 eggplant, weighing
   about 1 pound, peeled
   and cut into 1-inch
   cubes

1 pound tomatoes, peeled
   and chopped
1 teaspoon chopped fresh
   hot red or green
   pepper
Salt

Sauté the bacon in the oil or butter in a heavy casserole. Add the onion and garlic and cook until the onion is tender but not browned. Add the eggplant and the tomatoes and cook, covered for 15 minutes. Uncover and cook for 15 minutes longer, or until most of the liquid has evaporated. Season with the hot pepper and salt to taste. Serves 6.

Berehein na Forno   St. Maarten
Eggplant in Coconut Cream

1 large eggplant,
  weighing about
  1-pound
1 tablespoon butter,
  softened
3 large onions, finely
  chopped
1 teaspoon dried hot red
  peppers, crumbled, *or*

1 fresh hot red pepper,
  seeded and chopped
Salt, freshly ground
  pepper
2 cups coconut cream
  (see Index)

Peel the eggplant and slice thinly. Butter an oven-proof dish and arrange the eggplant slices in it. Cover with the onions, sprinkle with the peppers, season to taste with salt and pepper and pour the coconut cream over it. Cover the dish with a lid, or with foil, and bake in a 350° oven for 45 minutes. Uncover and bake for 10 minutes longer. Serves 4 to 6.

Baked Pawpaw   Jamaica

Papaya is known as pawpaw in Jamaica. When ripe it is eaten as a fruit, when unripe as a vegetable.

1 green (unripe) papaya,
  weighing about
  5 pounds
4 tablespoons unsalted
  butter
1 large onion, finely
  chopped

2 medium tomatoes,
  peeled and chopped
Salt, freshly ground
  pepper
1 cup bread crumbs
½ cup grated
  Parmesan cheese

Cut the unpeeled papaya in half, lengthwise. Scoop out and discard the seeds. Drop the fruit into boiling salted water and cook until tender, 15 to 20 minutes. Lift out and drain. Carefully scoop out the flesh, reserving the shells. Heat 2 tablespoons of butter in a frying pan and sauté the onion until tender but not browned. Add the tomatoes, salt and pepper to taste and the papaya mashed. Mix thoroughly. Stuff the shells with the mixture, sprinkle with the bread crumbs and cheese and dot with the remaining 2 tablespoons of butter. Bake in a 400° oven on a cookie sheet until the tops are browned. Serves 6.

VARIATION: Boiled papaya is also popular as a vegetable. Choose a green (unripe) papaya weighing 2 to 3 pounds. Wash, peel and slice it crosswise. Remove and discard the seeds. Put it into a saucepan with enough salted water to cover. Cover and simmer 15 minutes or until tender. Serve with melted butter and freshly ground pepper. Serves 4 to 6.

Banane Jaune Avec
Sauce Blanche   *Martinique*

Green Bananas with White Sauce

3 large green plantains, or 6 fairly small green bananas	1½ cups milk
	Salt, white pepper to taste
3 tablespoons unsalted butter	⅛ teaspoon grated nutmeg
3 tablespoons all-purpose flour	½ cup grated gruyère cheese (optional)

Peel the plantains or bananas by cutting through the skin lengthwise with a sharp knife in 3 places, then peeling off the skin. Cut the plantains in half cross-wise. The bananas should be left whole. Put into a saucepan with salted water to cover and cook until tender, about 30 minutes for the plantains, 15 minutes for bananas.

Heat the butter in a small saucepan and stir in the flour. Cook stirring constantly with a wooden spoon for a minute or two. Heat the milk and pour all at once into the butter-flour mixture. Cook, stirring until the sauce is smooth and thick. Season to taste with salt and pepper; add the nutmeg. Arrange the bananas or plantains in a serving dish and pour the sauce over them. Serves 6.

If liked, ½ cup grated gruyère cheese may be added to the white sauce, stirred in with the seasonings.

Breadfruit Stuffed with Saltfish and Ackee   *Jamaica*

1 pound salt codfish	1 breadfruit, peeled, or
2 dozen fresh ackees, or	1-pound 10-ounce can
1-pound 2-ounce can	breadfruit, drained
4 ounces salt pork, diced	and mashed
1 large onion, finely	Butter
chopped	

Soak the salt cod in cold water. The length of time will depend on the hardness and saltiness of the fish. Drain, and cook in fresh cold water. Simmer until tender, adding the fresh ackees 15 minutes before the fish is done. Drain. Fry the salt pork in a large frying pan until all the fat is rendered out. Add the onion and sauté until tender. Flake the fish and add to the skillet with the cooked ackees. If using canned ackees, drain and add them at this point. Cook until heated through.

If using fresh breadfruit, rub the breadfruit with butter and wrap in aluminum foil. While the fish is cooking, bake the breadfruit in a 350° oven until tender, about 45 minutes. Allow to cool a little. Remove the core and, if necessary a little of the flesh from the stem end. Stuff with the fish mixture. Rub more butter on the outside and return to the oven for about 15 minutes, or until heated through. If using canned breadfruit, line a buttered casserole with the mashed breadfruit, fill with the fish mixture, and top with more breadfruit. Dot with butter and bake in a 350° oven for 30 minutes, or until heated through. Serves 6.

Breadfruit may also be stuffed with the filling used for Deep Dish Meat Pie, St. Thomas, either of the Cuban Picadillos, or the beef filling for Keshy Yena, Curaçao. Run Down, Jamaica, can also be used, as well as the following stuffing. (See recipes in Index.)

SALTFISH STUFFING

2 tablespoons butter
1 medium onion, finely
  chopped
½ pound salt codfish,
  cooked and flaked
½ pound pork, cooked
  and chopped
1 fresh hot red pepper,
  seeded and chopped

½ cup brown sauce, or
  gravy
1 tablespoon chopped
  chives
½ teaspoon each
  thyme and marjoram
Salt, freshly ground
  pepper

Heat the butter in a frying pan and sauté the onion until tender. Add all the rest of the ingredients, mixing well. Use as a stuffing for breadfruit.

Chou Palmiste
en Sauce Blanche   *Martinique-Guadeloupe*

Palm Hearts in White Sauce

2 14-ounce cans palm
  hearts
3 tablespoons sweet
  butter
3 tablespoons all-purpose
  flour
1 cup milk

½ cup heavy cream
Salt, white pepper to
  taste
½ cup freshly grated
  Parmesan or gruyère
  cheese

Heat the palm hearts in their own liquid. Drain thoroughly and chop coarsely. Place in a buttered oven-proof dish.

Meanwhile melt the butter in a small saucepan, stir in the flour and cook over low heat, stirring constantly for about a minute. Heat the milk and cream together and pour on to the butter-flour mixture, stirring constantly until smooth. Season to taste with salt and pepper and pour over the palm hearts. Top with the grated cheese and run under a broiler until the cheese is lightly browned. Serves 6.

VARIATION: Heat the palm hearts, cut into lengthwise pieces and serve with a freshly made tomato sauce and freshly grated Parmesan or gruyére cheese.

Concombre en daube   *Martinique*
Stewed Cucumbers

3 medium-sized cucumbers	1 pound tomatoes, about 3 medium, peeled and chopped
3 tablespoons olive, or vegetable, oil	Salt, freshly ground pepper
1 medium onion, finely chopped	Pinch sugar

Peel the cucumbers and cut into halves, lengthwise. Scrape out the seeds and cut the cucumbers into 1-inch crosswise slices. Set aside. Heat the oil in a saucepan and sauté the onion until tender, but not browned. Add the tomatoes, salt and pepper to taste, and sugar. Add the cucumbers, stir to mix, cover and simmer very gently for 45 minutes. Serves 6.

Concombres en Salade   *Martinique*
Cucumber Salad

2 medium-sized cucumbers	1 tablespoon lime, or lemon juice
1 teaspoon salt	1 or 2 teaspoons fresh hot pepper, seeded and finely chopped
1 large clove garlic, crushed	

Peel the cucumbers and cut into halves lengthwise. Scrape out the seeds. Chop the cucumbers coarsely and mix with the salt. Allow to stand for 10 minutes, then drain thoroughly. Toss with the garlic, lime juice and hot peppers. Serves 4.

Coo-Coo

Though Coo-Coo is traditionally credited to Barbados, it turns up in a great many islands including Jamaica, Trinidad, and Tobago. In the Netherlands Antilles and the Virgin Islands it is called Funchi or Fungi, and is cooked without the okras, sometimes even without butter, though this produces a rather dull dish. There is also a sweet fungi, popular in the Virgin Islands, (see Desserts).

Coo-Coo in Barbados is served with the island specialty, steamed flying fish, but it is also served in other islands as a starchy vegetable with any meat or fish, and sometimes with tomato sauce. The word coo-coo means a cooked side dish, and in addition to corn meal coo-coo there are Conquintay (plantain flour) Coo-Coo, Breadfruit Coo-Coo, Cassava Coo-Coo, an interesting corn meal and coconut version from Grenada, and one from Trinidad made with fresh sweet corn.

Cold Coo-Coo can be cut into slices and fried in butter or vegetable oil.

Breadfruit Coo-Coo   *Barbados*

1 breadfruit, about
   2-pounds, or a
   1-pound 10-ounce can
½ pound salt beef,
   coarsely chopped
1 onion, finely chopped
½ teaspoon thyme
1 bay leaf

1 sprig parsley
2 or 3 stalks of chives
6 tablespoons unsalted
   butter
Salt, freshly ground
   pepper to taste
A little chicken stock

Peel the breadfruit, cut out the core, and cut up roughly. If using canned breadfruit, drain and chop coarsely. Put on to cook with the salt beef and onion, with the thyme, bay leaf, parsley and chive tied up in a piece of cheesecloth, in enough water to cover. Cook until breadfruit is tender. Drain, remove and discard *bouquet garni* and mash in 4 tablespoons of the butter, over very low heat, adding a little chicken stock if necessary to achieve a smooth mixture with the consistency of rather stiff mashed potatoes. Season to taste with salt and pepper. Turn into a buttered basin to mold, then turn out onto a warmed serving platter. Garnish with the remaining 2 tablespoons of butter. Serves 6 as a vegetable dish.

Coo-Coo   *Barbados*

12 small, young okras	2 cups yellow corn meal
6 cups water	3 tablespoons unsalted
Salt to taste	butter

Wash the okras, cut off the stems and slice crosswise, about ¼-inch thick. Bring the water to a boil, add salt and okras and cook, covered, for 10 minutes. Pour the corn meal into the water and okras in a slow, steady stream, stirring with a wooden spoon. Cook, stirring constantly, over medium heat until the mixture is thick and smooth, about five minutes. Turn into a greased basin to mold, then turn out onto a warmed serving platter and spread the butter on top, or turn out directly onto a warmed platter without molding. Serve hot. Serves 6 as a vegetable dish.

Conquintay Coo-Coo   *Trinidad*

This is made with plantain flour, sometimes available in Health Food stores and specialty shops, often sold as banana flour. However, it is easy enough to make at home.

1 cup conquintay flour   **Salt to taste**
1 cup water   **4 tablespoons butter**

Bring the water to a boil, add salt, remove from heat and gradually pour in the conquintay flour, stirring all the time with a wooden spoon until thick and smooth. Return to the heat and bring to a boil, stirring constantly. Cook for 2 or 3 minutes. Stir in the butter and serve. Serves 4 to 6 as a vegetable dish.

To make the flour, peel and slice green plantains, place on a cookie sheet and dry in a very slow oven until they are quite crisp. Put through a food mill or grate in an electric blender as fine as possible. Sift through a hair sieve. Store in a covered glass jar.

Coo-Coo   *Tobago*

12 small, young okras   1 pound sweet potatoes,
6 cups chicken, or beef,   peeled, cooked and
   stock   sliced
Salt to taste   2 medium tomatoes,
2 cups yellow corn meal   peeled and sliced
2 tablespoons unsalted   2 pimientos, sliced
   butter   Lettuce for garnish

Wash the okras, cut off stems and slice crosswise, about ¼-inch thick. Bring the stock to a boil, add salt to taste, and add okras, and cook, covered, for 10 minutes. Pour the corn meal into the water and okras in a slow, steady stream, stirring with a wooden spoon. Cook, stirring constantly, over medium heat until the mixture is thick and smooth, about five minutes. Put the butter into a warmed basin, add the coo-coo and shake until it forms a ball and absorbs the butter. Turn onto a warmed serving platter and decorate with the sweet potatoes, tomatoes, pimientos and lettuce. Serves 6.

Cassava Coo-Coo   *Windward Islands*

*This dish occurs in Brazil as Angú de Farinha de Man-
dioca. Since cassava (manihot utilissima) is originally
from Brazil and was taken to the Asiatic tropics by the
Portuguese in the 17th century, this is obviously a dish
native to the Indians of Brazil, and it may well have spread
to the Caribbean long before the West discovered the
Americas.*

6 cups water	2 cups cassava meal
Salt to taste	

Bring the water to a boil in a heavy saucepan, add salt
and pour in the cassava meal in a slow, steady stream.
Cook, stirring constantly with a wooden spoon, until the
mixture is thick and smooth, about 10 minutes. Serves 6.
Serve as a starchy vegetable with any meat or fish dish.

Corn and Coconut Coo-Coo   *Grenada*

4 cups freshly made	Salt to taste
coconut milk (see	2 cups yellow corn meal
Index)	

Put the coconut milk on to boil with salt to taste in a
heavy saucepan. When boiling pour in the corn meal in
a slow, steady stream, stirring constantly with a wooden
spoon. Cook until the mixture is thick and smooth. Serves
6 as a vegetable dish.

Lavina's Codfish Coo-Coo   *Jamaica*

2 tablespoons lard or	1 pound cooked,
butter	shredded salt codfish
2 ounces ham or bacon,	1 fresh hot red or green
chopped	pepper, seeded and
4 cups water	chopped
2 cups yellow corn meal	Salt to taste

Heat the lard in a large saucepan. Fry the ham or bacon
in it, add the water and bring to a rolling boil. Pour in the
corn meal in a slow, steady stream and cook, stirring
constantly with a wooden spoon over medium heat until
the mixture is smooth and thick. Add the codfish and hot
pepper and cook until the fish is heated through. Season
to taste with salt if necessary. Serves 4 as a luncheon dish.

Sweet Corn Coo-Coo   *Trinidad*

12 small young okras   2 cups fresh sweet corn,
2 cups water   grated
Salt to taste   2 tablespoons butter

Wash the okras, cut off stems and slice crosswise, about
¼-inch thick. Bring the water to a boil, add salt and okras
and cook, covered, for 10 minutes. Add the corn and
cook, stirring, until the mixture is thick and creamy. Stir
in the butter and serve hot. Serves 6.

Colombo de Giraumon   *Martinique-Guadeloupe*

Pumpkin Curry

2 tablespoons vegetable   2 medium tomatoes,
   oil   peeled and chopped
2 tablespoons unsalted   1 pound West Indian
   butter   pumpkin (calabaza), or
¼ pound bacon,   use Hubbard squash,
   chopped   peeled and cut into 1-
1 medium onion, chopped   inch cubes
1 bell pepper, seeded and   Salt, freshly ground
   chopped   pepper to taste
1 teaspoon curry powder   1 large clove garlic,
¼ teaspoon ground   crushed
   cloves

Heat the oil and butter in a heavy saucepan, add the bacon, onion and pepper and cook, stirring from time to time, until the onion is tender but not browned. Add the curry powder and cook, stirring for a minute or two. Add the cloves, tomatoes, pumpkin, salt and pepper, stir to mix, cover and cook on the lowest possible heat, stirring occasionally to prevent the mixture from burning. When the pumpkin is very tender and almost reduced to a purée, stir in the garlic and cook, uncovered for a minute or so longer.

Serve by itself or as an accompaniment to any plainly cooked meat or poultry. Serves 6.

Congris   *Cuba*

Red Beans and Rice

This is the popular rice and bean dish of the eastern part of the island, a specialty of Santiago de Cuba.

2 tablespoons achiote lard (see Index)

1 medium onion, finely chopped

1 clove garlic, minced

1 green bell pepper, seeded and chopped

2 medium tomatoes, peeled, seeded and chopped

Salt, freshly ground pepper to taste

2 cups cooked California pink beans (frijoles colorados) or red kidney beans

1 cup raw rice

2 cups cold water

Heat the lard in a heavy, covered casserole or saucepan, add the onion and garlic, and sauté until the onion is tender but not browned. Add the pepper and tomatoes and cook, stirring, until the mixture is thick and well blended. Season to taste with salt and pepper. Stir in the beans, mixing well. Add the rice and water, mixing lightly. Cover and cook over very low heat until the rice is tender and all the water absorbed, about 20 minutes. The rice should be fluffy and dry. Serves 4 to 6.

Christophene au Gratin   *Martinique*

Chayote with Cheese and Onion Stuffing

3 large chayotes (see
   Glossary), each
   weighing about
   ¾-pound
5 tablespoons unsalted
   butter

1 large onion, finely
   chopped
Salt, freshly ground
   pepper
1 cup plus 3 tablespoons
   grated Parmesan
   cheese

Boil the whole chayotes in salted water until tender, about
30 minutes. Remove from the saucepan, and when cool
enough to handle, cut into halves lengthwise. Scoop out
the pulp, including the edible seed, mash and set aside.
Reserve the shells.

   Heat 3 tablespoons of the butter in a frying pan and
sauté the onion until tender but not browned. Add the
mashed chayote pulp, salt and pepper to taste and cook,
stirring, for a few minutes to dry the mixture out a little.
Off the heat, add the cup of cheese, stirring to mix well.
Stuff the shells with the mixture, dot with the remaining
2 tablespoons butter and sprinkle with the extra cheese.
Place on a baking sheet and bake in a 350° oven for 15
minutes, or until the tops are lightly browned. Serve as
a luncheon or supper dish. Serves 6.

VARIATION: This vegetable is also popular as a salad in
Martinique. For Christophene en Salade (Chayote Salad),
peel 2 large chayotes and cut lengthwise into 4 pieces.
Do not remove edible seed. Boil in salted water for 20
minutes, or until tender. Drain thorough and when cool
cut into ½-inch crosswise slices and toss gently with Sauce
Vinaigrette (see Index), and ½ cup chopped shallots. Serve
on lettuce leaves. Serves 6.

Foo-Foo
Trinidad-Barbados

Pounded Green Plantain Balls

3 green plantains,   Salt
  unpeeled

Cook the plantains in unsalted water until tender, about
half an hour. When soft, peel, chop coarsely, and pound
in a mortar until smooth, moistening the pestle with water
from time to time as it gets sticky. Season with salt to
taste, and form into small balls. Keep warm. Serve with
Callaloo (see Index) or any creole soup. Serves 6.

Dal
Trinidad

Split Pea or Lentil Purée

*Dal is the Hindi name for all the legumes. The spelling
varies, but dal is the closest. In Trinidad, where split peas,
or less popularly, brown lentils, are the favorite dal, it is
also spelled dhal or dholl.*

2 cups split peas, or   2 tablespoons coconut oil,
  lentils   ghee, or vegetable oil
4 cups water   2 cloves garlic, chopped
1 teaspoon ground   1 teaspoon cumin seeds
  turmeric
Salt
1 medium onion, finely
  chopped

Soak the peas or lentils overnight, unless they are the
quick-cooking variety, in which case omit this step. Add
the tumeric to the peas and cook, covered, at a simmer
until they are tender. Season to taste with salt and stir in
the onion. Remove from the heat. Heat the oil in a small
pan and add the garlic and cumin. Sauté until the garlic
is dark brown. Strain the oil into the peas. Stir, cover and
let stand for a minute or two. Serve with boiled rice.

Serves 6 to 8. The dal should have about the consistency of mashed potatoes. If it seems too watery, simmer, uncovered, for part of the cooking time.

Frijoles Negros   *Cuba*

Black Beans

Black beans and white rice are a great favorite in Havana, either served separately, or together as Moros y Christianos (Moors and Christians).

2 cups black beans	1 clove garlic, minced
4 cups cold water	1 green bell pepper,
¼ cup olive oil	seeded and chopped
2 ounces salt pork,	1 bay leaf
chopped	Salt, freshly ground
1 medium onion, finely	pepper to taste
chopped	

Wash the beans thoroughly, but do not soak them. Put them into a large saucepan with the cold water, cover and simmer gently until they are tender, about 1½ to 2 hours. Add a little hot water from time to time as necessary.

Heat the oil in a frying pan and try out the salt pork. Add the onions, garlic, and pepper and sauté until the onion is tender but not browned. Add to the beans with the bay leaf and salt and pepper to taste. At this point the beans should still have quite a lot of liquid. Simmer, partially covered, for half an hour longer, stirring once or twice. Crush a spoonful or so of the beans to thicken the sauce, remove the bay leaf and serve. The beans should not be dry, but neither should the sauce be abundant. Serves 6 to 8.

VARIATION: Frijoles Colorados (Red Beans) are popular in the eastern part of Cuba. The beans most popularly used are California pink beans, or red kidney beans. They are cooked in the same way as Frijoles Negros (Black Beans) except that lard is used instead of olive oil. Some cooks like to use achiote lard (see Index).

Daube de Giraumon

Martinique-Guadeloupe

Seasoned West Indian Pumpkin

1½-pounds West
  Indian pumpkin
  (calabaza), or use
  Hubbard squash
2 tablespoons all-purpose
  flour
¼ cup vegetable oil
4 ounces salt pork, cut
  into ¼-inch cubes
2 cloves garlic, minced

1 tablespoon parsley,
  finely chopped
½ teaspoon marjoram
½ teaspoon thyme
1 bay leaf
Salt, freshly ground
  pepper
1 tablespoon white wine
  vinegar

Peel the pumpkin and cut into 1-inch cubes. Toss the pumpkin pieces in the flour, using up all the flour. Heat the oil in a heavy saucepan and add the pumpkin pieces and the salt pork. Sauté for about 10 minutes stirring from time to time. Add the garlic, parsely, marjoram, thyme, bay leaf, salt and pepper, and sauté for a minute or two longer. Add 1½ cups of hot water, half a cup at a time, stirring occasionally, and cook with the saucepan partially covered, until the pumpkin is tender and there is a fairly thick sauce. Just before serving stir in the vinegar. Serve as a starchy vegetable with meats or poultry. Serves 6.

Fried Ripe Plantains

All Islands

When plantains are ripe their skins are quite black, but they must still be cooked before they can be eaten. They are served, fried, with almost any meat or fish dish in the islands, though with some dishes, such as Picadillo in Cuba, they are traditional. In Guadeloupe they are often served as a dessert, in which case they are sprinkled with sugar after they are fried, then flamed with rhum vieux.

In French they are bananes frites, in the Spanish-speaking islands, plátano frito.

3 large, ripe plantains
Butter, or vegetable oil

Cut off both ends of the plantains, peel and halve lengthwise. Ripe plantains can usually be peeled as easily as ripe bananas. If there is any difficulty, cut through the skins lengthwise on the ridges, with a small sharp knife, and peel the segments. Slice the plantains in halves crosswise, giving 12 slices in all. Heat the butter or oil in a large, heavy frying pan and sauté the pieces until browned on both sides. Drain on paper towels and serve immediately. Serves 6.

If bananas are used as a substitute, use them when they are ripe, but still firm and the skins yellow, not black.

Funchi   *Netherlands Antilles*

Corn Meal Pudding

4 cups water	**2 cups yellow corn meal**
1 tablespoon salt	**4 tablespoons sweet butter**

Bring the water and salt to a rolling boil, pour in the cornmeal in a slow, steady stream and cook, stirring, over medium heat until the corn meal is thick and smooth, about 5 minutes. Beat in the butter, and turn out on to a warmed serving dish. Serves 6.

Jug Jug   *Barbados*

It is said that Jug Jug is derived from haggis, and was created by Scots who were exiled to Barbados after the Monmouth Rebellion of 1685. Millet, called guinea corn in Barbados, is used for what has become a Christmas, rather than a New Year dish, as haggis is. If Jug Jug is haggis transported, then like all dishes arriving in the Caribbean it has changed a great deal from the original.

4 ounces lean corned beef, cut into ½-inch cubes

4 ounces lean pork, cut into ½-inch cubes

4 cups (1 pound, about) fresh green pigeon peas, or use canned, drained peas (see Glossary)

2 medium onions, finely chopped

1 tablespoon finely chopped parsley

½ cup celery, with leaves, very finely chopped

½ teaspoon dried thyme, crumbled

2 scallions, finely chopped, using green and white parts

½ cup ground millet

Salt, freshly ground pepper

3 tablespoons unsalted butter

Put the meats on to cook in a heavy saucepan with water to cover and simmer, covered, for 1 hour. Add the pigeon peas, if they are fresh, and cook until both meats and peas are tender, about 20 minutes. If using canned peas, add when meats are tender and cook only long enough to heat through.

Strain the meat and pea mixture and set aside. Return the stock to the saucepan with the onions, parsley, celery, thyme, scallions, millet and salt and pepper to taste. Cook for about 15 minutes over low heat, stirring constantly. Mince the meat and pea mixture and add to the millet and cook, stirring, for 20 to 30 minutes, until the mixture is fairly stiff. Stir in 1 tablespoon of the butter. Turn the mixture out onto a warmed serving dish and mold into a smooth shape. Spread with the rest of the butter. Traditionally this is served as an accompaniment to ham or roast chicken. Serves 4 to 6 according to appetite.

If fresh pigeon peas are not available, dried ones may be used. In which case use 2 cups and put them on to cook with the meats adding a little hot water during the cooking if the peas absorb the liquid too fast.

Frijoles Negros Pascualas   *Cuba*
Holiday Black Beans

2 cups black beans
1 cup peanut oil
1 medium onion, finely
 chopped
4 cloves garlic, minced
1 fresh hot green pepper,
 seeded and chopped
½ teaspoon dried
 orégano, crumbled

½ teaspoon ground
 cumin
1 bay leaf
Salt to taste
¼ cup cider or
 distilled white vinegar
4-ounce jar of pimientos
 and juice from jar
1 tablespoon sugar, or to
 taste
1 tablespoon cornstarch

Wash the beans thoroughly, drain, and place in a heavy, covered casserole or saucepan with 4 cups cold water. Cover and simmer gently until the beans are tender, 1½ to 2 hours, adding a little hot water from time to time as necessary. Heat the oil in a heavy frying pan and sauté the onion, garlic and pepper until the onion is tender, but not browned. Add the orégano, cumin and bay leaf, season to taste with salt and stir into the beans, which should have quite a lot of liquid. Cook, stirring from time to time, for half an hour longer then add the vinegar, the pimientos with their juice, and the sugar. Mix the cornstarch with a tablespoon of cold water and stir into the beans. Cook, stirring from time to time for 5 minutes longer. Serves 6 to 8.

These beans are particularly good served with Salsa Roja para Frijoles Negros (Red Sauce for Black Beans).

Giraumon Boulli   *Martinique-Guadeloupe*

Boiled West Indian Pumpkin

1½ pounds West
  Indian pumpkin
  (calabaza) or use
  Hubbard squash
Salt
2 tablespoons vegetable
  oil
2 cloves garlic, chopped
4 scallions chopped, using
  green and white parts

¼ teaspoon thyme
1 fresh hot red or green
  pepper, seeded and
  chopped
2 basil leaves, chopped
Freshly ground pepper
½ cup buttered bread
  crumbs (optional)
½ cup grated
  Parmesan cheese
  (optional)

Peel the pumpkin, remove any seeds and string, cut into
1-inch slices and cook in salted water to cover until tender,
about 20 minutes. Drain thoroughly and mash. Set aside.

Heat the oil in a saucepan, add the garlic, scallions,
thyme, hot pepper, and basil. Sauté until the scallions are
tender but not browned. Season to taste with salt and
pepper, add the pumpkin, mixing thoroughly and cook
until heated through. If liked, turn into a buttered baking
dish, sprinkle with the buttered crumbs and cheese and
run under a broiler until the cheese melts and browns.
Serve as a starchy vegetable with meats, or poultry. Serves
6.

La Salade de Leyritz   *Northern Martinique*

Salad Leyritz

4 green (unripe) bananas
Salt
Vinaigrette dressing (see
  below)
1 large tomato, peeled,
  seeded and coarsely
  chopped

1 medium cucumber,
  peeled and coarsely
  chopped
1 cup sliced celery
2 medium carrots,
  scraped and shredded
1 medium avocado, sliced
Lettuce

Peel the green bananas by cutting through the skin, length-wise, in 2 or 3 places, then peeling the skin off in sections. Put the bananas into a saucepan with enough cold, salted water to cover, and cook, covered until they are tender, 10 to 15 minutes. Drain, cool and cut crosswise into ½-inch slices. Mix all the ingredients, except the lettuce, lightly together, with the vinaigrette dressing. Line a salad bowl with lettuce and fill with the banana mixture. Serves 6 to 8.

VINAIGRETTE:

½ cup olive, or
   vegetable, oil
2 tablespoons white wine
   vinegar
2 teaspoons prepared
   mustard, preferably
   Dijon

1 clove garlic, crushed
   (optional)
Salt, freshly ground
   pepper

Beat all the ingredients together with a fork.

Matété de Fruit à Pain   *Guadeloupe*

1 breadfruit, weighing
   about 1 pound, peeled
   and cut into 1-inch
   cubes, or use canned
   breadfruit
2 ounces salt pork, or
   corned beef, cut into
   ¼-inch cubes, or a
   pig's tail, chopped
1 tablespoon chives,
   finely chopped
2 cloves garlic, crushed

1 teaspoon parsley,
   chopped
¼ teaspoon thyme
1 fresh hot red or green
   pepper, seeded and
   chopped
Salt, freshly ground
   pepper
1 tablespoon vegetable
   oil, or lard
1 tablespoon lime juice

Put the breadfruit into a heavy saucepan with the meat, and enough water to cover. Cook, covered, at a gentle simmer until the breadfruit is half done, about 15 minutes.

Add the chives, garlic, parsley, thyme, hot pepper, salt, and freshly ground pepper and continue cooking, partially covered until the breadfruit is tender. Add the oil and lime juice, and continue cooking for 5 minutes or so longer, stirring constantly with a wooden spoon. The breadfruit will partly disintegrate forming a thick, creamy sauce for the pieces of it that remain whole. Serve as a starchy vegetable with meat or poultry, or by itself. Serves 6.

Moros y Cristianos   *Cuba*

Moors and Christians

Leftover Frijoles Negros (Black Beans) may be used for this recipe.

2 tablespoons olive oil
1 medium onion, finely
    chopped
1 clove garlic, minced
1 small green bell pepper,
    seeded and finely
    chopped

2 medium tomatoes,
    peeled, seeded and
    chopped
Salt, freshly ground
    pepper
2 cups cooked black
    beans
1 cup raw rice
2 cups cold water

Heat the oil in a heavy, covered casserole or saucepan, add the onion, garlic and pepper and sauté until the onion is tender. Add the tomatoes and cook, stirring, until the mixture is well blended and quite thick. Season to taste with salt and pepper. Stir in the beans, mixing well. Add the rice and water, mixing lightly. Cover and cook over very low heat until the rice is tender and all the water absorbed. Serves 4 to 6.

This is often served with fried egg and fried, ripe plantains.

Otro Arroz Blanco   *Dominican Republic*

Another white rice

2 cups long-grain rice
3 tablespoons lard or
  vegetable oil

Salt to taste
3 cups boiling water

Wash the rice thoroughly in several waters, drain and
allow to dry. In a heavy saucepan with a tight-fitting lid,
melt the lard or oil. Add the rice and cook, stirring until
the rice has absorbed the fat, taking care not to let the
rice brown. Add the salt and boiling water, cover, and
cook on the lowest possible heat until the rice is tender
and all the liquid absorbed, 20 to 30 minutes. Serves 6.

Mrs. Bessie Byam's
Rice and Peas   *Trinidad*

*This recipe given me by a friend, Mrs. Byam of Trinidad,
is particularly good, and because of the amount of meat,
is a meal in itself.*

½ pound smoked ham
  hocks
1 pound lean beef, chuck
  or shin, cut into 1-inch
  cubes
1 teaspoon salt
1 teaspoon crushed garlic
1 teaspoon ground cloves
2 tablespoons vegetable
  oil
½ cup tomatoes,
  peeled, seeded and
  chopped
½ cup chopped bell
  green pepper

1 fresh hot green pepper,
  seeded and chopped
½ cup coarsely
  chopped onions
2 cups fresh or canned
  pigeon peas
2 cups long-grain rice,
  washed
3 cups chicken or beef
  stock, about

Soak ham hocks overnight in water to cover. Drain. Cut meat off the bones in 1-inch pieces. Mix with the beef and season with salt, garlic and cloves. Heat the oil in a heavy, covered casserole and sauté the meat until browned. Add a cup of water and simmer, covered, until the meats are tender, about 1½ hours, adding a little water from time to time if necessary.

Measure the liquid. Add the tomatoes, sweet and hot peppers, onions, pigeon peas and rice. Make up the quantity of liquid to 4 cups with stock, or water, bring to a boil, cover and cook over very low heat until the rice is tender and all the liquid absorbed. Serves 6.

Serve with Mrs. Bessie Byam's Mango Relish (see Index).

Fresh pigeon peas can sometimes be bought at Latin American markets, but the season is quite short. Canned fresh pigeon peas can be bought in tropical food markets often labelled in Spanish, gandules verdes. Dried peas can also be used, in which case reduce the amount to 1 cup, soak overnight, and cook together with the meats.

Palmito Guisado   *Dominican Republic*

Stewed Palm Hearts

2 tablespoons vegetable oil
4 ounces lean boiled ham, cut into ½-inch cubes
2 cloves garlic, minced
1 fresh hot red or green pepper, seeded and chopped
2 tablespoons chopped chives
2 tablespoons tomato purée
3 medium tomatoes, peeled and coarsely chopped

1 tablespoon distilled white vinegar
Salt, freshly ground pepper to taste
2 14-ounce cans palm hearts, drained and coarsely chopped
1 tablespoon chopped pimiento-stuffed green olives
1 tablespoon chopped capers, preferably Spanish
Freshly grated Parmesan cheese
1 tablespoon chopped parsley

Heat the oil in a heavy 12-inch frying pan and sauté the
ham, garlic and hot pepper for a few minutes. Add the
chives, tomato purée and tomatoes, parsley, vinegar, salt
and pepper and cook until the mixture is thick and well
blended. Add the palm hearts and cook just long enough
to heat them through. Add the olives and capers and cook
for a minute or two longer. Serve accompanied by a bowl
of grated Parmesan cheese. Serves 6.

Palmito Revuelto
Con Huevos   *Dominican Republic*

Hearts of Palm Scrambled with Eggs

Cook the hearts of palm as in the recipe for Palmito Guis-
ado.
    Lightly beat 6 eggs and scramble them into the palm
hearts mixture. Cook just long enough for the eggs to set,
stirring with a wooden spoon to reach the entire surface
of the pan, about 3 or 4 minutes. Serves 6.

VARIATION: Heat the palm hearts in their own liquid. Drain
thoroughly, and chop coarsely. Heat 2 tablespoons of butter in a heavy frying pan, add the palm hearts, and season
to taste with salt and white pepper. Pour in 6 lightly beaten
eggs and cook, stirring with a wooden spoon to reach
the entire surface of the pan until the eggs are set, about
3 or 4 minutes. Serves 6.

Pepinos en Salso de Naranja   *Puerto Rico*

Stewed Cucumbers in Orange Sauce

3 cucumbers, about
  8-inches long
3 tablespoons butter
1 tablespoon flour
1 cup fresh orange juice,
  strained

Salt, freshly ground
  white pepper
1 teaspoon grated orange
  rind

Peel the cucumbers, cut in half lengthwise, scrape out the seeds with a spoon and cut into ½-inch crosswise slices. Drop into boiling salted water and cook for 5 minutes. Drain. Place in a warmed vegetable dish. Melt the butter in a small saucepan. Stir in the flour and cook without letting the flour take on any color, for a minute or two. Add the orange juice, stir and cook until smooth and thickened. Season to taste with salt and pepper, add rind, mix thoroughly and pour over the cucumbers. Serves 4.

Pois et Riz   *Guadeloupe*

Rice and Beans

This is the recipe for rice and red beans as they are cooked by Mme. Jean-Noel Villahaut Ces François at her restaurant Aux Raisins Clairs *in Guadeloupe. The large red kidney beans may be used, but the smaller type, sometimes called California pink, is to be preferred. This very simple form of rice and peas is delicious with either meat or fish.*

1 cup red beans	Sprig of thyme
1 small onion, finely chopped	1 fresh, hot red or green pepper (optional)
1 clove garlic, crushed	1½ cups long-grain rice
1 bay leaf	

Wash the beans thoroughly, drain and put into a heavy saucepan, large enough to hold both beans and rice. Add the onion, garlic, bay leaf, thyme and hot pepper, left whole. Add enough cold water to cover the beans by about 2-inches. Bring to a boil, lower and heat and cook, covered, at a gentle simmer until the beans are almost tender. If necessary add a little hot water from time to time. Drain the beans. Reserve the liquid. Remove the bay leaf and pepper and discard. Measure the liquid and add enough water to bring the quantity up to 3 cups. Return the beans and liquid to the saucepan. Wash the rice several times in cold water, drain, then add to the beans. Stir once, then bring to a boil, lower the heat and cook, covered for 20 minutes, or until the rice is just tender and all the liquid absorbed. Serves 6 to 8.

Pois et Riz Collés   *Haïti*

Rice and Beans Together

1 cup California pink
   beans, or red kidney
   beans
2 tablespoons vegetable
   oil
2 slices bacon, chopped,
   or 1 ounce salt pork,
   cut into ¼-inch dice
1 medium onion, finely
   chopped

¼ cup chopped
   shallots
1 fresh hot green pepper,
   seeded and chopped
Salt to taste
2 cups long-grain rice
1 tablespoon unsalted
   butter

Put the beans into a large, heavy saucepan with water to cover by about three inches. Bring to a boil, cover and cook over low heat until the beans are tender, 1½ to 2 hours. Drain, set the beans aside, and measure the liquid. There should be 4 cups. Add water to make up the quantity, if necessary, or if there is too much liquid, reduce it over brisk heat. Rinse out and dry the saucepan.

Heat the oil in the saucepan and fry the bacon, or salt pork dice until crisp. Add the onion, shallots and hot pepper and sauté until the onion is tender but not browned. Add the beans and season to taste with salt and cook, stirring, for a minute or two. Add the bean water, bring to a boil, pour in the rice, lower the heat, cover and cook until the water has evaporated and the rice is tender, about 20 minutes. Stir in the butter. Serves 6.

Pois Rouges en Sauce

Haïti

Red Beans in their Own Sauce

2 cups California pink beans, or red kidney beans	¼ cup chopped parsley, preferably flat Italian type
2 tablespoons unsalted butter	Salt, freshly ground pepper to taste
1 clove garlic, finely chopped	

Put the beans into a large, covered casserole with 7 cups of cold water. Bring to a boil, cover, lower the heat and simmer until the beans are tender, 1½ to 2 hours. Drain the beans and measure the liquid; there should be 3 cups. If there is too much liquid, reduce it quickly over brisk heat. If insufficient, make up the quantity with water. Measure 1½ cups of the cooked beans and reduce to a purée with 1 cup of the bean liquid. Stir the purée into the remaining 2 cups of bean liquid, together with the whole beans. Set aside.

Heat 1 tablespoon of the butter in a small frying pan and sauté the garlic and parsley being careful not to let the garlic burn. Stir into the beans and season to taste with salt and pepper. Cook very gently, stirring from time to time, until the sauce is thick and creamy. Stir in the remaining tablespoon of butter. Serves 6 to 8.

Okra in Tomato Sauce

St. Croix

1 pound young okra pods, or 2 10-ounce packages frozen okra	1 fresh hot green pepper, seeded and chopped
¼ cup olive oil	3 medium tomatoes, peeled and chopped or,
1 medium onion, finely chopped	1 cup canned Italian plum tomatoes, drained
1 clove garlic, chopped	
1 green bell pepper, seeded and chopped	Salt
	Pinch sugar

Wash the okras, pat dry with paper towels, and cut off the stem ends. If using frozen okra, thaw completely and pat dry. Heat the oil in a heavy frying pan, and sauté the okra until lightly browned all over. Lift out with a slotted spoon and transfer to a saucepan. In the oil remaining in the pan, sauté the onion, garlic and peppers until the onion is tender and very lightly browned. Add the tomatoes, salt, and sugar, and cook until the mixture is well blended, 2 or 3 minutes. Pour the tomato mixture over the okra, stir to mix, cover and cook until the okra is tender, about 5 minutes. Serves 6.

Pois Rouges Maçonne   *Guadeloupe*
Mashed Red Beans

It is impossible to translate this literally. It means red beans in the style of a mason's plaster, not a flattering description. It really does not have the consistency of plaster or wet concrete, but is a bit gloopy when contrasted with the very light texture of, say, Pois et Riz Collés. Whatever its name, it is a very good dish and an intersting example of the many forms rice and beans can take from island to island.

1 tablespoon peanut oil
2 slices bacon, coarsely chopped
1 medium onion, finely chopped
½ cup chopped shallots
1 clove garlic, minced
1½ cups California pink beans, or red kidney beans

1 fresh hot red or green pepper, seeded and chopped
1½ cups long-grain rice
Salt, freshly ground pepper to taste
1 teaspoon cassava meal, about

Heat the oil and sauté the bacon, onion, shallots and garlic until the onion is tender but not browned. Wash the beans, drain, and put into a heavy saucepan with the onion mixture. Add the hot pepper, pour in enough water to cover the beans by about 2-inches, bring to a boil, cover and simmer until the beans are just tender, about 1½ hours. Drain and measure the liquid. Make up the quantity to 4 cups.

Add the rice and liquid to beans, season to taste with salt and pepper, bring to a boil, lower the heat and cook, stirring frequently until the rice is tender and the liquid almost evaporated. Test a grain of rice from time to time and if the liquid is nearly gone and the rice still uncooked, add a little more water.

When the rice is tender, stir in the cassava meal and cook, stirring, until the cassava has thickened any remaining liquid. Serves 6.

Pois et Riz à L'Haïtienne   *Haïti*

Beans and Rice, Haitian style

1 cup California pink beans or red kidney beans	4 tablespoons lard, or butter
4 ounces salt pork, cut into ¼-inch dice	2 cups long-grain rice
Salt, freshly ground pepper to taste	Small pieces of crisply fried bacon, ham, sausage (optional)

Wash beans and drain. Place in a heavy covered casserole. Add 6 cups water, bring to a boil, cover and cook at a gentle simmer. When their skins wrinkle, add the salt pork, salt and pepper, and continue cooking until the beans are tender, 1½ to 2 hours. Drain. Reserve the liquid and set the beans aside. Rinse and dry the casserole.

Heat 1 tablespoon of the lard or butter in the casserole and stir in the rice, cooking until it has absorbed all the fat. Add 4 cups of the bean water, adding some plain water if necessary, bring to a boil, cover, reduce the heat as low as possible and cook until the rice is tender and all the liquid absorbed, 20 to 30 minutes. Gently fold in the bacon, ham and sausage, if liked. Heat the rest of the lard in a frying pan and fry the drained beans until they are thoroughly hot. Mound the rice in the center of a heated platter and arrange the beans round it to form a border. Serves 6.

Quingombós Guisados   *Puerto Rico*

Stewed Okra

1½ pounds young okra pods	1 recipe Sofrito (see Index)

Wash the okras and cut off the stem ends. If they are very young and small, leave them whole, older pods should be cut into ½-inch slices. Combine the okras and Sofrito in a saucepan, cover and simmer for 15 to 20 minutes, or until the okra is tender. Serves 6.

Serve with any plainly cooked meat or fish. Green beans may be cooked in the same way.

Ratatouille Créole   *Guadeloupe*

The special feature of this dish is the gros concombre, the enormous, light green cucumber of Guadeloupe and Martinique and some other islands. The cucumbers weigh a pound or more each but, apart from the size, differ very little from our cucumbers, which can be used instead. Simply choose the biggest ones available.

½ cup olive oil	½ pound green bell peppers, seeded and sliced
1 eggplant, weighing about 1 pound	
1 or 2 large cucumbers, weighing about 1 pound	½ pound ripe red bell peppers, seeded and sliced, or sliced canned pimientos
1 pound zucchini	
1 pound tomatoes, peeled and sliced	1 teaspoon sugar
	Salt, freshly ground pepper

Heat the oil preferably in an earthenware* casserole, or use any heavy saucepan or casserole large enough to hold all the ingredients comfortably. Peel the eggplant and cut into crosswise slices about ½-inch thick. Cut the widest of these in half. Arrange the eggplant slices in the casserole.

If the cucumbers are waxed, peel them and cut into ½-inch crosswise slices; otherwise leave unpeeled. Add to the casserole with the zucchini, washed, with the ends cut off, and sliced into ½-inch pieces. Add the tomatoes and the peppers. Season with the sugar, salt and pepper, cover and cook for 15 minutes. Uncover and cook for 15 minutes longer, or until most of the liquid has evaporated. Serves 6 to 8.

* If using earthenware make sure it is heavy enough not to crack over direct heat. Use one or more asbestos mats if necessary.

Stuffed Pawpaw   Jamaica

Papaya is known as pawpaw in Jamaica

1 green (unripe) papaya, weighing about 5 pounds	1 fresh hot red or green pepper, seeded and chopped
2 tablespoons vegetable oil	Salt, freshly ground pepper
1 large onion, finely chopped	1 tablespoon sweet butter
1 clove garlic chopped	4 tablespoons grated Parmesan cheese
1 pound lean ground beef	Tomato Sauce or Brown Sauce
3 medium tomatoes, peeled and chopped	

Wash the papaya, peel, cut in half lengthwise, and remove and discard the seeds. Drop the papaya halves into boiling, salted water and parboil for 10 minutes. Drain thoroughly and pat dry with paper towels. Heat the vegetable oil in a frying pan and add the onion, garlic and ground beef. Sauté for 15 minutes, stirring from time to time to break up the meat. Add the tomatoes, hot pepper and salt and pepper to taste and cook, stirring until the mixture is well blended and thick. Arrange the papaya halves in a greased baking pan and fill them with the meat mixture. Sprinkle with grated cheese and dot with butter. Bake in a 350° oven for 30-40 minutes. Serve with a Tomato Sauce or Brown Sauce served separately. Serves 6.

Riz au Djon-Djon   *Haïti*
Rice with Black Mushrooms

Rice is an immense favorite throughout the Caribbean and much ingenuity is shown in dishes that vary from island to island, or, as is the case with Riz au Djon-Djon, within themselves. In its simplest form it can accompany a main dish of fish or meat. A more elaborate version, accompanied by a green salad, can be served for lunch.

The mushrooms used are Haïtian black mushrooms, tiny, with inch-long inedible stalks. European dried mushrooms, such as German pfifferlinge, give almost the same taste to the dish, though it will lack the fine black color of the original.

1 cup dried mushrooms, about 1 ounce
4 tablespoons unsalted butter
2 cups long-grain rice
2 cloves garlic, finely chopped
½ teaspoon thyme
Salt, freshly ground pepper

If using Haïtian black mushrooms, remove the stems and soak them in 1 cup hot water. Soak the mushroom caps separately in another cup of hot water. If using European dried mushrooms, break them up coarsely and soak them in 2 cups hot water for half an hour. Discard the black mushroom stems, reserving the water which will be richly colored as much of the color is in the stems. Drain the caps, reserving the water. Drain the European mushrooms, reserving the water.

Heat the butter in a saucepan and sauté the rice with

the garlic until the butter is absorbed. Add the reserved 2 cups of mushroom liquor plus 2 cups more water to the rice with the mushrooms, thyme, and salt and pepper to taste. Bring to a boil, cover, and turn the heat as low as possible. Cook for 20 to 30 minutes, or until all the liquid is absorbed and the rice is tender. Serves 6.

VARIATION:

1 cup dried mushrooms, about 1 ounce	½ teaspoon thyme
2 tablespoons vegetable oil	A generous pinch of ground cloves
2 tablespoons unsalted butter	Salt, freshly ground pepper
1 ounce salt pork, cut into ¼-inch dice	4 ounces cooked, coarsely chopped corned pork, or 4 ounces coarsely chopped boiled ham
3 cloves garlic, finely chopped	
1 medium green bell pepper, seeded and chopped	4 ounces cooked salt codfish shredded, or 4 ounces cooked shrimp, coarsely chopped
1 tablespoon chopped chives	
	2 cups long-grain rice

Soak the mushrooms as in the recipe for Riz au Djon-Djon. Heat the oil and butter in a heavy saucepan and sauté the pieces of salt pork until they are crisp and brown. Add the garlic, bell pepper, chives, parsley, thyme, cloves, salt and pepper to taste, corned pork and codfish, and sauté lightly for a minute or two.

Add the rice, and stir for 2 or 3 minutes, or until the rice has absorbed the oil and butter, being careful not to let the rice brown. Add the mushrooms, 2 cups of mushroom liquid and 2 cups of water. Bring to a boil, cover and turn the heat as low as possible. Cook for 20 to 30 minutes, or until all the liquid is absorbed and the rice is tender. Serves 4.

Sancocho de Frijoles   *Dominican Republic*

Bean Stew

2 cups California pink
  beans, or red kidney
  beans
1 pound corned pork, cut
  into 1-inch cubes
3 quarts water
2 ounces salt pork, cut
  into ¼-inch cubes
2 medium onions, finely
  chopped
2 cloves garlic, minced
1 green bell pepper,
  seeded and coarsely
  chopped
1 fresh hot red or green
  pepper, seeded and
  chopped
1 pound longaniza
  sausage, skinned and
  coarsely chopped
2 medium tomatoes,
  peeled and chopped

1 bay leaf
¼ teaspoon orégano
1 teaspoon each parsley
  and fresh coriander,
  chopped
Salt and freshly ground
  pepper
1 pound each cassava
  root, white sweet
  potato and yam, peeled
  and cut into
  1-inch slices
2 ripe plantains, peeled
  and cut into ½-inch
  slices
2 tablespoons tomato
  paste
2 tablespoons vinegar,
  preferably cane vinegar
1 tablespoon Seville
  (bitter) orange juice

Wash the beans and put them with the corned pork and
the water into a soup kettle or heavy casserole big enough
to hold all the ingredients. Cover and simmer gently until
the beans are just tender, about 1 hour.

In a heavy frying pan try out the salt pork, and sauté
the onion, garlic, bell pepper, hot pepper and longaniza
sausage until the onion is tender but not browned. Add
the tomatoes, bay leaf, orégano, parsley and coriander
and cook, stirring frequently, until well blended. Season
to taste with salt and pepper. Add to the beans with the
cassava, sweet potato, yam and plantains and simmer
gently, partially covered, until the vegetables are tender,
stirring from time to time. Stir in the tomato paste, vinegar

and Seville orange juice and cook, stirring, for about 5 minutes, or until the sauce is thick and creamy. Serve with crusty bread and a green salad. Serves 6 to 8.

Rice and Peas

Jamaica

Fresh gungo peas (pigeon peas) are used when they are in season, but dried red beans are more usually the "peas" of Jamaican Rice and Peas.

1 cup California pink
  beans, or red kidney
  beans
2 tablespoons vegetable
  oil
1 medium onion, finely
  chopped

1 fresh hot red pepper,
  seeded and chopped
2 cups coconut milk (see
  Index)
½ teaspoon thyme
Salt, freshly ground
  pepper to taste
2 cups long-grain rice

Put the beans on to cook in a heavy, covered casserole or saucepan with enough cold water to cover by about 2 inches. Bring to a boil, cover, reduce the heat and cook at a gentle simmer until the beans are tender, adding hot water during the cooking if necessary. Drain the beans, measure the liquid and return both to the casserole.

Heat the oil in a frying pan and sauté the onion until it is golden. Add to the casserole with the hot pepper, coconut milk, thyme, salt and pepper to taste and the rice. Make up the quantity of liquid to 4 cups with cold water, if necessary. Cover and cook over very low heat for 20 to 30 minutes, or until the rice is tender and all the liquid absorbed. Serves 6.

If using fresh or canned gunga (pigeon peas) simply add with the rice. Do not cook them before hand. If using dried pigeon peas, cook exactly as the beans, using 1 cup.

Riz Créole

Martinique-Guadeloupe

Rice Creole Style

2 cups long-grained rice	1 tablespoon salt
6 cups water	

Wash the rice thoroughly in several waters. Drain. Put
the 6 cups of water on to boil with the salt and when it
comes to a rolling boil pour in the rice. Cook, uncovered,
at a vigorous simmer for 15 minutes. Drain, rinse quickly
under cold running water and return to the saucepan. Do
not add any water. Cook, covered, over very low heat
until the rice is tender and dry, about 20 minutes. Stir
with a two-pronged fork and serve. An asbestos mat or
two is helpful in preventing the rice from catching. Serves
6 to 8.

Some cooks add 2½ times the volume of water to rice,
(5 cups water to 2 cups rice), and cook the well washed
rice, covered, at a brisk simmer until the water has evaporated. The rice is then rinsed quickly in cold water,
returned to the saucepan and put over very low heat,
uncovered, to dry the grains.

Stuffed Cho-Cho   *Jamaica*

Chayote with Meat Stuffing

3 large chayotes (see
  Glossary), each
  weighing about
  ¾-pound
2 tablespoons vegetable
  oil
1 large onion, finely
  chopped
1 clove garlic, chopped
1 pound lean ground beef
1 tablespoon curry
  powder, or 1 fresh hot
  red pepper, seeded and
  chopped

3 medium tomatoes,
  peeled and chopped
Salt, freshly ground
  pepper
6 tablespoons grated
  Parmesan cheese
6 tablespoons bread
  crumbs
3 tablespoons sweet
  butter

Boil the whole chayotes in salted water until tender, about
30 minutes. Remove from the saucepan, and when cool
enough to handle, cut into halves lengthwise. Scoop out
the pulp, including the edible seed, mash and set aside.
Reserve the shells. Heat the oil in a frying pan and sauté
the onion, garlic and ground beef for 15 minutes, stirring
from time to time. Add the curry powder or hot pepper,
and cook for a few minutes longer. Add the tomatoes and
the chayote pulp. Cook, stirring, until the ingredients are
well blended, and the mixture is fairly dry. Season well
with salt and pepper, pack into the chayote shells, sprinkle
with cheese and bread crumbs, dot with butter and bake
in a 350° oven for 15 minutes, or until lightly browned.
Serve as a luncheon or supper dish. Serves 6.

Riz à L'Aubergine   *Haïti*

Rice with Eggplant

4 tablespoons sweet
butter
¼ cup vegetable oil
2-pound eggplant, peeled
and cut into
½-inch cubes
4 ounces bacon, coarsely
chopped

1 medium onion, finely
chopped
2 cups long-grain rice
Salt to taste
1½ cups tomato purée
4 ounces grated
Parmesan cheese

Heat the butter and oil in a large, heavy frying pan and
sauté the eggplant cubes over high heat until they are
golden brown, about 3 minutes. Set aside.

In a heavy, covered casserole try out the bacon. Add
the onion and sauté until it is tender but not browned. Add
4 cups of water, bring to a boil, pour in the rice; add salt
to taste and stir. Cover and cook over very low heat until
the rice is tender and all the liquid absorbed, 20 to 30
minutes.

Make a bed of the rice in an oven-proof platter, cover
with the eggplant, pour the tomato purée over the eggplant,
then sprinkle with the cheese. Run under a broiler until
the cheese melts and browns. Serves 6.

Sauces

Creole Sauce
Trinidad

This sauce, or one very like it, turns up in a number of the English-speaking islands.

3 tablespoons vegetable oil
1 medium onion, finely chopped
1 green bell pepper, seeded and chopped
3 tablespoons all-purpose flour
2 medium tomatoes, peeled and chopped
1 cup chicken stock, or dry white wine
Salt, freshly ground pepper
1 teaspoon lime juice
1 teaspoon vinegar
Hot Pepper Sauce to taste

Heat the oil in a saucepan, add the onion and pepper, and sauté until the onion is tender but not browned. Stir in the flour and cook, stirring constantly with a wooden spoon, for a minute or two until the flour is lightly browned. Add the tomatoes and stir to mix well. Gradually stir in the stock or wine, season to taste with salt and pepper and cook, stirring until the sauce has thickened. Add the lime juice and vinegar, and hot pepper sauce to taste. Adjust the seasoning. Makes about 2 cups.

Serve with suckling pig, any meats or poultry or fish. If serving with fish use dry white wine or fish stock instead of chicken stock.

Adobo   *Spanish-Speaking Islands*

Marinade for Roasting Pig

1 medium onion, very
   finely chopped
1 head garlic, peeled and
   crushed
2 tablespoons orégano
2 tablespoons salt

1 tablespoon freshly
   ground pepper
½ cup Seville (bitter)
   orange juice
½ cup peanut oil
   (optional)

Mix all the ingredients together and season the pig inside and outside with the adobo which should be left on overnight.

During roasting, baste the pig with the adobo and the meat's own juices and fat. If the peanut oil is omitted, increase the orange juice to ¾ cup. Makes enough for a 10 to 12-pound suckling pig.

Ajilimójili   *Puerto Rico*

Garlic and Pepper Sauce

3 fresh hot red peppers,
   seeded
3 ripe red bell peppers,
   seeded, or use
   4 pimientos
4 peppercorns
4 large cloves garlic,
   peeled

2 teaspoons salt
½ cup lime juice, or
   ¼ cup each lime
   juice and vinegar
½ cup olive oil

Pound the hot and sweet peppers with the peppercorns, garlic, and salt in a mortar. Transfer to a bowl and beat in the lime juice and oil, or combine the ingredients in an electric blender and reduce to a purée. Makes about 3 cups. Serve with suckling pig.

Curry Sauce
U.S. *Virgin Islands*

2 tablespoons unsalted butter
1 onion, finely chopped
1 small carrot, scraped and finely chopped
1 small stalk celery, chopped
2 tablespoons curry powder
½ teaspoon ground ginger

1 tablespoon all-purpose flour
Bay leaf
1 cup beef stock
Salt, freshly ground pepper
1 cup coconut milk, or light cream
1 teaspoon lime, or lemon, juice

In a heavy saucepan heat the butter and sauté the onion, carrot and celery until the onion is tender and lightly browned. Add the curry powder, ginger and flour and cook, stirring, for 3 or 4 minutes longer. Add the bay leaf and stock, season with salt and pepper, mix, cover and simmer gently for 30 minutes. Add the coconut milk and cook until heated through. Remove from the heat and stir in the lime juice.

   Makes about 2 cups.

Dr. Alex D. Hawkes' Pawpaw Applesauce
Jamaica

Many islands make a mock applesauce from papaya, known in Jamaica as pawpaw, or from chayote (christophene). This is one of my favorite versions.

2½ cups green
   (unripe) papaya,
   peeled, seeded and
   chopped

2 cups water
4 cloves
2 tablespoons sugar
⅓ cup lime juice

Put the papaya into a heavy saucepan with the water,
cloves, sugar and lime juice, cover and cook at a simmer
until the papaya is very soft and most of the liquid
absorbed, about 1 hour. Remove from heat. Discard the
cloves. Rub sauce through a sieve and serve hot or cold.
Makes about 2 cups.

This is excellent with suckling pig, or any meat, or
poultry.

Green Pawpaw Chutney   *Jamaica*

6 cups green (unripe)
   papaya, cut into
   1-inch cubes
2 cups finely chopped
   onion
1 cup seedless raisins
4 cloves garlic, chopped
6 fresh hot red peppers,
   seeded and chopped
4 red, or green bell
   peppers, seeded and
   chopped

¼ cup finely chopped
   fresh ginger root
½ teaspoon allspice
2 cups tomatoes, peeled
   and chopped
1 tablespoon salt
2 cups vinegar
2½ cups sugar

Put all the ingredients, except the sugar, into a large saucepan. Bring to a boil, lower the heat, cover and simmer
gently for 30 minutes. Add the sugar and cook, uncovered,
stirring from time to time until the mixture is thick, about
45 minutes. Makes about 8 cups.

Serve with cold meats, or with steak, lamb chops, roast
chicken. Makes 4 1-pint jars bottled while hot, sealed,
and stored for later use.

Hot Pepper Sauces

Every island has its hot pepper sauce. Indeed there are hot pepper sauces, all slightly different, from Mexico, where peppers were first cultivated as far back as 7000 B.C., all the way south to Argentina and Chile. The hot peppers of the Caribbean are very hot, and very flavorful. It is wise to remove the seeds which harbor a great deal of the heat, and wise to wash the hands after handling the peppers.

Hot Pepper Sauce   *Dominica*

½ pound yellow or red
  fresh hot peppers,
  seeded
1 medium onion, finely
  chopped
2 large cloves garlic,
  finely chopped

¼ cup green papaya,
  grated raw
½ teaspoon ground
  turmeric
1 teaspoon salt
¼ cup malt vinegar

Combine all the ingredients in an electric blender and reduce to purée. Pour into a saucepan and bring to a boil. Simmer for a minute or two. Pour into sterilized jars. Serve with any meat or fish. Makes about 1½ cups.

Hot Pepper Sauce   *St. Kitts*

½ cup seeded and
  finely chopped fresh
  hot peppers, preferably
  red

½ cup finely chopped
  onions
Salt

Combine the peppers and onions in a small, heavy saucepan and simmer over low heat. Do not add any water, the vegetables will give off enough liquid. When the mixture is thick, season with salt, cool and use as a sauce with any meat or fish. Makes about ½ cup.

Hot Pepper Sauce   *Trinidad*

1 small green pawpaw [papaya]
12 fresh hot red peppers, seeded and chopped
2 medium onions, finely chopped
2 cloves garlic, finely chopped

1 tablespoon salt
½ teaspoon ground turmeric
1 teaspoon curry powder
4 tablespoons dry mustard
2 cups malt vinegar

Put the papaya into a saucepan with enough cold water to cover, bring to a boil, cover and simmer until tender, about 15 minutes. Cool, peel and chop coarsely. Return to the saucepan with the hot peppers, onions, garlic, salt, turmeric, curry powder and the mustard mixed with the vinegar. Stir and simmer gently, uncovered, for 15 minutes. Cool and seal in sterilized jars. Makes about 4 cups.

If liked the turmeric and curry powder may be omitted.

Hot Pepper Sauce   *St. Lucia*

2 tablespoons vegetable oil
1 large onion, finely chopped
2 cloves garlic, chopped
3 scallions, chopped, using the green and white parts

1 christophene (see Glossary), weighing about ½ pound
12 fresh hot peppers, preferably red, seeded and chopped
Salt
1 cup malt vinegar

Heat the oil in a frying pan and sauté the onion, garlic and scallions until very lightly browned. Put the christophene into a saucepan with cold water to cover, and simmer, covered until tender, about 20 minutes. Drain, cool, peel and chop coarsely, using the edible seed. Combine all the ingredients in an electric blender, or put the solids through the fine blade of a food mill then mix with the vinegar. Season to taste with salt. Serve with any meat or fish. Makes about 2 cups.

Sauce Piquante

Martinique

Hot Sauce

½ cup hot water
1 cup finely chopped
  shallots
¼ cup chopped chives
2 cloves garlic, minced
1 or more fresh hot green
  peppers, finely
  chopped

3 tablespoons lime juice
Salt, freshly ground
  pepper

Pour the hot water over the shallots, chives, garlic, and hot pepper and mix well. Stir in the lime juice, season to taste with salt and pepper and allow to stand for 1 hour before using. Makes 2 cups.

Sauce Ti-Malice

Haïti

Hot Pepper Sauce

1 cup finely chopped
  onions
½ cup shallots, finely
  chopped
½ cup lime juice
2 cloves garlic, finely
  chopped

2 teaspoons finely
  chopped fresh hot
  peppers, red or yellow
  preferably
Salt, freshly ground
  pepper to taste
¼ cup olive oil

Mix the onions and shallots with the lime juice and allow to stand for about 1 hour. Pour into a small saucepan, add all the other ingredients and bring to a boil. Stir, remove from the heat and allow to cool. Serve cold with Griots de Porc (see Index). Makes about 2½ cups.

Saus di Promente Pica

Saba

Hot Pepper Sauce

Ideally for this sauce a mixture of hot peppers, green, yellow and red, is used. If this is not possible, use whatever hot peppers are available. There is a subtle difference in flavor between the pepper in its green, midway, and ripe stages, but not enough to outlaw the making of a one-color sauce.

1 tablespoon each of green, yellow, and red fresh, hot peppers, seeded and finely chopped
½ cup finely chopped onion
1 teaspoon finely chopped garlic
½ cup vinegar
½ cup water
1 teaspoon salt
1 teaspoon vegetable oil

Combine the peppers, onions, and garlic in a bowl. Bring the vinegar, water and salt to a boil and pour over the pepper mixture, stirring to mix well. Allow to cool then trickle the oil so that it floats on the surface of the sauce. The sauce will keep for 3 or 4 weeks if covered and refrigerated, but it is best eaten fresh as an accompaniment to any meat or fish dish.

A small amount will enliven a bland soup or plain vegetable. Makes about 1½ cups.

Mango or Green Pawpaw Chutney

St. Kitts

2 pounds hard, green (unripe) mangoes, or 2 pounds unripe pawpaw
8 ounces (about 1 cup) golden raisins, coarsely chopped
4 ounces cashew nuts, coarsely chopped

2 ounces fresh ginger root, finely chopped
3 cloves garlic, minced
2 fresh hot red peppers, chopped
2 cups light brown sugar
2 cups malt vinegar
Salt to taste

Peel the mangoes or pawpaw and cut into 1-inch cubes. Put into a heavy saucepan with all the other ingredients, mix thoroughly and simmer, stirring from time to time, until the mixture has thickened, about half an hour. Pour into sterilized jars. Makes about 2 1-pint jars.

Use with curries and cold meats.

Mango Sauce

3 cups chopped half-ripe mangoes
1 cup water
1 cup sugar

⅛ teaspoon ground ginger
⅛ teaspoon ground cinnamon
Pinch of salt

Put the mangoes and water in a saucepan and cook, covered, until the mangoes are soft. Add the sugar, ginger, cinnamon and pinch of salt and cook, uncovered, stirring from time to time for 10 minutes longer. Or until the sauce is thick and well blended. Makes about 2½ cups.

This sauce is good with meat. Or served with cookies as a desert.

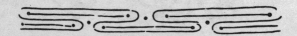

Lemon Butter Sauce   *U.S. Virgin Islands*

1 cup unsalted butter   1 tablespoon lemon juice
½ teaspoon salt

In a double boiler, over hot water but off the heat, stir
the butter with a wooden spoon until it is creamy. Add
the salt, continue stirring, and gradually add a tablespoon
of lemon juice. Serve at once with Danish fish pudding.
Makes 1 cup.

Mango Chutney   *Jamaica*

2 pounds hard, green
   (unripe) mangoes,
   preferably a fleshy type
2 tablespoons salt
½ pound ripe
   tamarinds (see
   Glossary)
2 cups vinegar,
   preferably Pickapepper
   cane vinegar, otherwise
   malt vinegar

3 cups West Indian
   brown sugar, or any
   light brown sugar
½ cup peeled and
   chopped fresh ginger
   root
½ cup seedless raisins
1 teaspoon ground
   allspice
1 ounce hot dried red
   peppers, seeded and
   roughly crumbled

Peel the mangoes and cut the flesh off the seeds into pieces
about 1-by-2 inches. Mix with the salt and set aside for
2 hours. Pick the shell off the tamarinds, or use tamarind
pulp, if available. Cover with ½ cup boiling water, allow
to stand for about half an hour then force the pulp through
a sieve. Discard the seeds. Drain the mangoes thoroughly,
discard liquid and put into a large, heavy saucepan with
the other ingredients and simmer, stirring from time to
time until the mixture is thick and the mangoes are tender,
about half an hour. The mango pieces should not disintegrate. Pour into sterilized jars. Makes about 3 1-pint
jars.
   Use with curries and cold meats.

Nicole Scott's Sauce Ti-Malice   *Haïti*

Hot Sauce

½ cup vinegar,
  preferably cane vinegar
3 tablespoons lime, or
  lemon, juice
½ tablespoon salt
1 medium onion, finely
  chopped
1 carrot, scraped and
  very finely diced
1 cup finely chopped
  cabbage
3 radishes, finely
  chopped

1 clove garlic, crushed
Salt, freshly ground
  pepper to taste
1 tablespoon tomato paste
1 fresh hot pepper,
  seeded and crushed, or
  1 teaspoon hot pepper
  sauce
2 tablespoons olive, or
  salad, oil

Combine all the ingredients in a bowl and allow to stand
for 1 hour before using. Serve with Griots de Porc, or any
meat, or suckling pig.

Makes about 3½ cups.

Pepper Wine   *Jamaica*

6 whole fresh hot red
  peppers

1 pint light rum, or dry
  sherry

Put the whole peppers into a glass jar and pour in the rum
or sherry. Cover tightly with the lid and allow to stand
10 days before using. Use a few drops in soups or sauce.
Pepper vinegar is made in the same way. Makes about 1
pint.

If fresh peppers are not available, whole, hot dried
peppers may be used.

Mojo para
Puerco Asado

Dominican Republic

Sauce for Roast Suckling Pig

⅔ cup peanut oil
½ cup scallions, finely
   chopped
6 cloves garlic, crushed
1 teaspoon fresh hot red
   or green pepper,
   seeded and chopped

6 tablespoons vinegar,
   preferably cane or malt
6 tablespoons Seville
   (bitter) orange juice
Salt, freshly ground
   pepper

Heat the oil in a saucepan, add the scallions and garlic and sauté until the scallions are tender, but not browned. Add the rest of the ingredients and simmer gently for 2 or 3 minutes. Serve with the suckling pig. Makes about 2 cups.

If liked, pour all the fat from the pan in which the pig was roasted, deglaze the pan with the orange juice, scraping to take up all the brown bits, and add this to the sauce.

Orange juice may be used if Seville orange juice is not available.

Mrs. Lilian Johnston's
Chilli Sauce

St. Kitts

6 pounds tomatoes,
   peeled and finely
   chopped
1 pound onions, finely
   chopped
1 cup sugar

2 tablespoons salt
1 pint malt vinegar
1 tablespoon seeded and
   finely chopped hot
   peppers, preferably red

Combine all the ingredients in a kettle and bring to a boil. Lower the heat and cook, stirring, until the mixture is quite thick. Pour into sterilized jars and seal. Makes about 3 pints.

Mango Relish

These fresh mango chutneys are closely related and obviously derive from an Indian original. They are good with curry and make an excellent accompaniment to boiled, baked or grilled fish or meat, especially cold meat. The Rougail de Mangues Vertes was traditionally served as an hors d'oeuvre in Martinique and Guadeloupe but unfortunately it seems to have lost much of its popularity. This is a pity, as it makes an unusual and refreshing beginning to a meal.

Mrs. Bessie Byam's Mango Relish

Trinidad

2 hard, green (unripe) mangoes, weighing 1 pound each
1 teaspoon finely chopped garlic
1 teaspoon salt
1 teaspoon fresh hot red or green pepper, seeded and finely chopped
1 tablespoon olive oil

Peel the mangoes and grate down to the seeds, or cut off the flesh and chop fine. Add the garlic, salt, and hot pepper, mixing thoroughly. Place in a clean jar, and top with the oil. Cover tightly and refrigerate until ready to use. This relish will keep for several days, but is essentially meant to be eaten quite soon after it is made.

Makes about 2 cups.

Traditionally eaten with Rice and Peas, it is good with curry and with any plainly cooked fish or meat, especially cold meat.

Rougail de Mangues Vertes

Martinique-Guadeloupe

Green Mango Relish

2 hard, green (unripe)
  mangoes, weighing
  1 pound each
2 teaspoons grated onion
½ teaspoon finely
  chopped fresh hot red
  pepper, or cayenne
  pepper to taste

1 tablespoon peanut oil
Salt, freshly ground
  pepper to taste
Chopped parsley

Peel the mangoes, chop flesh coarsely and put through a sieve. Add the grated onion, hot pepper, salt and pepper to taste, and the oil. Garnish with parsley. Makes about 2 cups.

In the past this fresh chutney was served as an hors d'oeuvre. It is also good with curry, or fish, or with meat, especially cold meat.

Salsa Criolla Cocida

Dominican Republic

Cooked Tomato Sauce, Creole Style

3 tablespoons vegetable
  or olive oil
1 medium onion, finely
  chopped
1 large tomato, peeled
  and chopped

1 fresh hot pepper,
  seeded and finely
  chopped
Salt, freshly ground
  pepper
1 tablespoon vinegar

Heat the oil in a small saucepan and sauté the onion until tender but not browned. Add the tomato, hot pepper, salt and pepper to taste and cook, stirring, for about 5 minutes or until well blended and fairly thick. Stir in the vinegar, mixing thoroughly. Makes about 1 cup. Serve with any meat or fish.

Salsa Criolla Cruda   *Dominican Republic*

Uncooked Tomato Sauce, Creole Style

1 medium onion, finely
  chopped
1 large tomato, peeled
  and chopped
1 hot green pepper,
  seeded and finely
  chopped
2 cloves garlic, minced

1 tablespoon chopped
  parsley, or fresh green
  coriander
Salt, freshly ground
  pepper
¾ cup olive oil
¼ cup vinegar

Combine all the ingredients in a bowl and allow to stand
for about 15 minutes before using for the flavor to develop.
Serve with any meat or fish, or with eggs. It is especially
good with grilled or broiled lobsters or spiny (rock) lobsters. Makes about 2 cups.

Salsa de Tomate   *Dominican Republic*

Tomato Sauce

3 pounds tomatoes,
  peeled, seeded and
  chopped
½ cup olive oil
Bay leaf

1 teaspoon sugar
Salt, freshly ground
  pepper
2 cloves garlic, minced

Put the tomatoes in a heavy saucepan and cook over low
heat, stirring from time to time with a wooden spoon until
some of the liquid has evaporated and the mixture is get-
ting thick. Stir in the oil, and add the remaining ingredients. Cook, stirring, for 5 minutes. Cool and use in soups,
casseroles, with fish and shellfish or stirred into cooked
beans. Makes about 5 cups.

   This sauce will keep, refrigerated, for several weeks
and is extremely useful to have on hand.

Salsa Rojo Para Frijoles Negros *Cuba*
Sweet Pepper Sauce for Black Beans

This is an exceptionally good sweet pepper and tomato sauce dating back to the beginning of this century. Traditionally it is served with cuban black beans, but may be used with any meat or fish.

1 cup olive oil
1½ cups tomatoes,
  peeled and chopped
2 cloves garlic, crushed
6 grinds black pepper, or
  ¼ teaspoon
½ teaspoon Spanish
  (hot) paprika, or
  cayenne
¼ teaspoon orégano

½ teaspoon sugar
Salt to taste
½ cup tomato purée
2 cups pimientos,
  chopped and the liquid
  from the can
¼ cup vinegar,
  preferably cane vinegar

Heat the oil in a saucepan and add the tomatoes. Cook, stirring with a wooden spoon until the tomatoes have disintegrated, about 5 minutes. Add all the rest of the ingredients, except the vinegar, and cook, stirring from time to time over low heat until the sauce is thick. Remove from the heat and stir in the vinegar. Makes about 4 cups.

Sauce Piquante   *St. Martin*
Hot Sauce

2 tablespoons capers
2 tablespoons chopped
  cornichon (French
  gherkins)
1 clove garlic, finely
  chopped
1 fresh red hot pepper,
  seeded and finely
  chopped

2 tablespoons chopped
  parsley
Salt, freshly ground
  pepper to taste
¾ cup olive oil,
  preferably French
¼ cup red wine
  vinegar

Mix all the ingredients together thoroughly. Serve with cold meats, hors d'oeuvres, or with plainly cooked meats, fish and shellfish. Makes about 1½ cups.

Sauce Vinaigrette   *French Islands*

French Dressing

¼ cup cane or white wine vinegar, or lime, or lemon juice, or a mixture of both
Salt
Freshly ground pepper
Pinch sugar
½ teaspoon Dijon mustard (optional)
¾ cup olive, or salad oil

Combine the vinegar, or juice, salt and pepper to taste, and the sugar in a bowl, together with the mustard, if liked. Beat with a fork until the salt has dissolved. Beat in the oil to blend throughly. Makes one cup.

Salsa Tártara   *Dominican Republic*

Tartare Sauce

2 cups mayonnaise
2 tablespoons finely chopped capers
½ cup finely chopped pickled cucumbers
1 tablespoon finely chopped onion
1 tablespoon chopped chives
1 tablespoon finely chopped parsley
1 hard-boiled egg, finely chopped
½ cup finely chopped black olives
1 tablespoon prepared mustard
Salt, freshly ground pepper

Mix all the ingredients together. Serve with Camarones Rellenos (see Index) and with fried fish and shellfish. Makes about 3½ cups.

Sauce Créole   *Martinique*

Creole Sauce

*This sauce is used for lobsters and crayfish, and any
plainly cooked fish.*

1 cup tomato purée
1 fresh hot green pepper,
  seeded and chopped
1 medium onion, finely
  chopped
1 tablespoon finely
  chopped celery
Salt, freshly ground
  pepper to taste

2 scallions, finely
  chopped and using
  both green and white
  parts
1 tablespoon thinly sliced
  pimiento-stuffed olives
¼ cup lime juice

Combine all the ingredients, stirring to mix well. Serve
at once, or refrigerate until ready to use. The sauce will
keep for about a week refrigerated. Makes about 2 cups.

Breads, Puddings and Desserts

Arrowroot Custard

St. Vincent

2 tablespoons arrowroot
2 cups evaporated milk
¼ cup sugar

½ teaspoon vanilla
3 eggs, well beaten

Mix the arrowroot and the milk together in a saucepan, add the sugar, and cook, stirring constantly, with a wooden spoon, over low heat until the mixture is thickened. Add the vanilla and the eggs and continue cooking, stirring constantly, over very low heat for about 5 minutes longer. Cool. Refrigerate before serving with stewed fruit, fruit pies, sliced mangoes, or any dessert in place of cream. Makes about 2¾ cups.

Baigner

Dominica

Fritters

*Northernmost of the British Windward Islands, Dominica
lies midway between French Martinique and Guadeloupe,
was named by Columbus for Sunday, the day on which
he sighted the island, and was fought over by England
and France. A French patois is still spoken by many of
the islanders even now, which explains how beignets have
become Baigner, a popular dessert.*

2¼ cups all-purpose flour	2 eggs, lightly beaten
1 teaspoon cinnamon	Vegetable oil for deep frying
½ cup water	Sugar
1 teaspoon vanilla	

Sift the flour with the cinnamon into a mixing bowl. Add
the water and vanilla, blending a batter. Add the eggs.
Deep fry by the tablespoon in hot oil (375° on a frying
thermometer). Drain on paper towels. Roll the fritters in
sugar.
  Serves 4 to 6.

Bakes

Trinidad

Fried Biscuits

2 cups all-purpose flour	2 teaspoons sugar
2 teaspoons baking powder	2 tablespoons lard
½ teaspoon salt	¼ cup water
	Oil for frying

Sift the flour, baking powder, salt and sugar together into
a bowl. Rub in the lard until the mixture is crumbly. Add
the water and stir to make a soft dough. Knead lightly on
a floured board, adding a little more flour if necessary.

Pinch off pieces of dough (about 2 tablespoons each) and roll into balls. Flatten into circles about ½-inch thick. Fry in a little hot oil in a large, heavy frying pan until golden on both sides, or bake on a hot, greased griddle. Makes about 10. Serve warm as bread.

Baked Bananas Flambée   *Antigua*

4 large bananas, peeled
  and sliced lengthwise
½ cup brown sugar
¼ cup lime juice

½ cup light rum
1 teaspoon ground
  allspice
4 tablespoons unsalted
  butter

Arrange the bananas in a well-buttered shallow fireproof serving dish. Sprinkle with the sugar, lime juice, half of the rum and the allspice. Dot with the butter. Bake in a 400° oven for 15 minutes, basting 2 or 3 times during the cooking. At the moment of serving, heat the other half of the rum, pour over the bananas and set alight. Serves 4.

Banana Bread   *Jamaica*

½ cup unsalted butter
½ cup sugar
1 egg
2 cups all-purpose flour
1 tablespoon baking
  powder
½ teaspoon salt

½ teaspoon nutmeg
2 large, ripe bananas
  (about 1 pound)
1 teaspoon vanilla
½ cup seedless raisins
½ cup coarsely
  chopped pecans

Cream butter and sugar together in a mixing bowl until light and fluffy. Add the egg and beat thoroughly. Sift the flour, baking powder, salt and nutmeg into another bowl. Mash the bananas and add the vanilla. Add the sifted ingredients and the banana alternately to the egg-butter-sugar mixture, beating after each addition until thoroughly blended. Toss the raisins with a teaspoon of flour and add them, with the pecans, to the batter, mixing well. Pour into a greased 9-by-5-inch loaf pan. Bake in a 350° oven for about 1 hour, or until a cake tester comes out clean. Makes one 9-inch loaf.

Banane Céleste   *Martinique*

6 ounces cream cheese
¼ cup brown sugar
¾ teaspoon cinnamon

4 large ripe bananas,
    peeled and halved
    lengthwise
4 tablespoons unsalted
    butter
¼ cup heavy cream

Mix the cream cheese, sugar and ½ teaspoon of the cinnamon together until well blended. Set aside. Heat the butter in a heavy skillet and sauté the banana halves until they are lightly browned on both sides. Lay 4 of the halves in a buttered shallow fire-proof serving dish. Spread half the cream cheese mixture on the bananas and top with the remaining 4 banana halves. Spread them with the rest of the cream cheese mixture. Pour the cream over them. Bake in a 350° oven for about 15 minutes, or until the cream cheese mixture is golden brown. Sprinkle with the remaining ¼ teaspoon of cinnamon and serve immediately. Serves 4.

Banana Coconut Custard   *St. Kitts*

2 cups evaporated milk
4 eggs, lightly beaten
½ cup sugar
Pinch salt
1 cup finely grated fresh
    coconut

1 cup sliced ripe bananas
½ teaspoon vanilla
1 tablespoon unsalted
    butter

Combine all the ingredients, except the butter. Butter a 1½ quart soufflé dish and pour in the custard mixture. Bake in a 350° oven until firm, about 50 minutes. Serves 4 to 6.

Banana Whip and Fruit Cream *Anguilla*

Many dishes can be quite accurately assigned to individual islands, but others have spread to so many islands that their actual birthplace is lost. Banana Whip and Fruit Cream could be attributed in a general sort of way to the English-speaking islands.

4 large ripe bananas	¼ cup light rum
¼ cup sugar, or to taste	3 egg whites
½ cup orange juice	Pinch salt

Peel the bananas and mash them with the sugar, orange juice and rum, adding more sugar if liked. Beat the egg whites with the salt until they stand in peaks. Fold the white into the banana mixture, lightly but thoroughly. Chill for several hours in the refrigerator until lightly set. Serve with Fruit Cream. Serves 6.

FRUIT CREAM

4 egg yolks	1 cup orange juice
3 tablespoons sugar	

Beat the egg yolk with the sugar until pale yellow. Transfer to a heavy saucepan, add the orange juice and cook over low heat, beating constantly with a wire whisk until the mixture begins to foam up. Remove immediately from the heat as the mixture must not be allowed to boil. Chill for several hours before using. Serve with Banana Whip (see Index). Serves 6.

Fruit Cream may be used instead of whipped cream, or custard, on puddings, or stewed fruits such as guavas.

Other fruit juices may be used to flavor Fruit Cream.
Adjust the amount of sugar to taste.

Beignets de Banane   *Martinique*

Banana Fritters

3 large ripe bananas	2 tablespoons sugar
⅓ cup dark rum	1 teaspoon vanilla

BATTER:

2 cups all-purpose flour	¾ cup milk
1 tablespoon sugar	1 tablespoon rum
½ teaspoon salt	Vegetable oil for deep
1 teaspoon baking	frying
powder	Vanilla sugar flavored
1 tablespoon melted	with ground cinnamon
unsalted butter	
1 egg	

Peel the bananas and cut into halves lengthwise; cut each
half into 4 equal pieces. Place in a bowl. Combine the
rum, sugar and vanilla and pour over the banana slices.
Leave for 1 hour, turning the pieces occasionally.

To make the batter, sift the flour, sugar, salt and baking
powder together, into a mixing bowl. Add the butter, egg,
milk and rum, mixing to a smooth paste. Let the batter
stand until the bananas are ready. Dip the banana pieces
in the batter, and fry in deep oil (375° on a frying thermometer) until they are golden brown all over. Drain on
paper towels. Sprinkle with the Vanilla Sugar. Serves 4
to 6.

To make vanilla sugar, drop a vanilla bean, 1 to 2 inches
long, into a jar of sugar. Keep the jar tightly closed and
add more sugar from time to time as it is used, until the
bean had lost all flavor. Add ground cinnamon to taste to
the vanilla sugar before sprinkling it on the beignets.

Bienmesabe
Puerto Rico

Coconut Cream Sauce

This is a sweeter, less rich, version of the Cuban dessert sauce, Coquimol. It crops up in various versions wherever Spanish is spoken.

2 cups sugar
1 cup water
1 cup coconut milk (see Index)

6 egg yolks
Slices of sponge cake, or lady fingers
Sherry (optional)

Boil the sugar and water together until it forms a syrup at the thread stage. Remove from the heat, stir the coconut milk into the syrup, mixing thoroughly. Beat the egg yolks and add them to the mixture, stirring constantly over gentle heat until thickened. Do not let it boil. To serve, pour over sponge cake or lady fingers. If liked, the cake may be sprinkled with sherry before the sauce is poured on. Makes about 2 cups sauce.

Boija
St. Croix

Coconut Corn Bread

2¼-ounce packets active dry yeast
3 cups all-purpose flour
2 cups corn meal
1 cup finely grated coconut
2 large ripe bananas, mashed

½ cup sweet butter, melted and cooled
½ cup sugar
½ teaspoon ground allspice
1 teaspoon salt
Water to mix

Dissolve the yeast in 1 cup of lukewarm water. Pour into a mixing bowl and add half the flour to make a sponge. Cover with a cloth and leave in a warm place to rise until double in bulk, about 1½ hours. Add all the rest of the ingredients and enough water, about 1 cup, to make a stiff batter, beating thoroughly with a wooden spoon to incorporate the sponge evenly. Pour into 2 greased 9-by-5-by-3-inch loaf pans. Cover loosely with a cloth and leave in a warm place to rise until double in bulk, about ½ hour. Bake in a 350° oven for 45 minutes to 1 hour, or until the bread begins to shrink from the sides of the pan and the top is lightly browned. Let cool few minutes in pan. Then turn out on cake rack to complete cooling. Makes two 9-inch loaves.

Bolo di Rom   *Curaçao*

Rum Cake

8 tablespoons unsalted butter	2 teaspoons grated lime, or lemon, rind
1 cup sugar	1½ cups all-purpose flour
4 large eggs	½ cup yellow corn meal
¼ cup dark rum	2 teaspoons baking powder
3 tablespoons lime, or lemon, juice	

Cream the butter and sugar together in a large bowl until light and fluffy. Beat in the eggs one by one, then add the rum, lime or lemon juice and grated rind. Sift the flour, corn meal and baking powder together and beat ½ cup at a time, into the egg and butter mixture. Pour the batter into a buttered 8-inch round cake pan.

Bake in a 350° oven, about 1 hour, or until a cake tester inserted into the center of the cake comes out clean. Let the cake cool completely before removing it from the pan.

If liked, sprinkle ½ cup semi-sweet chocolate bits over the cake and place under a broiler for 1 of 2 minutes to melt the chocolate, or sift confectioners' sugar over the top while the cake is still warm, or pour 2 tablespoons dark rum over the cake while it is still hot. Let cool before cutting. Makes 6 to 8 servings.

Boniatillo

Cuba

Sweet Potato Paste

This is made with boniatos, the white sweet potato, either the pink or white skinned variety.

1 pound sweet potatoes, peeled and sliced	Peel of 1 lime
1½ cups sugar	2-inch stick of cinnamon
½ cup water	3 egg yolks, beaten
	¼ cup sherry

Boil the sweet potatoes in water to cover until tender, about 25 minutes. Drain and mash. Makes about 2 cups. In the meantime make a syrup with the sugar, water, lime peel and cinnamon. Boil in a heavy saucepan until it reaches the soft ball stage (250° on a candy thermometer). Remove the peel and cinnamon and mix the syrup with the sweet potatoes. Cook in a heavy saucepan over low heat, stirring constantly until the mixture forms a thick paste. Off the heat, stir in the egg yolks and mix well. Return to the heat and cook, stirring, for 2 or 3 minutes. Remove from heat and add sherry. Cool. Serve as a dessert with a sauce, or with cream, or use as a base in other desserts such as Sweet Potato Cake. Makes about 3 cups.

Cafiroleta

Cuba

Mix equal quantities of Boniatillo (Sweet Potato Paste) and Coquimol (Coconut Cream Sauce) together and serve as a dessert.

Carrot Dumplings   *Montserrat*

⅔ cup all-purpose
   flour
½ teaspoon salt
1 teaspoon baking
   powder

3 tablespoons unsalted
   butter
½ cup finely grated
   carrot

Sift the flour, salt, and baking powder into a bowl. Rub
in the butter with the fingertips until the mixture is crumbly. Add the carrot, and enough cold water to make a
fairly stiff dough. Turn out onto a floured board and knead
lightly. Form into balls about 1½-inches in diameter. Drop
them into soup and simmer for 15 minutes, or cook separately in boiling salted water. Makes about 12 dumplings.

Carrot Pudding
with Rum Sauce   *English-speaking Islands*

*Carrot pudding turns up in all the English-speaking islands
and is probably derived from Gajar Halva, the Indian
carrot dessert, though like all derived dishes in the islands,
it has taken on its own character.*

1 cup seedless raisins
½ cup dark rum
8 tablespoons unsalted
   butter
½ cup sugar
2 cups finely grated raw
   carrots

1 cup all-purpose flour
½ teaspoon salt
2 teaspoons baking
   powder
1 teaspoon allspice
2 eggs, well-beaten

Soak the raisins in the rum for at least an hour. Cream
the butter with the sugar, add the carrots, the rum and
the raisins, and mix well. Sift the flour with the salt,
baking powder and allspice. Add all to the carrot mixture

and blend. Fold in the eggs. Pour into a buttered 1-quart soufflé dish.

Bake in a 350° oven for 40 minutes, or until a cake tester comes out clean. Serve warm with hot Rum Sauce, or with sauce and pudding chilled, as preferred. Serves 4 to 6.

RUM SAUCE:

2 tablespoons cornstarch
¼ cup sugar

1 cup dark rum
1 cup orange juice

Mix the cornstarch with 1 cup of cold water in a small, heavy saucepan. Add the sugar and cook, stirring, until the sauce has thickened. Off the heat stir in the rum and orange juice. Return to the heat and cook, stirring, for about 5 minutes, or until all the alcohol in the rum has evaporated. Serve hot or chilled. Makes about 3 cups.

The pudding is sometimes made with wine and served with a wine sauce. Dry red wine or sherry may both be used. The raisins should be soaked in wine instead of rum and served with the following sauce.

WINE SAUCE:

2 tablespoons sugar
1 cup water

1 tablespoon arrowroot,
    or cornstarch
2 cups dry red wine

Stir the sugar into the water over low heat until dissolved. Cool. Mix with the arrowroot or cornstarch, then stir in the wine and cook over low heat, stirring constantly, until thickened. Makes about 3 cups.

Coconut Bread   *Trinidad*

3 cups all-purpose flour
1 tablespoon baking
  powder
1 teaspoon salt
1 cup sugar
2 cups finely grated fresh
  coconut

1 egg, well-beaten
1 cup evaporated milk
1 teaspoon vanilla
4 ounces unsalted butter,
  melted and cooled
Sugar

Sift the flour, baking powder, and salt together. Mix in
the sugar and coconut. Add the egg, milk, vanilla and
butter, mixing lightly but thoroughly. Divide the mixture
between 2 greased 9-by-5-inch loaf pans. Fill each about
⅔ full. Sprinkle with sugar and bake in a 350° oven for
about 55 minutes, or until a cake tester comes out clean.
Let loaves cool partially in pans. Then turn out on cake
rack. Makes 2 9-inch loaves.

Coconut Milk Sherbet   *Barbados*

1 medium sized coconut
  (about 1½ pounds)
2 cups warm milk
1 cup sugar

¼ cup water
Pinch cream of tartar
2 drops almond extract

Puncture 2 of the eyes of the coconut and drain out the
coconut water. Split the shell and take out the meat. Pare
the brown skin from a piece of coconut about 4-inches
square and grate it on the coarse side of a hand grater.
There should be 1 cup of grated coconut. Spread the coconut on a cookie sheet or shallow baking pan and toast in
a 325° oven for about 15 minutes, or until lightly browned.
Remove from oven and set aside.

   Finely grate the rest of the coconut, unpeeled, in the
usual way for making coconut milk, or reduce in an electric blender with the warm milk. Squeeze through a kitchen
towel to extract all the liquid. Set aside.

In a small, heavy saucepan combine the sugar, water and cream of tartar and cook, stirring from time to time until the sugar is dissolved and the syrup clear. Combine the syrup, almond extract, coconut milk, and toasted coconut in a large bowl, stirring to mix well. Pour into 2 ice cube trays with the dividers removed. Freeze for 3 to 4 hours, stirring every half hour to break up the solid particles that form on the bottom and sides of the trays. The finished sherbet should have a fine, snowy texture. Serve in parfait glasses or dessert dishes. Makes about 1 quart.

Coconut Pie

St. Kitts

2 large eggs
¼ cup sugar
½ cup freshly grated
  coconut, or canned
  shredded moist coconut
½ cup evaporated milk

½ cup coconut milk
  (see Index)
1 tablespoon unsalted
  butter, melted
8-inch pie shell, unbaked

Beat the eggs and sugar together until light and fluffy. Add the grated coconut, the evaporated milk and coconut milk and butter. Pour into the pie shell. Bake in a 450° oven for 10 minutes, then reduce the heat to 350° and bake for 25 to to 30 minutes longer, or until the custard is set and the pastry is lightly browned. Serves 4.

Coconut Soufflé

Jamaica

1 envelope (1 tablespoon)
  unflavoured gelatin
4 eggs, separated
¼ cup sugar
1 cup coconut cream

1 cup finely grated fresh
  coconut
Grated rind 1 lime
½ cup coarsely grated
  fresh coconut

Pour ¼ cup cold water into a small, heavy saucepan, sprinkle the gelatin on top of the water and let if soften for a few minutes. Place over very low heat and stirring constantly with a wooden spoon, dissolve the gelatin. Set aside.

Put the egg yolks into the top of a double boiler, away from heat, and add the sugar, beating constantly until the yolks are lemon colored and form a ribbon. Heat the coconut cream separately. Set the egg yolks over hot water and low heat and pour in the coconut cream, beating constantly. Stir until the mixture forms a custard thick enough to coat the spoon. Remove from the heat and stir in the finely grated coconut, lime rind, and gelatin. Cool.

Beat the egg whites until stiff and fold into the cooled custard. Pour into a 1-quart soufflé dish and refrigerate for several hours, or until firm. Meanwhile, spread the coarsely grated coconut on a cookie sheet and toast for 10 minutes in a 325° oven, or until light brown. Cool. Sprinkle over the soufflé and serve. Serves 6.

Coco Quemado   *Cuba*

Coconut Pudding

2 cups sugar	1 teaspoon ground
1 cup water	cinnamon
4 cups grated coconut	½ cup dry sherry
4 egg yolks, lightly	
beaten	

Cook the sugar and water together to form a syrup at the thread stage. Add the coconut, then stir in the egg yolks. Add the cinnamon and sherry and cook over low heat, stirring constantly with a wooden spoon until the mixture is thick.

Pour into a flame-proof serving dish. Run under a broiler to brown the top. Serve with plain or whipped cream. Serves 6.

Coquimol   *Cuba*

Coconut Cream Sauce

*This is very similar to the Puerto Rican coconut sauce
Bienmesabe though rather richer.*

Water from 1 coconut	6 egg yolks
1 cup sugar	1 teaspoon vanilla
2 cups rich coconut milk made from 1 coconut and 1 cup light cream (see Index)	2 tablespoons light rum (optional)

Make the coconut water up to 1 cup, adding plain water
if necessary. Combine the coconut water and sugar in a
saucepan and cook, stirring, until the sugar is dissolved.
Continue cooking over brisk heat until the syrup reaches
the soft ball stage, or 230° on a candy thermometer. Remove
from the heat and pour in the coconut milk, stirring constantly. Beat the egg yolks lightly. Stir about ½ cup of the
hot syrup into the eggs, then pour this into the syrup
stirring constantly with a wooden spoon. Cook over low
heat, stirring, for about 5 minutes, or until the sauce has
thickened. Remove from the heat, cool slightly, and stir
in the vanilla and the rum, if liked. Makes about 2 cups.

Serve over cake, or instead of whipped cream with
desserts such as Gâteau de Patate or Bolo di Rom.

Cold Rum Soufflé   *Jamaica*

*This is a domestic version of the very good cold rum
soufflé developed by the chef at the Jamaica Inn, Ocho
Rios. In my experience, it is important to use Appleton
Estate rum for the right flavor. However, this is a matter
of taste, and any good island rum may be substituted.*

1 tablespoon cornstarch
2 tablespoons cold water
1 cup evaporated milk,
   or light cream
4 eggs, separated
½ cup sugar

1 envelope (1 tablespoon)
   unflavored gelatin
½ teaspoon vanilla
½ cup Appleton Estate
   rum, or other island
   rum
Pinch salt

Mix the cornstarch with the water and stir into the evaporated milk, or cream and cook, stirring constantly, over low heat until thickened. Set aside. Beat the egg yolks with the sugar until they are lemon colored and form a ribbon. Sprinkle the gelatin on ¼ cup cold water to soften. Add the gelatin and the egg mixture to the milk mixture and cook, stirring, over very low heat for 5 minutes. Remove from the heat, add the vanilla and rum, stirring to blend well. Add the salt to the egg whites and beat until they stand in peaks. Fold into the yolk mixture. Pour into a 1½-quart soufflé dish, or glass serving bowl, and chill in the refrigerator until set. Serves 6.

Corn Meal Pone

Trinidad and Barbados

½ pound pumpkin,
   peeled
2 cups finely grated fresh
   coconut
¼ cup sugar
1 teaspoon ground
   allspice

½ teaspoon salt
2 ounces seedless raisins
1 cup corn meal
2 tablespoons butter,
   melted
Milk to mix

Grate the raw pumpkin and mix with the coconut, sugar, allspice, salt, raisins and corn meal. Stir in the butter. Add enough milk to make a fairly stiff batter, and beat for a minute or two. Pour into a shallow, greased baking pan and bake in a 350° oven for about half an hour, or until a cake tester comes out clean. This can be eaten as a sweet bread, or as a pudding. Serves 6.

Corn Pone

Barbados

1 tablespoon, plus ½ pound butter, softened
8-inch springform cake pan
2 cups yellow corn meal
2 cups all-purpose flour
Pinch salt
1 cup sugar

1 teaspoon vanilla
½ teaspoon grated nutmeg
6 eggs, lightly beaten
1 cup milk
2 tablespoons light rum
1 cup seedless raisins
¼ cup coarsely chopped candied cherries

Butter the cake pan with the tablespoon of butter and set aside. Sift the corn meal, flour and salt together. Cream the half pound of butter and the sugar together, then add 2 tablespoons of the corn meal and flour mixture. Add the vanilla, nutmeg and eggs, beating the mixture constantly. Beat in 1 cup of the corn meal and flour, then ¼ cup of the milk, then more corn meal and flour, and milk until all are used up. Add the rum, raisins, and cherries. Mix and pour the batter into the prepared cake pan. Bake in the middle of a 350° oven for 1½ hours, or until the top is golden and a toothpick inserted in the center comes out clean. Let cool for 5 minutes before removing sides of springform. Slide on to a cake rack to cool. Makes 6 to 8 servings.

Dal Puri   *Trinidad*

Split Pea Stuffed Bread

½ cup split peas
1 tablespoon massala
  (curry powder)
1 teaspoon ground cumin
Salt, freshly ground
  pepper
1 small onion, finely
  chopped

1 clove garlic, crushed
2 cups all-purpose flour
1 teaspoon baking
  powder
1 tablespoon vegetable oil
Extra ghee or oil for
  frying puris

Soak the peas overnight and drain unless they are the quick-cooking variety, in which case omit this step. Put the peas into a saucepan with enough water to cover and stir in the massala (curry powder). Simmer, covered, until tender. Add the cumin, salt and freshly ground pepper to taste, the onion and garlic, and stir to mix well. The mixture should be fairly dry. Set aside.

Sift the flour with baking powder and ½ teaspoon of salt. Add the oil to ½ cup of water and stir in to the flour to make a stiff dough. Add a little more water if necessary, but keep the dough stiff, not soft. Knead thoroughly, cover with a cloth and allow to stand for 1 hour. Knead again and divide into 4 equal sized balls. Allow to rest for 10 minutes, then roll out lightly. Put ¼ of the split pea mixture in the center of each circle of dough, moisten the edges with water and gather up the dough to cover the split peas, sealing it firmly. Roll the filled puris out very carefully to ¼-inch thickness. This is rather tricky as the stuffing mixture bursts out if the dough is rolled too heavily. Using a pastry brush, paint the puri with ghee or oil and cook on a hot, greased griddle, turning frequently and brushing with more ghee or oil. Cook until lightly browned and puffy, about 10 minutes. Eat as a snack, or as an accompaniment to a main dish. Makes 4.

Daube de Banane

Martinique

Banana Pudding

4 tablespoons unsalted butter	1 cup sugar-cane syrup (see Glossary)
6 large bananas, peeled and halved lengthwise	1 cup sweet red wine
	½ teaspoon cinnamon

Heat the butter in a flameproof serving dish and sauté the bananas until they are lightly browned on both sides. Combine the cane syrup, wine, and cinnamon in a saucepan and heat through, stirring to mix well. Pour over the bananas and simmer over very low heat for 15 minutes. Serves 6.

Dumplins

Antigua

2 cups all-purpose flour	2 tablespoons sweet butter
1 tablespoon baking powder	½ teaspoon salt

Sift the flour, salt and baking powder into a bowl. Rub in the butter with the fingertips until the mixture is crumbly. Add enough cold water to make a fairly stiff dough. Turn out on a flour board and knead until smooth. Shape into balls about 1½ inches in diameter, and flatten. Drop into boiling salted water to cover and cook for about 10 minutes. Makes about 18 dumplins. The dumplins may be dropped into a soup or stew instead of being cooked separately.

Farine Dumplings   *St. Vincent*

Cassava Meal Dumplings

1 cup water	½ teaspoon salt
2 cups cassava meal (farine)	¼ cup sugar (optional)
1 egg, well beaten	Oil for frying
2 tablespoons unsalted butter	

Mix the water and the cassava meal together in a sauce-pan, then cook, over low heat, stirring constantly with a wooden spoon until the cassava turns clear. Remove from the heat, cool slightly, and stir in the egg, butter, salt and sugar, if liked. Allow to cool completely. Heat oil in a frying pan and drop the cassava mixture into the pan by tablespoonful. Fry until golden brown on both sides. Drain on paper towels. Serve hot as an accompaniment to meat or fish dishes.
    Serves 6.

Flan de Coco   *Puerto Rico*

Coconut Custard

1¾ cups sugar	1 cup coconut milk (see Index)
6 eggs, lightly beaten	1 cup freshly grated coconut
2 cups evaporated milk	

Put 1 cup of the sugar into a small, heavy saucepan and set it over a medium heat. Cook, stirring with a wooden spoon until the sugar caramelizes. Have ready a 2-quart porcelain mold warmed with boiling water, and dried. Pour in the caramel, turning the mold so that the caramel coats the bottom and an inch or so of the sides. Set aside.
    Add the remaining ¾ cup sugar to the eggs. Pour the evaporated milk and coconut milk into a saucepan, bring

to scalding point and slowly pour into the egg mixture, stirring with a wooden spoon or wire whisk. Add the coconut and pour into the caramelized mold. Set the mold in a pan of hot water in a 350° oven and bake for 1 hour, or until a toothpick inserted into the custard comes out clean. Cool thoroughly and unmold onto a serving platter. If any caramel is left in the mold, add a little hot water and set the mold on an asbestos mat over medium heat until the caramel dissolves. Pour over the custard. Serves 6 to 8.

Floating Islands   *Jamaica*

This is a very popular dessert that crops up on a number of islands. Both Jamaica and Barbados think of it as local. It is a very old recipe.

3 eggs, separated	½ cup heavy cream
¼ cup sugar	¼ cup light Jamaica
2 cups light cream	rum, such as Appleton
1 teaspoon vanilla	Estate
¼ cup guava jelly	1 tablespoon sugar

Combine the egg yolks and sugar in the top of a double boiler away from any heat and beat until the yolks are light and lemon colored. Scald the cream and pour into the egg mixture in a steady stream, beating constantly. Place over water in lower half of boiler and cook over gentle heat, stirring constantly, until the mixture thickens and coats the spoon. Do not let it boil. Cool, stir in the vanilla, pour into a serving dish and refrigerate.

Let the guava jelly stand at room temperature. Beat lightly with a fork to soften. Beat the egg whites until they stand in stiff peaks. Fold in the guava jelly. Drop by spoonfuls onto the custard to make the islands. Whip the cream with the sugar. Add the rum when the cream is stiff and whip for a few seconds longer. Serve separately, or spoon round the outer edge of the custard. Serves 6.

Floats   *Trinidad*
Fried Yeast Biscuits

These fried biscuits are an essential part of the traditional Trinidadian dish, Accra (Codfish Cakes) and Floats.

¼ cup lukewarm
   water
1 packet (¼-ounce)
   active dry yeast
3½ cups all-purpose
   flour
1 teaspoon salt

1 teaspoon sugar
½ cup lard, chilled
   and cut into ¼-inch
   dice
2 cups vegetable oil

Pour the water into a small bowl and sprinkle the yeast over it. Let it stand for a few minutes, then stir to dissolve. Set aside in a warm, draft-free place. Sift the flour, salt and sugar together into a bowl. Rub the lard into the flour until the mixture is crumbly. Add the yeast and enough lukewarm water to make a fairly soft dough. Knead on a lightly floured board until the dough is smooth and elastic, about 5 minutes. Return to the bowl, cover and leave in a warm, draft-free place until it has doubled in bulk, about 1 hour. Pinch off pieces of the dough and roll into small balls about 1½-inches in diameter. Arrange on a baking sheet and leave in a warm draft-free place until they have doubled in bulk, about 45 minutes to an hour. Then roll the balls out thin. Heat the oil in a large, heavy frying pan and fry the floats until they are golden brown, about 3 minutes on each side. Drain on paper towels. Serve warm with Accra (see Index). They may also be served with any other codfish cakes, or as a bread, since they are quite delicious. Makes about 18.

Figues Bananes Fourrées   *Haïti*
Stuffed Bananas

In the French-speaking islands the bananas known as figues are simply our dessert bananas as distinct from the plantain known as banane. The banane must be cooked before it can be eaten. In addition to figues, there are a great many varieties of eating banana less suited to this sort of presentation.

2 tablespoons seedless raisins	½ cup confectioners' sugar
¼ cup dark rum	3 tablespoons coarsely chopped peanuts
3 very large bananas	12 glacé cherries (candied cherries)
¼ cup lemon juice	
8 tablespoons unsalted butter	

Put the raisins to soak in 2 tablespoons of the rum. Peel the bananas and cut into halves lengthwise, then cross-wise. Sprinkle with the lemon juice to prevent them turning brown. Cream the butter with the sugar until it is very pale and smooth. Beat in the remaining 2 tablespoons of rum. Scoop out a cavity about ¼ inch deep the length of each half banana and stuff with the rum butter cream. Sprinkle with the peanuts, garnish with the raisins and any rum they have have not absorbed, and decorate with the glacé cherries. Refrigerate for 2 to 3 hours before serving. Serves 6.

Gâteau patate   *Martinique*
Sweet Potato Cake

2 pounds sweet potatoes
2 tablespoons unsalted
  butter
¾ cup dark brown
  sugar
¼ cup dark, island
  rum
4 eggs
½ cup milk
Grated rind 1 lime

1 tablespoon lime juice
½ teaspoon each
  cinnamon and nutmeg,
  ground
½ teaspoon salt
2 teaspoons baking
  powder

Peel and slice the sweet potatoes and cook with enough water to cover until tender, about 25 minutes. Drain and mash. While still warm mix in the butter, sugar and rum. Beat in the eggs, 1 by 1. Then add the milk, grated rind and lime juice. Sift together the cinnamon, nutmeg, salt and baking powder and mix thoroughly into the sweet potatoes.

Pour into a greased 9-by-5-loaf pan. Bake for about 1 hour in a 350° oven or until a cake tester comes out clean. Let cool few minutes in the pan then turn onto cake rack to cool. Makes 1 loaf cake.

A very similar cake bread is also found in Trinidad, usually with the addition to the batter of a quarter of a cup of raisins.

Gâteau de Patate   *Haïti*
Sweet Potato Cake

2 pounds sweet potatoes
1 large banana
4 tablespoons butter,
  melted and cooled
3 eggs, well-beaten
1 cup sugar

1 cup evaporated milk
¼ cup seedless raisins
½ cup molasses
¼ teaspoon each
  ground nutmeg and
  cinnamon
½ teaspoon vanilla

Peel and slice the sweet potatoes and cook in water to cover until tender, about 25 minutes. Drain and mash. Peel and mash the banana and add to the sweet potatoes. Add all the other ingredients, mixing thoroughly. Pour into a greased 9-by-5 loaf pan and bake in the center of a 350° oven for 1½ hours. Let cool few minutes in the pan then turn onto cake rack to cool. Makes 1 loaf cake.

This is a cross between a pudding and a bread and is delicious for tea time. Served with rum flavoured whipped cream or with a rich coconut cream, it makes a splendid dessert. A little rum may be poured over the cake at serving time with advantage.

Gâteau Maïs   *Martinique*

Corn Cake

CAKE:

1 quart milk	4 tablespoons unsalted butter
¼ cup sugar	
1 teaspoon vanilla	¼ cup *rhum vieux*, or use a dark rum like Myer's
1 cup golden seedless raisins	
1 cup yellow corn meal	1 tablespoon ground cinnamon

CARAMEL SAUCE:

1 cup sugar	3 tablespoons unsalted butter
¼ cup water	
Pinch cream of tartar	½ cup evaporated milk

FOR THE CAKE BATTER: bring the milk, sugar, vanilla and raisins to a boil in a large saucepan, and add the corn meal, a little at a time, stirring constantly until it is quite stiff. Remove from the heat. Stir in the butter and the rum. Pour into a buttered mold and refrigerate for 2 or 3 hours, or until the cake is thoroughly chilled. Unmold onto a serving platter and sprinkle with the cinnamon. Serve with the Caramel Sauce. Serves 6.

FOR THE CARAMEL SAUCE: combine the sugar and water in a heavy saucepan and cook, stirring, over brisk heat until the sugar dissolves. Stir in the cream of tartar and continue to cook, stirring, until the sugar has caramelized to a deep golden brown. Meanwhile, combine the butter and milk in a small saucepan, and heat until the butter has dissolved and the milk has reached scalding point. Pour into the caramel mixture, over low heat, and stir until the caramel has dissolved and the sauce is smooth. Pour into a sauceboat and serve warm with the cake.

Gingerbread   *Jamaica*

2 cups all-purpose flour
1 tablespoon baking
   powder
½ teaspoon baking
   soda
1 teaspoon allspice,
   ground
½ teaspoon salt
8 ounces unsalted butter
½ cup dark brown
   sugar

1 cup molasses
1 cup evaporated milk
2 eggs, well-beaten
1 ounce freshly grated
   ginger root, or 2
   teaspoons ground
   Jamaica ginger
3 ounces finely chopped
   crystallized ginger

Sift the flour, baking powder, soda, allspice and salt together. Melt the butter, cook, and mix with the sugar, molasses, milk and eggs. Add to the flour, blending thoroughly. Fold both the grated and the crystallised ginger into the mixture. Pour into a greased 9-by-5-inch loaf pan and bake in a 350° oven for about 35 minutes, or until a cake tester comes out clean. If using ground ginger instead of freshly grated ginger, sift with the dry ingredients. Bakes 1 loaf gingerbread.

Ginger Mousse
Jamaica

This mousse is frequently credited to Trinidad but I am inclined to think it is Jamaican in origin, especially as Jamaican ginger is justly famous.

1 envelope (1 tablespoon) unflavored gelatin	Pinch salt
¼ cup cold water	½ cup rum, preferably a light Jamaican rum
2 cups evaporated milk	1 cup finely chopped crystallized ginger
4 eggs, separated	
½ cup sugar	

Soften the gelatin in the water. Scald the milk and stir in the gelatin to dissolve. Remove from heat. Beat the egg yolks with the sugar until they are pale yellow and form a ribbon. Pour the egg mixture into the milk, stirring constantly with a wooden spoon. Cook, stirring, over very low heat until the custard is thick enough to coat the spoon. Remove from the heat. Beat the egg whites with a pinch of salt until they stand in peaks. Add the rum and the ginger to the cooled custard, mixing well. Stir in a quarter of the egg whites, then fold in the rest gently but thoroughly. Pour into a serving bowl and refrigerate until set. Serves 6.

Gratin d'Ananas au Rhum
Martinique

Pineapple Gratin with Rum

1 cup sugar	1 cup heavy cream
4 egg yolks from large eggs	½ cup dark rum
2 whole large eggs	2 cups coarsely chopped pineapple
1 cup, less 3 tablespoons, all-purpose flour	½ cup toasted slivered almonds
2 cups milk	1 cup sifted confectioners' sugar
1 teaspoon vanilla	

Make a thick crème pâtissière: place the sugar and egg yolks in a heavy saucepan and beat until the mixture is pale yellow and forms a ribbon. Beat in the 2 whole eggs, then the flour. Place over very low heat and cook, stirring until the mixture is lukewarm. Meanwhile bring the milk to a boil. Pour it into the egg mixture, stirring vigorously with a wire whisk. Continue to cook, stirring, for about 3 minutes, or until the mixture is thick and smooth. Remove from the heat and stir in the vanilla, add the cream and the rum. Strain into a bowl.

Butter a gratin dish (shallow ovenware) and pour in half the cream. Cover with the pineapple and top with the rest of the cream. Sprinkle with the almonds and the confectioners' sugar and rum under a broiler for a minute or two to brown the top. Serves 6 to 8.

Guava Pie   *Jamaica*

2 cans (2-pounds 2-ounces each) guava shells
6 tablespoons lime, or lemon, juice
1 tablespoon arrowroot

1 9-inch baked pie shell using short-crusty pastry (see recipe for Mango Pie)
1 cup heavy cream

Drain the liquid from the guava shells, measure, and pour into a small saucepan. Set the shells aside. Bring the guava juice to a boil and reduce to 1 cup. Add the lime juice. Dissolve the arrowroot in a little cold water, stir into the guava juice and cook over low heat, stirring constantly, until the mixture thickens lightly. Remove from the heat.

Spread a thin layer of this glaze over the bottom of the pie crust. Arrange the guava shells, cut side down, in the pie crust in decorative circles. Pour the rest of the glaze over them and cool to room temperature. Whip the cream and serve separately with the pie. Serves 6.

Ice Creams

Ice cream is extremely popular throughout the island and good use is made of the fruits that occur in lavish profusion. These recipes, with the exception of Avocado Ice Cream which is from Jamaica, are all from Grenada and are made on the basis of an egg custard.

BASIC CUSTARD FOR ICE CREAM:

4 eggs	**2 cups milk**
½ cup sugar	**½ teaspoon vanilla**

Beat the eggs lightly with the sugar. Scald the milk and stir into the eggs. Cook the egg mixture in the top of a double boiler over hot water, stirring constantly until the mixture coats the spoon. Cool. Add the vanilla. With the addition of fruit pulp, this makes enough ice cream for 6 to 8 servings.

Avocado Ice Cream

Peel and mash 2 medium-sized avocado pears with ¼ cup sugar and a squeeze of lime juice. Mix with the Basic Custard. Turn into a freezing tray and freeze to a mush. Remove from refrigerator, beat well and return to freezing compartment.

Banana Ice Cream

Peel 3 fully ripe bananas and mash. Mix with the Basic Custard. Freeze as above.

Coconut Ice Cream

Add 1 cup coconut milk and 1 cup heavy cream to the Basic Custard. Freeze as above.

Top ice cream with grated coconut (toasted with sugar in a 350° oven for 15 minutes and cooled before using).

Guava Ice Cream

Mix 1 cup stewed sweetened guava purée with Basic Custard. Freeze as above.

Mango Ice Cream

Mix 1 cup mango pulp with ¼ cup of sugar. Mix thoroughly with Basic Custard. Freeze as above.

Pawpaw Ice Cream

Mix 1 cup of mashed pawpaw (papaya) with ¼ cup sugar and 1 tablespoon lime juice. Mix thoroughly with Basic Custard. Freeze as above.

Pineapple Ice Cream

Mix 1 cup crushed pineapple with ¼ cup sugar. Mix thoroughly with Basic Custard. Freeze as above.

Soursop Ice Cream

Mix 2 cups of soursop (Guanábana) juice with 1 cup of heavy cream. Add ½ cup sugar, stir well and freeze as above. No custard is used in this recipe, just the soursop juice, cream and sugar.

Le Gâteau Martiniquais   *Martinique*

Martinique Sweet Potato Cake

The sweet potatoes used in this cake are the white type, either red or white skinned, called boniatos in Latin American markets. They are true sweet potatoes, but are less sweet and have firmer flesh than the orange sweet potato, known as Louisiana yam, which may also be used. The term yam is mistakenly used, since yams and sweet potatoes come from entirely different botanical families. If the Louisiana yam is used, the cake will need longer cooking time.

2 pounds sweet potatoes	Pinch salt
1¼ cups sugar	3 eggs, well beaten
4 tablespoons unsalted butter	2 tablespoons dark rum, preferably Martinique *vieux rhum*
2 cups coconut cream (see Index)	

Peel and slice the sweet potatoes, and put on to cook with enough cold water to cover in a large saucepan. Cook, covered, until the sweet potatoes are tender, about 20 minutes. Drain very thoroughly. Return to the saucepan and mash with the sugar, butter, coconut cream and salt. Beat in the eggs. Pour into a buttered 9-inch round cake pan and bake in a 400° oven until a cake tester comes out clean, about 2 hours. Remove from the oven and pour the rum over the cake. Allow to stand about 5 minutes in the cake pan then turn out to cool. When cool, refrigerate.

GLACAGE AU CHOCOLAT:

Chocolate-butter Icing

3 ounces semi-sweet chocolate	3 tablespoons dark rum, preferably Martinique *vieux rhum*
	4 ounces unsalted butter

To make the icing, put the chocolate into the top of a double boiler, over hot water, with the rum, and cook, stirring, until the chocolate is smooth. Remove from the heat, but do not take the chocolate off the hot water. Using a wire whisk, beat in the butter, a tablespoon at a time. Place the mixture over cold water, and continue to beat until it is cool. Allow to stand until it is thick. Spread over the cake, frosting top and sides. Return to the refrigerator until ready to serve. Serves 6 to 8.

In Martinique the cake is sometimes made without any baking. In this case it is essential to use the white (boniato) sweet potato. When the sweet potato is cooked, it should be drained, mashed and then dried slightly over low heat. Omit the eggs, and use only 1 cup of the very richest coconut cream. Combine with mashed potatoes. Pour into a buttered mold. Do not douse with rum. Chill thoroughly until the cake is set. (It is helpful to line the mold with buttered waxed paper.)

Turn cake out, frost and return to the refrigerator until immediately before serving.

Lime Pie   *St. Kitts*

2 tablespoons cornstarch
2 cups water
1 tablespoon unsalted
   butter
2 eggs, well beaten
1 cup strained fresh lime
   juice

2 tablespoons finely
   grated lime rind
1 cup sugar
9-inch baked pie shell

Mix the cornstarch to a paste with a little of the water. Add the rest of the water and pour into a saucepan. Cook, stirring with a wooden spoon, over low heat until thickened. Stir in the butter. Remove from the heat and cool slightly. Stir in the eggs, the lime juice and rind, and the sugar. Cook, stirring, over very low heat for about 5 minutes, or until the mixture has thickened. Pour into the pie shell and chill. Serve with whipped cream, or Arrowroot Custard. Serves 6.

If liked the pie may be topped with meringue.

FOR MERINGUE:

3 egg whites　　　　　　　　　Pinch salt
3 tablespoons sugar

Beat egg whites, sugar and salt together until the whites stand in peaks. Drop by spoonfuls to cover the pie filling. Bake in a 325° oven for 15 minutes, or until the meringue is delicately browned.

Lime Soufflé　　　　　　　　　　　*Barbados*

1 envelope (1 tablespoon)　　　　1½ cups sugar
　unflavoured gelatin　　　　　　4 tablespoons finely
1 cup strained fresh lime　　　　　grated lime rind
　juice　　　　　　　　　　　　Pinch salt
1 tablespoon cornstarch　　　　　½ cup coarsely grated
¼ cup water　　　　　　　　　　fresh coconut, or
1 cup evaporated milk　　　　　　canned shredded moist
4 eggs, separated　　　　　　　　coconut

Soften the gelatin in the lime juice and set aside. Mix the cornstarch with the water. Pour the milk into a saucepan and stir the cornstarch into it. Cook over low heat, stirring constantly with a wooden spoon, until the mixture is smooth and thickened. Beat the egg yolks until blended, then beat in the sugar gradually. Stir into the milk mixture and cook, stirring constantly, until the custard is thick, about 5 minutes. Stir in the gelatin and lime juice, and cook just long enough to dissolve the gelatin. Stir in 3 tablespoons of the grated rind. Cool. Beat the egg whites with the salt until they stand in peaks. Fold gently into the custard. Pour into a 6-cup soufflé mold or glass serving dish, and chill in the refrigerator until set.

Before serving, spread the coconut in a baking pan and

toast it in a 325° oven, for 10 to 15 minutes, or until light brown. Cool, and sprinkle on the soufflé with the remaining tablespoon of lime rind. Serves 6.

Lime Soufflé   *Tobago*

3 tablespoons unsalted
  butter
3 tablespoons all-purpose
  flour
½ cup evaporated milk
¾ cup sugar
½ cup strained fresh
  lime juice

3 tablespoons finely
  grated lime rind
4 eggs, separated and 1
  extra egg white
Pinch salt

Heat the butter in a saucepan, add the flour and cook, stirring with a wooden spoon, for 1 or 2 minutes without letting the mixture take on any color. Add the milk, and sugar, and cook, stirring, for 3 or 4 minutes longer. Stir in the lime juice and rind, and mix well. Allow to cool for a few minutes then beat in the egg yolks, one by one. Beat the egg whites with the salt until they stand in peaks. Stir 2 tablespoons of the beaten whites into the soufflé mixture, then gently fold in the rest of egg whites. Pour into a buttered 6-cup soufflé mold. Bake in a 375° oven for 30 to 35 minutes or until done. Serve immediately. Serves 6.

Mango Sherbet   *Jamaica*

1 envelope (1 tablespoon)
  unflavored gelatin
3 cups sieved mango
  purée

½ cup sugar
3 tablespoons lime juice

Sprinkle the gelatin on ⅓ cup cold water, then dissolve, stirring, over low heat. Cool. Mix mango purée, sugar, lime juice and gelatin. Chill until the mixture is syrupy. Beat until light and fluffy. Serve with whipped cream, or ice cream. Serves 6.

Mango Cream   *Jamaica*

1 envelope (1 tablespoon) unflavored gelatin	½ cup sugar
2 cups mango purée	1 tablespoon lime juice
	1 cup heavy cream

Sprinkle the gelatin on ⅓ cup cold water, then dissolve, stirring, over low heat. Cool. Mix the mango purée, sugar, lime juice and gelatin. Whip the cream until stiff, then fold lightly but thoroughly into the mango mixture. Pour into a mold rinsed out with cold water. Refrigerate until set. Unmold and serve plain, or garnished with slices of mango. Serves 6.

Mango Ice Cream   *Jamaica*

1 large, fleshy mango weighing about 1½ pounds	½ cup water
	¼ cup lime juice
½ cup sugar	1 cup heavy cream

Peel the mango, cut off the flesh and chop fine. There should be about 2 cups. Make a syrup with the sugar and water simmered together for 5 minutes. Cool. Add to the mango with the lime juice, mixing thoroughly. Whip the cream until stiff and fold into the mango mixture. Freeze in refrigerator ice trays with the cube dividers removed, at the coldest temperature available. Stir after 1 hour, and again at the end of the second hour. The ice cream should be ready in about 2½ hours from beginning of freezing. Makes 2 ice trays, 6 or more servings.

Mango Fool   *English-speaking Islands*

3 cups mango purée,   ½ cup sugar
  sieved   3 cups stiffly whipped
1 tablespoon lime juice   cream, chilled

Season the mango purée with sugar and lime juice. Chill
thoroughly. Just before serving fold in the whipped cream.
Blend lightly so that the mixture is not quite uniform in
appearance, but has discernable streaks of cream and
mango. Serves 6.

    If liked the cream may be flavoured with 3 tablespoons
of light rum.

Mango Pie   *English-speaking Islands*

SHORT CRUST PASTRY FOR 9-INCH PIE PLATE:

1½ cups all-purpose   2 tablespoons lard,
  flour   chilled and cut into
1 tablespoon sugar   small pieces
¼ teaspoon salt   3 tablespoons cold water
6 tablespoons unsalted
  butter, chilled and cut
  into small pieces

Sift the flour, sugar and salt together into a large bowl.
Rub the fat into the flour with the fingertips until the
mixture is crumbly. Sprinkle water over the mixture and
mix lightly to a stiffish dough. Gather into a ball, wrap in
waxed paper and chill until firm enough to roll out. Turn
on to a floured board and roll out into a circle large enough
to line the pie plate. Brush the pie plate with melted butter.
Roll the pastry round the rolling pin and unroll it into the
pie plate. Press the pastry lightly into the sides of the pan,
and over the rim. Trim away any excess, and crimp the
edges with a fork or the fingers. Prick the bottom with a
fork. Bake shell on the center shelf of an oven preheated

to 350° for 25 minutes, or until golden brown. If air bubbles form, prick bottom of shell 2 or 3 times during the first 10 minutes of baking. Cool before chilling.

FILLING FOR PIE:

Large, fleshy mango, weighing about 1½ pounds	½ cup sugar
	¼ cup water
	1 tablespoon arrowroot
3 tablespoons lime juice	

Carefully peel the mango. Feel with the tip of a small, sharp knife where the seed is, and cut off 2 slices lengthwise, down each side of the mango as close to the seed as possible. Cut each slice into lengthwise strips about ¼-inch thick, sprinkle with a little of the lime juice and set aside. Cut all the remaining flesh off the seed. There should be about 1 cup of pulp. Put the pulp into a saucepan with the sugar, remaining lime juice and water and cook until soft, about 10 minutes. Rub through a sieve, return to the saucepan and stir in the arrowroot mixed with a little cold water, and cook until thickened, stirring constantly. Cool slightly. Arrange the mango slices in the baked pastry shell in an overlapping pattern, using the shorter pieces to fill in at the sides. Spoon the purée over these pieces evenly. Chill well before serving. Serve plain, or with custard, whipped cream, or ice cream to taste. Serves 6.

Mango Ice   *Jamaica*

2 cups sieved mango purée	½ cup water
	1 egg white
2 tablespoons lime juice	
¼ cup sugar	

Mix the mango purée with the lime juice. Simmer the sugar and water together for 5 minutes to make a syrup. Cool. Add to the mango purée, mixing thoroughly. Beat the egg white until it stands in peaks. Fold into the mango mixture. Freeze until firm, about 3 hours in refrigerator ice trays. Every half hour during the freezing process, stir the mixture, scraping into the center the ice crystals that form around the edge of the tray. The finished ice should have a snowy texture. Makes 2 ice trays, 6 or more servings.

Mango Mousse   *Barbados*

Ripe mangoes, weighing about 4 pounds
½ cup lime juice
½ cup granulated sugar

1 envelope (1 tablespoon) unflavored gelatin
2 egg whites
Pinch of salt
½ cup heavy cream

Peel the mangoes, cut the flesh off the seeds, and purée in an electric blender with the lime juice, being careful not to overblend. There will be 5 cups of purée. Stir in the sugar. Dissolve the gelatin in ¼ cup hot water, cool, and stir into the mango purée. Beat the egg whites with the salt until they stand in peaks. Whip the cream until it is stiff. Fold the cream into the egg whites, then fold this mixture gently into the mango purée. Pour into a large serving dish, or into individual dishes, and refrigerate for 2 to 3 hours, or until set. Serves 6 to 8.

Mousse à L'ananas   *Martinique*

Pineapple Mousse

2 cups unsweetened pineapple juice
1 cup sugar, or less to taste

6 tablespoons cornstarch
6 egg whites
Pinch salt

Pour the pineapple juice into a saucepan, and add the sugar. Use a little of the juice to dissolve the cornstarch, then add the cornstarch to the saucepan and cook, stirring constantly with a wooden spoon over low heat for 5 minutes. Cool. Beat the egg whites with the salt until they stand in peaks. Fold into the mixture, gently but thoroughly. Turn into a serving dish and refrigerate. Serve with Crème Anglaise.

CREAM ANGLAISE:

Custard Sauce

6 egg yolks
¼ cup sugar
⅛ teaspoon salt
2 cups light cream

1 teaspoon vanilla
1 cup coarsely chopped
   pineapple

In the top of a double boiler, but not over any heat, beat the egg yolks, sugar, and salt together until the mixture is pale yellow and forms a ribbon. Scald the cream and pour it slowly into the egg mixture, stirring constantly with a wooden spoon or wire whisk. Pour hot, not boiling water into the lower part of the double boiler. Replace the top part with the custard and cook, stirring constantly over very low heat so that the water does not boil, until the mixture thickens and coats the spoon. Remove from the heat and stir until slightly cooled. Strain, and add the vanilla and pineapple. Chill and serve as a sauce with the mousse. Serves 6 to 8.

Mrs. Roy Lyons' Mango Cheese

Jamaica

Jamaicans insist that you must use No. 11 mangoes for this recipe to succeed. I have tried it with several types of mango and report success. However, if it is overcooked the mango paste turns into what Jamaicans graphically call tie-teeth.

Juicy-type mangoes   Lime juice (optional)
Sugar

Peel the mangoes, cut off the flesh and push through a sieve to remove any stringy part. To each cup of purée add 1 cup of sugar and 1 teaspoon lime juice, if liked. Cook in a heavy saucepan over medium heat, stirring constantly with a wooden spoon. When the bubbles grow smaller and a spoon drawn across the bottom of the pan leaves a clean wake, the mango should be tested: drop a little onto an ice cube, if it sets, turn the mango cheese into a damp mold and when cool, turn out. In Latin America this is eaten with fresh cheese and crackers. It may be eaten by itself or with plain cake or cookies.

Orange Bread

Barbados

2 cups all-purpose flour
4 teaspoons baking
  powder
½ cup sugar
½ teaspoon salt
1 tablespoon grated
  orange rind

1 egg, well beaten
1 cup orange juice
4 tablespoons unsalted
  butter, melted

Sift the flour, baking powder, sugar, salt and orange rind together. Mix the egg with the orange juice and butter and fold into the flour. Pour the batter into a greased 9-by-5-loaf pan and bake in a 350° oven, for 30 minutes, or until a cake tester comes out clean. Makes 1 loaf.

Pan de Maíz   *Dominican Republic*

Corn Bread

2½ cups yellow corn
  meal
1½ cups all-purpose
  flour
3 tablespoons baking
  powder*
1 teaspoon salt
8 ounces unsalted butter
2 cups finely grated fresh
  coconut

½ teaspoon aniseed
  (optional)
½ cup evaporated
  milk, or heavy cream
½ cup coconut milk
  (see Index)
4 eggs, well-beaten

Sift the dry ingredients together. Cream the butter until light and fluffy and gradually blend into the cornmeal and flour. Add the coconut and the aniseed, if liked. Add the evaporated milk or cream, coconut milk, and the eggs. Mix well, beating for a minute or two. Grease two 9-by-5-loaf pans. Spoon the mixture, which should be very soft, into the pans. Bake in the center of a 350° oven for 30 minutes, or until the bread shrinks slightly from the sides of the tin and is golden brown. This is very good sliced, toasted and buttered. Makes 2 loaves.

*This amount of baking powder may look alarming but it is needed as the corn meal is very dense in texture.

Pain de Patates Douces   *Haïti*

Sweet Potato Bread

4 cups sweet potatoes,
  (about 2 pounds)
8 tablespoons unsalted
  butter, melted and
  cooled
¾ cup each milk, and
  coconut milk (see
  Index)
1 cup molasses

1 large banana, mashed
½ teaspoon each
  ground cinnamon and
  nutmeg
½ teaspoon salt
1 teaspoon vanilla
Grated rind of 1 lime
½ cup raisins
  (optional)
½ cup sugar

Peel the sweet potatoes, chop coarsely and grate in a
blender, bit by bit, to a medium consistency. Put into a
large mixing bowl and add all the other ingredients, mixing
thoroughly. Pour into a greased rectangular baking dish.
Bake in a 400° oven for about 45 minutes. Serve at room
temperature from the baking dish. Makes 6 to 8 servings.

Pan Dulce de Maíz   *Dominican Republic*

Sweet Corn Bread

3 cups yellow corn meal
1 cup all-purpose flour
3 tablespoons baking
  powder*
½ teaspoon each
  ground cinnamon,
  nutmeg and cloves
½ cup sugar
1 teaspoon salt
6 tablespoons each of
  butter and lard

½ cup each milk and
  coconut milk (see
  Index)
4 eggs, well-beaten
Grated rind of 1 lime, or
  lemon
2 cups finely grated fresh
  coconut
8 ounces mixed fruits and
  peels (Glacé Cake Mix)

Sift all the dry ingredients, including the spices, together.
Cream the butter and lard until light and fluffy and add
to the corn meal mixture. Add the milk, coconut milk,
eggs and grated rind. Mix in the grated coconut and the
fruits and peels, lightly floured. Mix well and pour into 2
greased 9-by-5-loaf pans. Bake for about 35 minutes in
the center of a 350° oven, or until a cake tester comes out
clean. Makes 2 loaves.

*This amount of baking powder may look alarming but is needed as the corn
meal is very dense in texture.

Pastel de Batata   *Cuba*

Sweet Potato Cake

8 tablespoons unsalted butter	2 eggs, separated
2 cups sweet potato paste (Boniatillo) (see Index)	1 cup cake flour
½ teaspoon vanilla	2 teaspoons baking powder
	Pinch of salt

Melt the butter, and beat it into the sweet potato paste.
Add the vanilla. Beat the egg yolks thoroughly and add.
Sift the flour with the baking powder and add. Beat the
egg whites with a pinch of salt until stiff and fold into the
potato mixture gently but thoroughly. Pour into a buttered
2-quart soufflé dish, and bake in a 350° oven for about 45
minutes, or until a cake tester comes out clean. This can
be served as a sweet bread, or with rum flavored whipped
cream as a dessert. Makes 6 to 8 servings.

Piña con Ron   *Puerto Rico*

Pineapple with Rum

*I first encountered this way of serving pineapple in Puerto
Rico, but later met with it in other islands. In Martinique*

rhum vieux *is poured over the fruit with a generous, unmeasured hand, giving the pineapple a very heady flavor. The lighter Puerto Rican rum is also extremely pleasant.*

1 small, ripe pineapple   Rum

Cut the pineapple lengthwise into thirds, slicing through the leaves, which should be left on. Carefully cut the flesh from each shell in 1 piece. Cut off the core by slicing lengthwise. Halve the flesh lengthwise then cut crosswise into bite-size pieces. Replace in the pineapple shells. Pour on rum to taste. Serves 3.

Pitch Lake Pudding   *Barbados*

This Bajan pudding which sometimes appears as Mousse Antillaise, is said to have been inspired by Trinidad's Pitch Lake, a seepage of natural asphalt. It makes an exceptionally good party dessert. The recipe can be successfully doubled.

1 cup unsweetened cocoa   5 eggs, separated
2 tablespoons instant   ¼ cup dark rum
  espresso coffee   Pinch of salt
1 cup superfine sugar   1 cup heavy cream

Place the cocoa in the top of a double boiler over hot water. Dissolve the coffee in ½ cup boiling water. Add the sugar and stir until dissolved. Stir this mixture gradually into the cocoa and cook, stirring with a wooden spoon over low heat for 5 minutes. Beat in the egg yolks, one at a time, beating vigorously after each addition. Remove from the heat and stir in the rum. Add the salt to the egg whites and beat until they stand in stiff peaks on the beater when it is lifted from the bowl. Fold into the cocoa mixture gently but thoroughly. Pour into a 1-

quart soufflé dish, or glass serving dish, and refrigerate overnight, or for several hours.

To serve, beat the cream until stiff and spread it over the mousse. The cream may be flavored and sweetened if liked, in which case add 1 tablespoon superfine sugar and 1 tablespoon dark rum. Serves 6.

Planter's Cake

Jamaica

CAKE:

5 large eggs, separated
1 tablespoon lime, or lemon, juice
1 teaspoon grated lime or lemon rind

1 cup sugar
Pinch salt
1 cup cake flour

Beat the egg yolks in a mixing bowl, with the lemon juice, until thick. Add the grated rind. Sift the sugar into the eggs and continue beating until the mixture forms a ribbon.

In a separate bowl, beat the egg whites with the salt until they stand in peaks. Combine the whites and yolks, folding the whites in with a spatula and using an undercutting motion. Sift the flour and cut into the egg mixture as lightly as possible, without beating.

Pour into two 9-inch layer pans and bake in a 350° oven for about 25 minutes, or until a toothpick inserted in the center comes out clean. Remove from oven and cool for about 5 minutes before turning out onto cake racks to cool.

RUM BUTTER CREAM FROSTING:

8 egg yolks
1 pound unsalted butter
1½ cups sugar
2 tablespoons instant espresso coffee

½ cup water
¼ cup dark rum

To make the frosting for the cake, beat the egg yolks in a large bowl until they are thick and lemon colored. Soften the butter at room temperature and cream it with the sugar until it is light and fluffy. Combine the espresso coffee and water in a small saucepan, bring to a boil. Pour the coffee into the egg yolks, beating constantly, then beat in the butter and sugar mixture to make a thick, smooth cream. Beat in the rum, a little at a time. Cover and chill until the cream is firm, about 30 minutes.

To assemble the cake, cut each of the cakes in half horizontally, so that there are 4 layers. Place a layer on a serving plate, and spread with a layer of the rum butter frosting. Set a second layer on top, and repeat until all the layers are in place then cover the top of the cake and sides with remaining frosting. Refrigerate until ready to serve. Makes one 9-inch round layer cake.

Pudding au Fruit à Pain   *Martinique*

Breadfruit Pudding

½ can (1-pound 10-ounce) breadfruit
½ cup sugar
4 tablespoons unsalted butter, melted and cooled
Grated rind of 1 lime, or lemon

2 tablespoons all-purpose flour
¼ cup Martinique *rhum vieux*, or a dark rum such as Myer's
½ teaspoon vanilla
2 cups milk
2 large eggs

Drain the breadfruit, divide in 2 equal parts. Store the second half in the can liquid in a covered container in the refrigerator. It will keep for a week or two. Mash the breadfruit until smooth. Add the sugar, butter, lime rind, and flour, mixing well. Stir in the rum, vanilla, milk and eggs beating until the mixture is smooth. Pour into a buttered mold or baking dish and cook for 1½ hours in a 350° oven, or until a toothpick inserted into the pudding comes out clean. Serve at room temperature with rum sauce, or any dessert sauce. Serves 6.

If using fresh breadfruit, peel, remove the core and cook 1 pound of the breadfruit in boiling salted water until tender, about 20 minutes. Drain and use as canned breadfruit.

I like to pour a jigger of *rhum vieux* over the pudding while it is still warm, then turn it out onto a serving platter, and when it is quite cold, mask it with a cup of heavy cream whipped with a tablespoon of sugar and a tablespoon of *rhum vieux*. It may be refrigerated, if liked. It is also delicious served with a very heavy coconut cream flavored with *rhum vieux* and a little sugar.

Pumpkin Buns   *Trinidad*

2 cups all-purpose flour
½ teaspoon salt
1 teaspoon ground
  allspice
1 teaspoon ground ginger
½ cup seedless raisins
½ ounce (2 packages)
  active dry yeast

½ cup lukewarm
  water
¼ cup sugar
1 cup cooked mashed
  West Indian pumpkin,
  or Hubbard squash
2 tablespoons unsalted
  butter
2 eggs, well-beaten
Grated rind of 1 lime

Sift the flour with the salt, allspice, and ginger into a mixing bowl. Add the raisins. Sprinkle the yeast on the lukewarm water and stir in the sugar. Set aside until it bubbles. Add the butter to the pumpkin while it is still warm, and stir to blend well. Make a well in the flour mixture and add the yeast, pumpkin, eggs and grated rind. Mix to a smooth dough, cover and set in a warm, draft-free place until doubled in bulk, about half an hour. Shape into 12 buns and place on a greased cookie sheet, leave to rise again in a warm draft-free place. Bake in a 400° oven for about 15 minutes or until done. Serve warm or at room temperature.

Pumpkin Bread   *Trinidad*

4 cups all-purpose flour
2 teaspoons salt
½ ounce (2 packages)
  active dry yeast
½ cup lukewarm
  water

1 teaspoon sugar
2 tablespoons unsalted
  butter
1 cup cooked mashed
  West Indian pumpkin,
  or Hubbard squash.

Sift the flour with the salt into a large bowl. Sprinkle the yeast on the lukewarm water and stir in the sugar. Set aside until it bubbles. Add the butter to the pumpkin while it is still warm and stir to blend well. Cool. Make a well in the flour, add the yeast, and pumpkin and mix to a soft dough, adding a little more water if necessary. Turn out on to a lightly floured board and knead until smooth, about 5 minutes. Place the dough in a greased bowl and cover with a towel. Set in a warm, draft-free place until it doubles in bulk, about 1 hour. Divide the dough into 2 equal parts and knead again until smooth. Shape into 2 loaves and place in 2 greased 9-by-5-inch loaf pans. Cover, and set them in a warm draft-free place until again doubled in bulk. Bake in a 400° oven until the loaves are browned on top and shrink away from the sides of the pans. Turn out and cool on a wire rack. If the loaves are done, the bottoms will sound hollow when tapped. Makes 2 loaves.

Pumpkin Tea Bread   *Trinidad*

2 cups all-purpose flour
1 tablespoon double-
  acting baking powder
½ teaspoon salt
8 tablespoons unsalted
  butter
¾ cup sugar
1 egg, well-beaten

1 teaspoon Angostura
  bitters
1 cup cooked mashed
  West Indian pumpkin,
  or Hubbard squash
½ cup glacé fruit mix,
  or seedless raisins

Sift the flour with the baking powder and salt into a bowl. In a separate bowl cream the butter and sugar until the mixture is light and fluffy. Add the egg and Angostura bitters, mixing well, then beat in the pumpkin and the flour alternatively until the batter is smooth. Toss the glacé fruits with a tablespoon of flour and stir into the batter. Pour into a buttered 9-by-5-inch loaf pan and bake in the middle of a 375° oven for about 30 minutes, or until a cake tester comes out clean. Makes 1 loaf.

Roti   *Trinidad*

Bread

Roti simply means bread, and this is the term most often used in Trinidad for parathas, which is what these are. They are of Indian origin, but like everything else in the Caribbean, have evolved from the original. One 12-inch roti makes a magnificent lunch when a generous dollop of curried chicken, kid, shrimp or potatoes is placed in the center, and the bread folded over it like an envelope. One can eat it with a knife and fork; fingers, however, are more fun. The 8-inch roti is served as a bread with curries. I have two versions of roti, one a little more elaborate than the other, both very good.

2 cups all-purpose flour	3 tablespoons butter, or
1 teaspoon baking	vegetable shortening
powder	Ghee (see Index)
1 teaspoon salt	Extra flour

Sift the flour, baking powder and salt into a bowl. Rub in the butter or shortening with the fingertips until the fat is in small flakes. Pour ¼ cup cold water over the flour and mix to make a fairly stiff dough. Add more water, 1 tablespoon at a time, until the dough holds together but is not sticky. Knead until smooth. Cover, and leave in a warm place for half an hour. Knead again for 3 or 4 minutes then divide into 4 equal balls. Roll out on a floured board into 12- or 8-inch rounds. Brush lightly all over with ghee, then sprinkle with flour. Fold in half, then in half again, to form a 4-layered quarter circle. Cover and leave for half an hour. Then shape roughly into a circle with the hands, and roll out on to a floured board into 12- or 8-inch rounds. Heat a cast-iron frying pan or griddle so that a little flour sprinkled on it will brown instantly, or a drop of water will sputter. Place 1 of the roti in the pan or on the griddle and cook for about a minute. Turn, and spread with a thin layer of ghee. Cook for 2 minutes, then spread again with ghee. Cook for 1 minute longer then turn. Cook for about a minute then remove from pan to a board. Hit with a wooden mallet all over until it is flaky. Wrap in a towel and keep warm until the other roti are cooked. Serve at once. Serves 4.

2 cups all-purpose flour	**Milk, or water to mix**
¼ teaspoon baking	**Ghee (see Index) or**
soda	**vegetable oil**
½ teaspoon salt	

Sift the flour, baking soda, and salt into a bowl. Add enough milk or water to mix to a stiff dough. Knead the dough thoroughly on a lightly floured board. Form into 4 balls and roll out into 8-inch circles. Brush all over with ghee or vegetable oil and fold into a ball again. Cover and allow to stand for about 15 minutes. Roll out again into 8-inch circles. Heat a cast-iron frying pan or griddle until a drop of water will sputter when dropped on it, or a little flour will brown instantly. Cook the roti for about 1 minute, turn, spread with ghee or vegetable oil and cook, turning frequently until the roti is baked. Remove from the pan and clap with both hands until pliable. Wrap in towel to keep warm until the other roti are cooked. Serve at once. Serves 4.

Surullitos
Corn Sticks

Puerto Rico

2 cups water
1 teaspoon salt
1½ cups yellow corn
  meal
Vegetable oil or lard for
  frying

1 cup grated Edam or
  mild Cheddar cheese,
  which are the nearest
  equivalents to the local
  cheese known as native
  cheese

Combine the water and salt in a saucepan and bring to a boil. Pour in the corn meal in a steady stream, and cook, stirring for about 5 minutes, or until the mixture is thick and smooth. Remove from the heat and stir in the cheese, mixing well. Cool. Take out by spoonfuls and form into cigar-shaped cylinders about 3-inches long and 1-inch in diameter. Heat oil or lard in a large, heavy frying pan and fry the corn sticks until golden brown all over. Drain on paper towels and keep warm until the mixture is used up. Serve warm as bread, or as an accompaniment to drinks. Makes about 24.

Sweet Cassava Bread

St. Kitts

2 cups finely grated
  cassava
1 teaspoon salt

1 cup freshly grated
  coconut
½ cup brown sugar

Mix the cassava and salt. Place in a damp kitchen towel or cloth, and wring out all the liquid. (The liquid can be used to make cassareep.) Spread half the cassava meal in the bottom of a small iron, or other heavy frying pan and pat down firmly. Cover with the coconut and the brown sugar. Add the rest of the cassava and pat down lightly. Bake in a 350° oven until lightly browned, about 20 minutes. Makes 6 servings.

Sweet Fungi

U.S. Virgin Islands

Corn Meal Pudding

4 cups water
Salt to taste
1 cup milk
2 tablespoons sugar
1 teaspoon vanilla, or
 ½ teaspoon ground
 cinnamon

1 cup seedless raisins,
 plumped in ½ cup
 hot water
2 cups yellow corn meal
2 tablespoons unsalted
 butter

Bring the water, salt, milk, sugar, vanilla or cinnamon and raisins to a boil. Pour in the cornmeal in a slow, steady stream and cook, stirring constantly with a wooden spoon over medium heat until the mixture is thick and smooth. Stir in the butter and turn out onto a warmed serving platter. Serves 6.

Sweet Potato Pone

U.S. Virgin Islands

2 pounds sweet potatoes
2 teaspoons brown sugar
4 tablespoons butter

⅓ cup orange juice
2 eggs, separated
½ cup dark rum
¼ teaspoon salt

Peel and slice the sweet potatoes and cook in water to cover until tender, about 20 minutes. Drain thoroughly and mash with the brown sugar and butter. Stir in the orange juice and the egg yolks, lightly beaten, and the rum. Beat the egg whites with the salt and fold into the sweet potato mixture, lightly but thoroughly. Pour into a 1-quart buttered soufflé dish, or pie dish and bake in a 350° oven until a cake tester comes out clean, about 30 minutes. Serves 6 to 8.

Sweet Potato and Coconut Bread

Barbados

1 pound white sweet
  potatoes
1 cup finely grated fresh
  coconut
2 tablespoons unsalted
  butter
1 teaspoon baking
  powder
½ teaspoon salt
¾ cup orange juice

¼ cup lime juice
2 eggs, well-beaten
¼ cup seedless raisins
¼ cup chopped
  crystallized ginger
¼ cup mixed fruits
  and peels (glacé cake
  mix)
¼ cup dark rum

Peel and grate the sweet potatoes. Mix with the coconut
in a large bowl. Soften the butter and beat in. Add the
allspice, baking powder and salt to the orange and lime
juice and add, stirring to mix thoroughly. Add the eggs,
raisins, ginger and mixed fruits and peels, again stirring
to mix thoroughly. Pour into a greased baking dish or loaf
pan and bake in a 350° oven for 1 hour, or until a cake
tester comes out clean. Pour the rum over the loaf while
it is still hot. Serve warm, as a pudding, from the baking
dish with whipped cream, or turn out of loaf pan, slice
and serve with butter as a sweet bread. Serves 6.

Tarta de Batata   *Dominican Republic*

Sweet Potato Tart

1½ cups coconut milk
  (see Index)
2 cups cooked, mashed
  sweet potato
½ teaspoon ground
  nutmeg
1 teaspoon ground
  cinnamon
2 tablespoons unsalted
  butter, melted and
  cooled

¼ cup superfine sugar
Grated rind 1 lime
4 eggs, lightly beaten
1 unbaked 9-inch pastry
  shell
1 teaspoon sugar
1 cup heavy cream
1 tablespoon light rum,
  such as Appleton
  Estate or Mount Gay

Mix the coconut milk and sweet potato thoroughly in a bowl with the nutmeg, cinnamon, butter, sugar and lime rind. Fold in the eggs. Pour the mixture into the pastry shell and bake in a 400° oven for 30 minutes or until set.

Add the sugar to the cream and beat until the cream is stiff. Add the rum, all at once, and beat for a minute or two longer. Transfer to a serving bowl. Serve the tart chilled, or at room temperature, accompanied by the bowl of cream. Serves 6.

Tarta de Ciruelas Pasas   *Dominican Republic*

Prune Tart

1 pound pitted prunes
¼ cup all-purpose
  flour
1 cup sugar
¼ teaspoon salt

½ teaspoon ground
  cinnamon
1 cup heavy cream
1 unbaked 9-inch pastry
  shell

Set aside 18 of the prunes. Finely chop the rest. Sift together the flour, sugar, salt and cinnamon. Stir in the cream. Add the chopped prunes and mix well. Turn into the unbaked pie shell. Decorate in a circle around the pie filling with the reserved whole prunes.

Bake in a 400° oven for 35 to 40 minutes, or until set. Serve with heavy cream, or whipped cream, if liked. Serves 6.

Tere Lomba's Budin de Pan   *Puerto Rico*
Tere Lomba's Bread Pudding

1-pound day old loaf sandwich bread	¼ teaspoon ground nutmeg
1 pint milk	8 tablespoons unsalted butter, melted
5 eggs, well beaten	¼ cup rum
1 cup sugar	1 pound Pasta de Guayaba (guava paste), cut into ¼-inch dice
1 teaspoon ground cinnamon	

Remove the crusts from the bread and cut it into cubes, place in a bowl and pour the milk over it. Allow to stand for 15 minutes. Stir in the eggs, sugar, cinnamon, nutmeg, butter and rum, mixing thoroughly. Fold in the guava dice. Pour the pudding into a caramelized 6-cup mold. Stand the mold in a baking pan containing 1-inch of water. Bake in a 350° oven for about 1 hour and 45 minutes, or until a cake tester comes out clean. Serves 6.

To caramelize the mold see Index for Flan de Coco (Coconut Custard).

Wilma's Sweet Cassava Bread   *St. Lucia*

2 cups cassava meal	1 cup grated coconut
¼ cup brown sugar	

Mix the cassava meal, sugar and coconut thoroughly. Grease a heavy, 10-inch skillet and when it is hot enough for a drop of cold water to sputter, add the cassava mixture, patting it down evenly. Cook over fairly brisk heat for about 1½ minutes, turn and cook other side, until lightly browned. This is pleasant by itself or with stewed fruit. Serves 2 to 4.

Drinks

Banana Daiquiri   *Cuba*

2 ounces light rum
½ ounce banana
  liqueur
½ ounce lime juice

½ small banana,
  peeled and coarsely
  chopped
½ cup crushed ice

Combine all the ingredients in an electric blender, and blend at high speed until smooth and frothy. Pour into a 6-ounce saucer champagne glass. Serves 1.

Batido de Piña   *Puerto Rico*
Fresh Pineapple Drink

4 ounces light rum
⅔ cup fresh pineapple,
  coarsely chopped

Superfine sugar to taste
½ cup finely crushed
  ice
Sprig fresh mint

Combine the rum and pineapple in an electric blender and blend on high speed until the pineapple is completely pulverized and the drink smooth. Taste, and blend in some sugar if necessary.

Put the ice into a goblet and pour in the liquor. Stir to mix. Decorate with the sprig of mint. Serves 1.

Blue Mountain Cocktail   *Jamaica*

1½ ounces light Jamaica rum	2 tablespoons orange juice
¾ ounce vodka	1 tablespoon lime juice
¾ ounce Tia Maria	3 or 4 ice cubes

Combine all the ingredients in a cocktail shaker and shake vigorously. Pour, unstrained, into an old-fashioned glass. Serves 1.

Cuban Cocktail   *Cuba*

2 ounces light rum	1 tablespoon lime juice
¾ ounce apricot brandy	3 or 4 ice cubes

Combine the ingredients in a cocktail shaker and shake vigorously. Strain into a cocktail glass, or pour, unstrained, into a small old-fashioned glass. Serves 1.

Cuban Special   *Cuba*

2 ounces light rum	1 tablespoon lime juice
1 teaspoon Curaçao	3 or 4 ice cubes
1 tablespoon pineapple juice	Stick pineapple
	Maraschino cherry

Combine the rum, Curaçao, pineapple and lime juices, and the ice cubes in a cocktail shaker and shake vigorously. Strain into a sour glass and decorate with the fruit, or pour, unstrained into a small old-fashioned glass and decorate with the fruit. Serves 1.

Curaçao Special

Curaçao

½ ounce light rum
½ ounce dark rum
½ ounce 151 proof rum
½ ounce sweet vermouth
½ ounce Curaçao
1 ounce orange juice
½ teaspoon lime juice
½ teaspoon Grenadine
½ cup finely crushed ice
1 tablespoon dry red wine
Slice of orange
Maraschino cherry

Combine the rums, vermouth, Curaçao, orange and lime juice and Grenadine in a mixing glass and stir to mix well. Put the ice into a goblet and pour the liquor over it. Stir. Carefully pour the red wine on top. Garnish with orange slice and cherry. Serves 1.

Ginger Beer

St. Kitts

This is a popular Christmas drink.

1 teaspoon active dry yeast
2 teaspoons all-purpose flour
2 ounces fresh ginger root, or use ground ginger
4 quarts boiling water
1½ pounds sugar
6 tablespoons lime juice
2 teaspoons grated lime rind
Slice toast

Mix the yeast and flour with ¼ cup lukewarm water, cover and leave in a warm place until it is bubbly. Peel the fresh ginger root and crush with the flat side of a cleaver. Put into a large crock and pour on the boiling water. Cool. Add the sugar, lime juice and rind, and stir to mix thoroughly. Spread the yeast on the slice of toast and add. Cover and stand in a warm place for 24 hours. Remove the toast. Strain, bottle and cork tightly. Wait 2 days before using. Serve in small tumblers, with or without ice cubes. Makes about 16 servings.

Ginger Beer   *Trinidad*

This drink is popular throughout the English-speaking islands, especially at Christmas time. The crystal clear ginger beer makes a pretty contrast to the pink of Sorrel Drink, also popular at Christmas.

1 ounce fresh ginger root, or use 1 tablespoon ground ginger	Peel 1 lime
	1 cup sugar
	4 cups boiling water
⅓ cup lime juice	1 teaspoon active dry yeast

Peel the ginger root and crush it lightly with the flat side of a cleaver. Combine the ginger, lime juice, peel, and sugar in a large bowl and pour the boiling water over them. Put the yeast into a small bowl with ¼ cup lukewarm water and let it stand for a few minutes, then stir to dissolve it completely. Let it stand in warm, draft-free place for about 5 minutes, or until it begins to bubble. Add it to the ginger mixture, and stir thoroughly. Cover the bowl and leave in a warm, draft-free place for a week, stirring every second day. Strain through a fine sieve, bottle, and let the beer stand at room temperature for 3 or 4 days longer. Chill, and serve, with or without ice in tumblers. A little rum may be added to the ginger beer, if liked. Makes 1 quart.

Daiquiri

Cuba

2 ounces light rum
2 tablespoons lime juice

1 teaspoon superfine
   sugar
3 or 4 ice cubes

Combine all the ingredients in a cocktail shaker, and shake vigorously. Strain into a thoroughly chilled 4-ounce cocktail glass. Serves 1.

El Jíbaro

Puerto Rico

1½ ounces orange
   juice
1½ ounces lemon juice
1½ ounces dark rum
2 or 3 cubes ice

1 ounce 151 proof rum
Dash of Grand Marnier
Lime slice
Mint leaves

Combine the orange and lemon juice, the dark rum and the ice cubes into a cocktail shaker and shake vigorously. Strain into a tumbler and add the 151 proof rum and Grand Marnier. Garnish with the lime slice and mint leaves. Serves 1.

Frozen Daiquiri

Cuba

3 ounces light rum
2 tablespoons lime juice

2 teaspoons superfine
   sugar
2 cups finely crushed ice

Place all the ingredients in an electric blender and blend on high speed until the contents have the consistency of snow. Serve immediately in a thoroughly chilled 6-ounce saucer champagne glass, with short drinking straws. Serves 1.

Hartley Augiste's Rum Punch   *Dominica*

*Dominica produces some glorious rum. The tiny moun-
tainous island lying between Martinique and Guadeloupe
also produces glorious limes, and is in fact the home of
Rose's lime juice. The combination of rum and lime produces the best rum punch I have ever had.*

2 ounces Dominica rum, or use a light rum from Martinique or Guadeloupe	3 teaspoons simple syrup
	2 or 3 dashes Angostura bitters
½ ounce lime juice	3 or 4 ice cubes
	Maraschino cherry

Combine the rum, lime juice, simple syrup, bitters and
ice in a cocktail shaker and shake vigorously. Strain over
ice cubes in a small tumbler. Serves 1.

Hot Buttered Rum   *Jamaica*

Cinnamon stick	6 ounces boiling cider, or apple juice
2 ounces light Jamaica rum	Nutmeg
1 square (½ teaspoon) sweet butter	

Put the cinnamon stick into an 8-ounce mug. Add the rum
and butter and pour on the hot cider. Stir and grate a little
nutmeg on top. Serves 1.

Kibra Hacha   *Curaçao*

*This drink is named after the tree which grows in Curaçao.
All the branches lean to one side. The significance of the
name applied to the drink escapes me.*

1½ ounces light rum	2 dashes Angostura
½ ounce Curaçao	bitters
1 teaspoon lime juice	3 or 4 ice cubes

Combine the rum, Curaçao, lime juice, and bitters in a mixing glass and stir well. Pour over the ice cubes in an old-fashioned glass. Serves 1.

Leo Byam's Cream Punch   *Trinidad*

Creole Eggnog

A friend, Leo Byam, gave me this excellent recipe for the traditional holiday eggnog. It is supposed to keep, if refrigerated, but I have never found that anyone gave it a chance.

6 medium eggs	1 teaspoon vanilla
2 8-ounce cans sweetened	Dash Angostura bitters
condensed milk	1 pint Trinidad rum, or
Grated peel 1 lime, or	more to taste
lemon	

Beat the eggs slightly in a large bowl. Add all the other ingredients, except the rum, and mix well. Add the rum, mixing thoroughly. Serve over crushed ice in punch cups. Makes 6 to 12 servings.

Mangoade   *Jamaica*

2 cups coarsely chopped	1 teaspoon grated orange
ripe mango	rind
¼ cup sugar, or to	2 cups orange juice
taste	½ cup lime juice
2 cups water	

Rub the mango through a sieve. Combine the sugar, water and orange rind in a saucepan and heat, stirring, until the sugar has dissolved. Cool and add to the mango purée and fruit juices. Refrigerate. Serve in tall glasses over ice cubes. Serves 6.

Mango Daiquiri   *Cuba*

4 ounces light rum	2 tablespoons lime juice
1 ounce Curaçao	1 tablespoon superfine
½ cup finely chopped	sugar
fresh mango	2 cups finely crushed ice

Place all the ingredients in an electric blender and blend at high speed until the contents have the consistency of snow. Pour into 2 thoroughly chilled 6-ounce champagne glasses and serve with short drinking straws. Serves 2.

Mauby   *St. Vincent*

So far as I have been able to find out mauby bark, some-times mawby, in Spanish maubí, is the bark of the algar-roba (carob) tree. It can be found in Puerto Rican or tropical markets. The drink made with the bark is popular as a refreshing soft drink in most of the islands.

3 ounces mauby bark	6 cloves
12 cups water	1-inch piece dried orange
4-inch piece stick	peel
cinnamon	4 cups brown sugar

Put the mauby bark into a saucepan with 2 cups of the water, the cinnamon, cloves, and orange peel and boil for about 20 minutes, or until the liquid is strongly flavored and bitter. Strain. Add the rest of the water and the sugar and stir to dissolve the sugar. Bottle, leaving the neck of the bottle empty so there will be space for fermentation. Seal the bottles and leave for 3 to 4 days. Strain and chill thoroughly before serving in tumblers. Makes about 4 quarts.

Noël's Planter's Punch from Mandeville

Jamaica

1½ ounces dark
  Jamaican rum
¾ ounce lime juice

3 ounces orange juice
½ cup crushed ice
Maraschino cherry

Combine all the ingredients in a cocktail shaker and shake vigorously. Strain into a tumbler and garnish with the cherry. Serves 1.

Peach Daiquiri

Cuba

2 ounces light rum
½ medium-sized ripe
  fresh peach, peeled and
  coarsely chopped

1 tablespoon superfine
  sugar
1 cup finely crushed ice

Combine all the ingredients in an electric blender and blend at high speed for about 30 seconds. Pour into a thoroughly chilled 6-ounce champagne glass and serve with short drinking straws. Serves 1.

Peanut Punch

Trinidad

2 tablespoons cornstarch
½ cup water
2 cups milk

6 tablespoons peanut
  butter
Sugar to taste

Mix the cornstarch and water in a small saucepan. Add the milk, peanut butter and sugar, to taste. Cook, stirring with a whisk, over moderate heat until thickened and thoroughly mixed. Cool and refrigerate. Serve in tumblers, with or without ice. Serves 2.

Though this is traditionally served as a soft drink, many Trinidadians find it improved, as indeed I do, by the addi-

tion of a good Trinidadian or similar rum. Add 4 ounces
(½ cup) rum to the above recipe and serve in tumblers
with ice cubes.

Pineapple Daiquiri   *Cuba*

2 ounces light rum   1 tablespoon lime juice
½ ounce Cointreau   Superfine sugar
½ cup pineapple juice   Ice cubes

Combine the rum, Cointreau, pineapple and lime juice in
an electric blender and blend quickly at high speed. Taste
and blend in a little superfine sugar, if necessary. Fill an
8- to 10-ounce old-fashioned glass with ice cubes and pour
in the Daiquiri. Serves 1.

Planter's Punch   *All Islands*

1½ ounces light rum   1 teaspoon lime juice
1½ ounces orange   4 ice cubes
  juice

Combine the rum, orange juice and lime juice in a cocktail
shaker with 3 of the ice cubes and shake vigorously. Place
the remaining ice cube in a sour glass and strain the punch
over it. Stir and serve. Serves 1.

Planter's Punch   *Jamaica*

2 tablespoons lime juice   Dash Angostura bitters
2 tablespoons simple   ½ cup finely crushed
  syrup   ice
3 ounces dark Jamaica   Maraschino cherry
  rum

Combine the lime juice, syrup, rum, bitters and crushed ice in a cocktail shaker and shake vigorously. Pour, unstrained, into a small tumbler. Decorate with the cherry. Serves 1.

Planter's Punch

Puerto Rico

2 tablespoons fresh lime
  juice
2 teaspoons superfine
  sugar
1½ ounces dark
  Puerto Rican rum
½ teaspoon Angostura
  bitters

½ cup crushed ice
Ice cubes
Carbonated water
1 to 2 tablespoons 151
  proof rum
Pineapple stick, slice of
  orange, maraschino
  cherry

Combine the lime juice, sugar, rum, bitters and crushed ice in a cocktail shaker and shake vigorously. Pour, unstrained, into a 10-ounce highball glass. Add ice cubes or a little carbonated water to taste. Invert a teaspoon in the glass and carefully pour in the 151 proof rum so that it floats on top of the drink. Garnish with the pineapple stick, slice of orange and cherry. Serves 1.

Piña Colada

Puerto Rico

4 ounces pineapple juice
2 ounces coconut cream
2 ounces golden rum

½ cup crushed ice
Pineapple stick
Maraschino cherry

Place all the ingredients, except the pineapple stick and cherry, in an electric blender, and blend for a few seconds. Pour, unstrained, into a highball glass and decorate with the pineapple stick and cherry. Serves 1.

Pineappleade   *St. Kitts*

1 medium-sized pineapple	2 cups sugar
½ cup lime juice	8 cups water

Peel the pineapple and grate fruit finely. Place in a bowl and pour the lime juice over it. Boil the sugar with 2 cups of the water for 5 minutes then pour over the fruit. Add the remaining 6 cups water, and stir to mix well. Let it stand for 1 hour. Strain, pressing the fruit down into the sieve to extract all the juice. Serve in tumblers with crushed ice, or add 1½ to 2 ounces rum to each serving. Makes about 2 quarts.

Punch au Lait de Coco   *Martinique*
Rum and Coconut Milk Punch

1½ ounces white rum, preferably Martinique *rhum blanc*	⅛ teaspoon vanilla
	4 ounces coconut milk
½ ounce jus de canne (cane syrup) (see Glossary)	½ cup finely crushed ice
	Nutmeg

Combine the rum, cane syrup, vanilla, coconut milk and ice in a cocktail shaker and shake vigorously. Pour, unstrained, into an 8-ounce goblet. Grate a little nutmeg on top. Serves 1.

If liked, the drink may be strained. Sweetened coconut milk, sold canned, may be used for this drink, in which case, omit the cane syrup.

Punch Blanc

Martinique-Guadeloupe

White Punch

This apéritif, perhaps the most popular in Martinique and Guadeloupe, is also known as Punch au Petit Citron Vert (Punch with Small Green Lime), usually shortened to Petit Punch, Little Punch. It is made with the local rhum agricole, a very gentle white rum, and jus de canne—pure cane syrup, which is now available from the islands, sometimes labelled cane juice, in a number of tropical markets, otherwise simple syrup is the best substitute, though it lacks the special flavor.

½ ounce cane syrup　　　　1 or 2 ice cubes
1½ ounces white rum　　　　Water
Small piece green lime
　peel

Pour the cane syrup and rum into a small glass, twist the peel to release the oil and drop it in, add an ice cube or two and water to taste. Stir gently. Serves 1.
　A more traditional way to drink the Petit Punch is to mix the syrup and rum together with the peel, but without ice, and drink this neat, followed by a glass of iced water.

Punch Vieux

Martinique-Guadeloupe

Old Punch

This is made with the smooth, dark, aged rum known as vieux (old, aged).

½ ounce cane syrup　　　　2 or 3 ice cubes
1½ ounces *rhum vieux*　　　Water

Pour the cane syrup and rum into a small glass, add an ice cube or two and water to taste. Stir gently. Serves 1.

Traditionally ice is seldom served with a vieux, however a newer fashion is to serve the drink in an old-fashioned glass over 3 or 4 ice cubes, with or without the jus de canne (cane syrup).

Refresco de Coco y Piña *Dominican Republic*

Coconut and Pineapple Drink

2 cups coconut milk (see Index)
2½ cups coarsely chopped pineapple

2 tablespoons superfine sugar
1 drop almond extract

Combine the coconut milk, pineapple, sugar and almond extract in an electric blender and blend at high speed until the mixture is very smooth and the pineapple completely pulverized.

Strain through a fine sieve, pour into a jug and refrigerate until thoroughly chilled. Serve in tumblers with or without ice cubes according to taste. Serves 3 to 4.

This may be served with the addition of 1½ ounces of light rum per serving, over 2 or 3 ice cubes, in an old-fashioned glass. Serves 6.

Refresco de Lechosa *Dominican Republic*

Milk and Papaya Drink

1 small ripe papaya, weighing about 12 ounces
½ cup coconut milk, or milk (see Index)
3 tablespoons lime juice

½ teaspoon grated lime rind
¼ cup superfine sugar
1 teaspoon vanilla
½ cup finely crushed ice
Lime slices for garnish

Peel the papaya, cut in half and remove the black seeds, and chop fruit coarsely. Combine the papaya, coconut milk, lime juice and rind, sugar, vanilla and ice in an electric blender and blend at high speed until the mixture is smooth and thick. Serve in chilled tumblers, garnished with lime slices. Serves 3 to 4.

Rum Cocktail   *English-speaking Islands*

2 ounces light or dark
   rum, according to taste
2 ounces milk
½ cup finely crushed
   ice
2 dashes Angostura
   bitters

1 teaspoon superfine
   sugar, if liked
Nutmeg or ground
   cinnamon

Combine the rum, milk, crushed ice, Angostura bitters and sugar in a mixing glass and swizzle to a foam. Pour into a sour, or small old-fashioned glass, or large cocktail glass, and grate a little fresh nutmeg on top, or sprinkle with cinnamon. Serves 1.

Rum Flip   *English-speaking Islands*

4 ounces light Jamaican,
   Trinidadian, or Bajan
   rum
1 egg, lightly beaten
1 teaspoon superfine
   sugar

2 dashes Angostura
   bitters
½ cup finely crushed
   ice
Nutmeg

Combine the rum, egg, sugar, bitters and ice in a cocktail shaker and shake vigorously. Pour, unstrained, into a small tumbler. Sprinkle with a little grated nutmeg. Serves 1.

Rum Float   *English-speaking Islands*

1 ounce simple syrup (see
   Index)
1 ounce ice water
2 ounces light or dark
   rum, according to taste

Dash Angostura bitters
Pinch cinnamon
Small piece lime rind

Pour the simple syrup and ice water into a 4-ounce old-
fashioned glass. Stir to mix. Float the rum on top by tilting
the glass a little and trickling the rum down the side.
Trickle the bitters down the side in the same way. Sprinkle
the surface with the cinnamon and gently lay the lime rind
on top. Serves 1.

Rum Neat   *English-speaking Islands*

*This is regarded as a splendid pick-up after a day's hard
work.*

2 to 3 ounces good, full-
   bodied island rum

Cold water

Pour the rum into a cocktail glass and sip slowly. Then
drink the same amount of cold water. Serves 1.

Rum Punch   *Antigua*

This is one of my favorite rum punches.

1 ounce lime juice
1 ounce orange juice
1 ounce pineapple juice
1 ounce Grenadine

2 ounces light rum,
   preferably local, or
   from Barbados or
   Trinidad
3 or 4 ice cubes
Nutmeg

Combine the juices, Grenadine, rum and ice cubes in a cocktail shaker and shake vigorously. Strain into a small tumbler and grate a little nutmeg on the top. Serves 1.

Rum Punch
Barbados

This punch follows a very old formula that is still popular both in the island and in England. It is charming in its simplicity and leaves the choice of rum, light or dark, up to the drinker.

One of sour—1 ounce
   lime juice
Two of sweet—2 ounces
   simple syrup (see
   Index)

Three of strong—3
   ounces rum, preferably
   Bajan rum
Four of weak—4 ounces
   water

Pour all the ingredients into a mixing glass and stir well. Chill, pour into a tumbler and serve with a dash of Angostura bitters and a grating of nutmeg. If liked, garnish with a sprig of mint, or a lime leaf. Serves 1.

Rum Sour
Jamaica

1½ ounces light
   Jamaica rum
¾ ounce lime juice
1 teaspoon sugar, or to
   taste

1 cup crushed ice
Slice of orange

Combine the rum, lime juice, sugar and ice in a cocktail shaker and shake vigorously. Strain into a sour glass and decorate with the slice of orange. Serves 1.

Shrub   *Martinique-Guadeloupe*

4 Seville (bitter) oranges   1 quart rhum vieux from
4 ounces (½ cup)   Martinique or
   granulated sugar   Guadeloupe, or use
¼ cup water   any dark rum

Using a vegetable peeler, peel the skins off the oranges
as thinly as possible. Boil the sugar with the water until
the sugar is dissolved. Pour out a little of the rum to make
room for the syrup and orange peel. Add the syrup and
peel to the rum bottle, re-cork and leave for 2 weeks.
   Strain and rebottle. Serve as a liqueur.

Simple Syrup

*Sugar does not dissolve readily in alcohol, and for this
reason superfine sugar is specified in drinks. Simple syrup
gives a much smoother drink and is very easy to make.*

2 cups granulated sugar   2 cups cold water

Combine the sugar and water in a bowl. Stir from time
to time until the sugar is dissolved. Use in drinks instead
of sugar ½ ounce (1 tablespoon) simple syrup equals 1½
teaspoons sugar.

Sorrel Cocktail   *Trinidad*

2 or 3 ice cubes   3 ounces sorrel drink (see
1½ ounces light   Index)
   Trinidad rum   Squeeze lime juice

Put the ice cubes into an old-fashioned glass. Add the rum
and sorrel drink. Add a squeeze of lime juice and stir.
Serves 1.

Sorrel Drink

Trinidad

This is made from the sepals of an annual plant called rosella or sorrel (see Glossary). Traditionally a Christmas drink in Trinidad, when the sorrel sepals are at their best, the drink can also be made with dried sorrel.

1 ounce dried sorrel
  sepals
3-inch piece stick
  cinnamon
Piece dried orange peel,
  about 3-by-1-inch
6 cloves
2 cups sugar
2 quarts boiling water

½ cup medium dark
  rum, preferably
  Trinidad rum, or use
  Appleton Estates or
  Mount Gay
1 teaspoon ground
  cinnamon (optional)
¼ teaspoon ground
  cloves (optional)

Put the sorrel, cinnamon, orange peel, cloves and sugar into a large jar or crock and pour the boiling water over them. Cool, cover loosely, and leave for 2 or 3 days at room temperature. Strain, add the rum, cinnamon and cloves and leave for another 2 days. Strain through a fine sieve lined with cheesecloth and serve in chilled glasses, with or without ice cubes. If preferred, the drink may be used after the first 2 or 3 days. Simply strain and add the rum, or not, as liked. Makes about 2 quarts.

Spanish Town

Jamaica

2 ounces light Jamaica
  rum
1 teaspoon Curaçao

½ cup finely crushed
  ice
Nutmeg

Combine the rum, Curaçao and ice in a cocktail shaker and shake vigorously. Pour, unstrained, into a small old-fashioned glass and grate a little nutmeg on top. Serves 1.

Stuyvesant Cooler

Curaçao

½ cup crushed ice
1½ ounces light rum
1½ ounces Curaçao

2 tablespoons lime juice
Slice orange
Maraschino cherry

Put the crushed ice into a goblet. Pour in the rum, Curaçao and lime juice. Stir to mix. Decorate with the orange slice and cherry. Serves 1.

Tamarinade

Jamaica

6 whole tamarinds,
  shelled

2 cups water
¼ cup sugar

Soak the tamarinds in the water for 30 minutes. Add the sugar stir to dissolve and let stand 5 minutes longer. Strain and chill thoroughly. Serve over ice cubes in small tumblers. Serves 2.

Glossary

Ackee, akee or ***achee*** is the fruit of a West African tree, Blighia sapida, named in honor of Captain Bligh who introduced it to Jamaica. A handsome evergreen, it bears a fruit whose scarlet shell and shiny black seeds alone would make the tree worth cultivating for its decorative aspect. The edible part, sometimes called Vegetable Brains, is the aril, which looks like a small brain, or scrambled eggs, according to the eye of the viewer. It had a delicate flavor and is best known in the Jamaican dish Saltfish and Ackee. Canned ackees from Jamaica are quite widely available in Latin American markets and specialty food shops.

Akkra, originally a West African fritter made from black-eyed peas (they are the Samsa of Upper Volta), are called Calas in the Dutch Islands, and are popular in Jamaica, as akkra where soy beans are also used. The name, changed to Accra, is also used for fritters made of a heavy batter into which other ingredients are mixed, the most popular being salt cod. These are called Stamp and Go in Jamaica, acrats de morue in Martinique and Guadeloupe and bacalaitos in Puerto Rico. In Haïti the name changes to marinades. The recipes differ sufficiently from island to island to make necessary the inclusion here of a wide selection.

Allspice, pimento, Jamaica pepper, the poivre de la Jam-
aïque, or toute-épice of the French islands, the pimienta
de Jamaica or pimienta gorda of the Spanish-speaking
islands, is the dark-brown berry of an evergreen tree,
which the Spaniards found growing all over Jamaica when
they first arrived in the Caribbean. When dried, the berries, which closely resemble peppercorns, have the combined flavor of nutmeg, cinnamon and clove. The Spaniards
were no botanists and seem to have called everything
pimienta, or pepper. The allspice tree is a bay, belonging
to the myrtle family. Allspice is available wherever spices
are sold.

Annatto, or *annotto,* are the seeds of a small, flowering
tree of tropical America, Bixa orellana. The Spanish name
achiote is sometimes corrupted to achote. The seeds are
also known as bija or bijol in some of the Spanish-speaking
islands. In the French and Dutch islands they are called
roucou. In the West Indies the orange pulp surrounding
the seed is used to color and flavor food, usually in the
form of Aceite or Manteca de Achiote (Annatto Oil or
Lard), see Index. In Latin America, especially in South-
eastern Mexico and Guatemala, the whole seed is ground
and used as a spice. Available in Latin American and some
Oriental markets.

Arrowroot, mostly imported from St. Vincent, is a white
starchy powder made from the underground rhizome of
the Maranta arundinacea. It is very popular as a thickening agent in Caribbean sauces and gravies to which it
gives a light and delicate quality. It is also used in desserts
and in the making of cakes and biscuits. It is widely available.

Avocado, Persea americana, first cultivated in Mexico as
far back as 7000 B.C. but now grown in most tropical and
semitropical countries. They are usually marketed unripe,
when they are hard to the touch, and should be kept until
the flesh yields when a gentle pressure is applied.

Banana and *Banana Leaves*. Bananas both green and ripe are used a great deal in West Indian cooking. They are used in appetizers, as a starchy vegetable when green, and in desserts. When plantains are not available, bananas make a good substitute. Banana leaves which can be 10-feet long and 2-feet wide, are used for wrapping such foods as conkies from Barbados and pasteles from Puerto Rico. Kitchen parchment and aluminum foil make adequate substitutes but do not add the delicate flavor that banana leaves give. They are sometimes available in specialty food shops.

Banana Pesé pressed plantain. See *Tostones de Plátano*.

Bay rum, Pimenta acris, is an evergreen tree native to West Africa and closely related to the West Indian, principally Jamaican, tree which produces allspice, and the West African tree which produces melegueta pepper. All these grow in the West Indies and some confusion arises between bay rum berries and leaves, known in the French islands as Bois d'Inde, and melegueta pepper known also as Guinea pepper or Grains of Paradise. Bay rum berries and melegueta peppercorns can be used interchangeably. There is no substitute.

Beans. English-speaking islanders use the terms peas and beans interchangeably, as do all English-speaking communities. However, their usage differs slightly from most others. Kidney beans in Jamaica are called peas. In Trinidad pigeon peas are often simply referred to as peas, in the way we use the term peas to mean green peas. The French islands use the term *pois*, peas, for the beans, such as kidney beans, that originate in Mexico. Cuba follows Mexican usage and calls its chuelas, while in the Dominican Republic both terms are used, though habichuelas occurs more frequently than frijoles. The only types of bean not available in ordinary groceries are the Pois de Bois of Guadeloupe, called Pois d'Angole in Martinique, which closely resemble pigeon peas.

Bitter or *Seville, orange,* also called sour and bigarade orange. It is not cultivated commercially in the United States but is grown extensively in Spain and throughout the West Indies. It is large, with a rough reddish-orange skin. The pulp is too acid to be eaten raw. The juice is used a great deal in meat and poultry dishes in the Caribbean, particularly in the Spanish-speaking islands. The oranges are also used to make marmalade, and can sometimes be found in specialty fruit shops. More frequently they can be found in Caribbean markets. The juice freezes successfully. A mixture of lime or lemon, and sweet orange juice can be used as a substitute but lacks the distinctive and pleasant flavor of the bitter orange.

Breadfruit are large green fruits, usually about 10-inches round, which hang lantern-like from handsome trees, Artocarpus communis, with large, dark-green, deeply indented leaves. Cultivated since time immemorial in the south Pacific, the trees were introduced to the West Indies by Captain Bligh in 1792. Breadfruit are increasingly available in markets selling tropical produce. However, canned breadfruit, available in specialty food shops, makes an excellent substitute. Breadfruit are not edible until cooked, when the flesh, yellowish-white, is a little like a rather dense potato. It can be used in place of any starchy vegetable, rice, or pasta, to accompany a main dish. It makes a fine soup.

Calabaza, or West Indian or Green pumpkin, is a squash, available in markets specializing in West Indian produce. The pumpkins, not to be confused with American pie pumpkin, come in a variety of sizes and shapes, usually large, and are generally not sold whole, but by the wedge. The yellow flesh has a delicate flavor and is used mainly in soups and as a vegetable. The best substitutes are Hubbard or butternut squash.

Callaloo, also spelled *calaloo, callilu, calalou and callau,* is the principal ingredient in, and the name of, what is probably, them most famous of all the island soups. The term applies to the leaves of two distinct types of plant which are used interchangeably. The first are the elephant-ear leaves of the diverse group of tropical plants with edible tubers classified as taro, but known in the Caribbean under a wide variety of names (see Taro). The other is Chinese spinach, Amaranthus gangeticus, sometimes sold as yin-choi or hon-toi-moi in Chinese markets, and as hiyu in Japanese markets. It is widely cultivated in India and Ceylon where it is known as bhaji, so that one finds it called both bhaji and callalo in many West Indian markets, especially in Jamaica and Trinidad, where there is a sizable Indian population.

Cane syrup. This is pure cane juice and is sold in Caribbean markets and sometimes in health food and specialty food shops. It is sometimes labelled cane juice. In the French islands, where it is used a great deal in rum drinks, it is called jus de canne. When it is not available use simple syrup (see Index).

Cassareep is the boiled down juice squeezed from grated cassava root, and when flavored with cinnamon, cloves and brown sugar is the essential ingredient in Pepperpot, an Amerindian stew originating in Guyana and popular in Trinidad, Barbados and other islands. Cassareep may be bought bottled in West Indian markets.

Cassava. Manihot utilissima, also called manioc, mandioca, yucca or yuca, is a tropical vegetable with a long tuberous root at least 2-inches in diameter and from 8- to 10-inches long. It is covered with a brown bark-like rather hairy skin, and the flesh is white and very hard. It can be cooked and eaten as a starchy vegetable. Cassava meal or flour for making bread or cakes, is obtained by washing, peeling and grating cassava, pressing out the juice, and drying the meal. It can be bought ready made as cassava or manioc meal. Tapioca and cassareep are both made from cassava. There are two varieties of the plant, bitter and sweet. Bitter cassava is poisonous until cooked.

It is used commercially, but is not sold in US markets. In the French island cassava meal is often called farine, a shortened form of farine de manioc.

*Chayote, cho-cho,*and *christophene*, are the Spanish, English and French names for a tropical squash, Sechium edule, originally from Mexico, but now widely grown in tropical regions throughout the world. The skin is rather prickly and there is a single, edible seed. The taste is rather like summer squash, but the texture is finer and quite crisp.

Chicharrones are fried pork cracklings and are available packaged in Latin American and Caribbean markets.

Chive, Allium schoenoprasum, the smallest and mildest of the onion family, is much used in island cooking, especially islands where the French have been. Known in English as chive, cive or sometimes simply herb, in French as ciboulette and oignon pays and in Spanish as cebollino, the chives of the West Indies are more fully flavored than ours, and may be a different species. Long established chives grown outdoors seem to acquire a flavor closer to that of the Caribbean herb. Scallions, using both white and green parts, also approximate the flavor.

Chorizo, a Spanish sausage used in the Spanish-speaking islands. Lightly smoked, and made from coarsely chopped pork, seasoned with hot peppers and garlic. It is available in links, or canned, in Latin American groceries.

Conch is a large Antillean marine mollusk of the gastropod class, 9-inches to a foot long, with a heavy spiral shell yellow shading to pink inside. The flesh is usually tenderized by pounding, before the mollusk is cooked. It is widely used in island cooking, in soups, stews and salads. The Carib name is lambi or lambie, and is used in many islands, both French and English. The Spanish name is concha, and the French conque. The English conch is pronounced conk as in the French.

Coriander. Coriandrum sativum, or Chinese parsley, also known as culantro, culantrillo, cilantro (Spanish), coriandre (French), yuen-sai (Chinese), and koyendoro (Japanese), is an annual herb originally from the Mediterranean area but now cultivated throughout the world. The green leaves, which rather resemble parsley, are used a great deal in the cooking of the Spanish-speaking islands. The seeds which can be bought packaged from supermarket spice shelves, are widely used in curries. Fresh coriander, available in Chinese and Latin American markets, is sold with its roots on. These should not be removed, and the plants should not be washed before storing. They should be wrapped in paper towels and placed in the refrigerator in a plastic bag, or put into a glass jar with cover. They should be washed and soaked for a few minutes in cold water just before using.

Court-bouillon. In the French islands this term is used to describe a fish poached in a special manner, and does not mean the classic poaching liquid of French cookery.

Crapaud is the French word used to describe the very large frogs found on the islands of Dominica and Montserrat. They are also known as mountain chicken.

Crayfish, crawfish, is the sea crayfish, or spiny or rock lobster, of the islands, which has meat in the tail and lacks the large claws of the lobster. It is often called lobster in the English-speaking islands and is langosta in Spanish, langouste in French.

Créole, criolla, are terms not easy to define. Créole and criolla dishes are the culinary result of the meeting of the techniques and raw materials of France and Spain, Africa and America, in the kitchen. Créole applies to the cuisines of Louisiana and the Gulf States, as well as to the French-speaking West Indies, while criolla applies to the Spanish-speaking West Indies and all of Latin America.

Curaçao is an orange liqueur made in the Dutch island of Curaçao from the peel of the bitter oranges that grow there.

Dal is the Hindi name for all the legumes. In Trinidad, however, dal, sometimes spelled dahl, usually means split peas. Gram, or channa, dal is chick pea.

Eggplant is also called garden egg, or melongene, in some of the English-speaking islands. It is known in the Spanish-speaking islands as berenjena, and in the French-speaking islands as aubergine and bélangère, the latter being a very large variety.

Escabeche is the Spanish for pickled, and is used to describe a method of cooking fish, poultry and game in which the food is cooked in oil and vinegar, or cooked and then pickled in an oil and vinegar marinade. In Jamaica escabeche has been transformed into escovitch and caveached fish.

Ginger root in its fresh form is popular in West Indian cookery. The root, usually about 3-inches long, is gnarled with a brown skin and moist, yellow flesh. Placed in a plastic bag, it will keep, refrigerated, for several weeks. It may be peeled and put in a jar of sherry, or salted water. It is available in oriental markets and specialty food shops. Ground ginger may be used as a substitute, though the flavor is less pungent.

Guava is the fruit of an evergreen tree native to tropical America. Guavas are usually about 5 or 6-inches in diameter with pale yellow skins and pink or white flesh. They may be eaten raw, but are also made into a paste, into jams and jellies, and are stewed. Cooked and with the seeds removed, the shells are sold canned.

Hearts of Palm are the tender hearts of palm trees, sold canned in slightly salted water. They are used fresh in the islands in salads and as a vegetable. The canned product is an excellent substitute. Called palmito in the Spanish-speaking islands, it is known in the French islands as chou palmiste, chou coco, and chou glouglou, according to the type of palm from which it comes.

Keshy Yena is a baked Edam or Gouda cheese with a variety of fillings. It originates in Curaçao and the name, which derives from the Spanish queso (cheese) and relleno (stuffed) is in Papiamento, the patois of the Netherlands Antilles that is a mixture of Portuguese, Spanish, Dutch, English and African words. Curiously enough the dish has been adopted by Chiapas and Yucatán in Mexico, where it was probably introduced some time in the last century by Dutch and German coffee men. It is called queso relleno there.

Mango, fruit of an evergreen tree native to Asia, but now cultivated in tropical and semitropical regions throughout the world. All mangoes are green when unripe, and vary in color when ripe from green-skinned to a deep rose red. The flesh varies from a light yellow to a deep orange yellow. Mangoes are ripe when the flesh yields to gentle pressure. They range in weight from about 10 ounces to about 4 pounds. They are used a great deal in island cooking, the hard, unripe mango for chutney and relishes, while ripe mangoes may be eaten by themselves, or made into jam, pies, ice cream and drinks.

Melegueta pepper or *Guinea pepper*, also known as *Grains of Paradise* are the small brown berries of the West African tree, Amomum melegueta.

Mountain chicken. See *Crapaud*.

Okra, which was introduced into the islands from Africa, though it is of tropical Asian origin, has a great many names. In English it may be okra, or ochro, ladyfingers, or bamie. In the Spanish-speaking islands variants stem from the standard Spanish, quimbombó. In Cuba and Puerto Rico, it is quingombó, and in the Dominican

Republic is it quimbombó or molondron. In the French-speaking islands it is gombo.

Papaya, Carica papaya, is the fruit of a woody, herbaceous plant that looks like a tree and is native to tropical America. It is hard and green when unripe, but changes to yellow or orange when ripe, and the fruit varies greatly in sizes from 6-inches to well over 1-foot. The immature fruit is used as a vegetable in island cooking. It tastes a little like summer squash. Green papaya is also used to make a chutney or relish, and makes a main dish when stuffed. Ripe, it is eaten as a melon, or in fruit salad. It is known as pawpaw in the English-speaking islands, as papaya in most Spanish-speaking islands, with the exception of Cuba where it is called fruta bomba and the Dominican Republic where it is called lechosa. In the French islands it is papaye.

Peppers. All peppers, both hot and sweet, originated in Mexico but have spread so widely all over the world that they are an accepted part of all kitchens. In the islands one finds the usual sweet green or red (ripe) bell peppers and the red pimiento. Any sweet pepper may be used in place of these. The hot peppers of the Caribbean have a very distinctive and splendid flavor, and are sometimes available crushed and bottled in vinegar. They are worth searching for in tropical markets. There is an island hot-pepper sauce from Jamaica, Pickapeppa Hot-Pepper Sauce, that is widely available. If found fresh they may be used to make Pepper Wine or Pepper Vinegar, preserving their distinctive flavor. Otherwise, any hot pepper may be used, fresh, canned or bottled.

Pigeon Peas are of African origin and are popular in West Indian cooking, both dried and fresh. They have a number of names: in Jamaica they are known as gungo, gunga or goongoo peas, while Trinidad recognizes them as pigeon peas, gungo peas and arhar dahl. The Spanish-speaking islands call them gandules. They are available in most groceries in the dried form, in Latin American and Caribbean markets canned, and fresh in many tropical markets.

Plantain, plátano Spanish, *banane* French, is a large member of the banana family, and must be cooked before eating. It is widely used in West Indian cooking both green, ripe, and semiripe, as an appetizer, in soups, as a starchy vegetable, and as a dessert.

Rosella, Hibiscus sabdariffa, a tropical plant grown for its fleshy red sepals which are used to make drinks, jam and jelly. It is available in the islands, fresh at Christmas time, but all year round in its dried form. It may be bought dried in tropical markets. It is also known as sorrel, and flor de Jamaica.

Salt codfish is very popular in all the islands. In the English-speaking islands it is usually called simply saltfish, and sometimes fish other than cod are used. In the Spanish-speaking islands it is bacalao, and in French morue.

Seville oranges, see *Bitter* or *Seville oranges*.

Shrob, shrub, is a liqueur made in the French islands, from rum and the peel of bitter oranges.

Sofrito is a basic tomato sauce originally used in Spanish cooking. It is derived from the Spanish verb sofreir which means to fry lightly. The Puerto Rican version differs quite considerably from the Spanish and is essential to the cooking of the island. It is also used on other Spanish-speaking islands. It can be made in quantity and stored in the refrigerator where it will keep for some weeks. See Index for recipe.

Soursop is the spiny dark green fruit of a tropical American tree, Annona muricata. The edible pulp is tart and delicately flavored. It is used mainly for drinks, ices and sherbets. It is guanábana in Spanish and corossol in

French. The frozen pulp is sometimes available in Latin American markets.

Sweet potato, Ipomoea batata, is originally from tropical America though its exact birth place is not known. Skin color is reddish brown, pink or white, and the flesh ranges from deep orange through yellow to white. Some confusion arises about sweet potatoes since the most widely available type in the U.S., with moist orange-yellow flesh and reddish brown skin, is also known as a Louisiana yam. Yams, however, are from an entirely different botanical group, the Dioscoreas. Two other sweet potatoes are available, both far less sweet than the Louisiana yam. One has fairly dry mealy flesh which is yellowish in color. The boniato, which is brown or pink skinned with white flesh, is only very slightly sweet. This is the preferred sweet potato of the islands.

Tamarind, Tamarindus indica, a large tropical tree whose seed pods contain a brown acid pulp, used principally in curries. The pulp may be bought in special food shops, especially those selling Indian foods.

Taro. Great confusion reigns among this group of tropical root vegetables, but if one bears in mind that, shape and name apart, they all taste much the same, the confusion clears up. Taro belongs to the arum family and is known in Jamaica, Barbados, and Trinidad as coco, eddo and baddo, the leaves being called callaloo. A closely related group, the malangas, cultivated in many of the islands, are found in markets as malaga, dasheen, tanier, tannia, and yautía. Their leaves are also known as callaloo. The roots which come in a wide range of sizes have rather rough brown skin and flesh which ranges from white to yellowish to gray-white and purplish. Any recipe for potatoes can be used for these tubers.

Tostones de Plátano, more often than not simply called tostones, are slices of green plantain partly fried, then flattened and fried until crusty and brown on both sides.

Popular in the Spanish-speaking islands, as an accompaniment to both meat and fish dishes, they are also served as an accompaniment to drinks. They are known as banane pesé, pressed plantain, in Haïti and always accompany griots, grillots.

Yams are the edible tubers of a number of plants of the Dioscorea family. They come in a great variety of sizes and shapes and may weigh as much as 100 pounds though most are about the size of a large potato and weigh 1 pound or less. The flesh is white or yellow and has a very pleasant rather nutlike flavor, and a texture rather like potatoes. They may be cooked according to any potato recipe. They are widely used in West Indian cooking and are available in all tropical markets. Yams should not be confused with the incorrectly named Louisiana yam, the orange fleshed sweet potato, as they belong to entirely different botanical families.

Yard-Long Beans, Vigna sesquipedalis, also known as Chinese beans, asparagus bean and, in the Netherlands Antilles, as boonchi are originally from tropical Asia, and can sometimes be found in oriental markets. The beans, which have a very delicate flavor somewhat akin to green beans, grow to a length of up to 4 feet, but are only about ½-inch round. They are flexible enough to wrap around the skewered meat and vegetables in the Aruba dish, Lamchi and Boonchi.

Note on the Availability of Foods Needed to Cook Caribbean Style:

Most of the ingredients called for in these recipes can be found in any supermarket or grocery. However, there are a few ingredients less widely available. Fortunately many of these are used not only in Caribbean cooking, but also in the cooking of Mexican, South American, Indian, and Middle Eastern dishes so that they can be found in a variety of specialty food stores. Because the Caribbean is multi-lingual, it is a good idea to be prepared to ask for the foods under more than one name. Consult the glossary for guidance in this regard.

Health food stores frequently carry items like millet, and canned coconut milk while most Latin American and Puerto Rican groceries and vegetable markets carry the special fruits and vegetables not ordinarily available.

The following is a list of stores and markets which accept mail orders for Caribbean foods, especially those that are canned or dried. Since stores frequently change their inventories, write the store nearest you for a list of what they carry. Where special Caribbean markets do not accept mail orders this has been indicated. Where stores carry only a few of the needed items, this has been noted. The list does not pretend to be complete since the merchandising scene is a constantly changing one. It is hoped that these guidelines will prove useful.

CALIFORNIA
San Francisco
Casa Lucas Market
2934 24th Street
San Francisco, California
   94110

Mi Rancho Market
3365 20th Street
San Francisco, California
   94110

WASHINGTON, D.C.
Pena's Spanish Store
1636 17th Street, N.W.
Washington, D.C. 20009

FLORIDA
Miami
The Delicatessen Burdine's
Dadeland
   Shopping Center
Miami, Florida 33156

Epicure Markets
1656 Alton Road
Miami Beach, Florida
   33139

Imperial Supermarket
5175 S.W. Eight Street
Miami, Florida 33134

ILLINOIS
Chicago
La Preferida Inc.
117-181 W. South Water
   Market
Chicago, Illinois 60608

Marshall Field & Company
111 N. State Street
Chicago, Illinois 60690

IOWA
Cedar Rapids
Swiss Colony
Lindale Plaza
Cedar Rapids, Iowa 53402

LOUISIANA
New Orleans
Central Grocery
923 Decatur Street
New Orleans, Louisiana
   70116

Progress Grocery
915 Decatur Street
New Orleans, Louisiana
   70116

MASSACHUSETTS
Cambridge
Cardullo's Gourmet Shop
6 Brattle Street
Cambridge, Massachusetts
   02138

MICHIGAN
Birmingham
Continental Gourmet
Shop
210 S. Woodward Avenue
Birmingham, Michigan
48010

Detroit
Delmar & Company
501 Monroe Avenue
Detroit, Michigan 48226

NEW YORK
New York
Casa Moneo Spanish
Imports
210 West 14th Street
New York, New York
10016

Kalustyan Orient Export
Trading Corporation
123 Lexington Avenue
New York, New York
(Tamarind pulp)

H. Roth and Son
1577 First Avenue
New York, New York
10028
(Cassava (manioc) meal,
tamarind pulp, etce-
tera)

OHIO
Cleveland
Spanish & American Food
Market
7001 Wade Park Avenue
Cleveland, Ohio 44103

TEXAS
Houston
Antone's Import Company
Box 3352
Houston, Texas 77001

Jim Jamail & Son
3114 Kirby Drive
Houston, Texas 77006

Pier 1 Imports
5403 South Rice Avenue
Houston, Texas 77006

TENNESSEE
Nashville
Morris Zager
221 6th Avenue N
Nashville, Tennessee
37219

CANADA
Woodward's
Chinook Center
Calgary 9, Alberta

S. Enkin, Inc.
1201 St. Lawrence Street
Montreal 129, Quebec

Index

About the Author

Elizabeth Lambert Ortiz is the author of THE COM-
PLETE BOOK OF MEXICAN COOKING, THE COM-
PLETE BOOK OF JAPANESE COOKING, and THE
BOOK OF LATIN AMERICAN COOKING. She has
traveled extensively in the American South, Central
America, the Caribbean, and the Far East and has studied
the foods and dishes unique to each area. As a journalist,
she has worked in Australia, England, Mexico, and the
United States and has written for *Gourmet* and *House
and Garden* about travel and food. She is married to a
retired United Nations official and lives in England.